STRANGERS IN THE HOUSE

STRANGERS
in the
HOUSE

A PRAIRIE STORY OF
BIGOTRY AND BELONGING

CANDACE SAVAGE

DAVID SUZUKI INSTITUTE

GREYSTONE BOOKS
Vancouver/Berkeley

Greystone Books Ltd.
greystonebooks.com
David Suzuki Institute
davidsuzukiinstitute.org

Cataloguing data available from Library and Archives Canada
ISBN 978-1-77164-204-0 (cloth)
ISBN 978-1-77164-205-7 (epub)

Editing by Nancy Flight
Copy editing by Paula Ayer
Proofreading by Dawn Loewen
Text design by Belle Wuthrich
Map by Eric Leinberger
Jacket photograph © Vladimir Kayukov / Shutterstock.com
Printed and bound in Canada on ancient-forest-friendly paper by Friesens

Every attempt has been made to trace ownership of copyrighted material. Information that will allow the publisher to rectify any credit or reference is welcome.

Greystone Books gratefully acknowledges the Musqueam, Squamish, and Tsleil-Waututh peoples on whose land our office is located.

Greystone Books thanks the Canada Council for the Arts, the British Columbia Arts Council, the Province of British Columbia through the Book Publishing Tax Credit, and the Government of Canada for supporting our publishing activities.

Canadä

BRITISH COLUMBIA

BRITISH COLUMBIA ARTS COUNCIL
An agency of the Province of British Columbia

Canada Council   Conseil des arts
for the Arts   du Canada

Le passé n'est jamais tout à fait le passé.
N'avez-vous pas senti comme il rôde partout,
Et tangible? Il est là, lucide, clairvoyant,
Non pas derrière nous, comme on croit, mais devant.

The past is never entirely past.
Haven't you sensed it prowling around,
Tangible? It is there, lucid, clairvoyant,
Not behind us, as we believe, but out in front.

HENRY BATAILLE
Le songe d'un soir d'amour, 1910

CONTENTS

Napoléon Sureau dit Blondin in 1898 or 1899, aged
about 20, and Clarissa Marie Parent in 1916, aged 18.
Courtesy of Lorena Martens.

PREFACE

DURING THE YEARS when this book was in the making, I often found myself called upon to describe it to friends. "I'm tracing the first people to live in my house, back in the 1920s," I'd explain. "Here in Saskatoon. They came from deep roots in French Canada. Napoléon Sureau dit Blondin and his wife, Clarissa Marie Parent." I'd let the syllables roll off my tongue in my most musical accent, a small flourish that never failed to give me pleasure.

"But your own name," one of those friends objected. "Savage. That doesn't sound very French. I know you live in the same house they once did, but do you inhabit their story? I mean, really, do you have skin in the game?"

I offered some kind of an answer and the talk turned to other things, but her question echoed in my thoughts for days. There I was, daring to represent the experience of people who had died before I was born and whose background was, in notable ways, different from my own. Apart from the coincidence of sequential cohabitation, what gave me a right—or even a reason—to delve into their story? It was a valid question and one worthy of consideration.

2   That exotic-sounding name, Sureau dit Blondin, was the most obvious sign of the distance between my subjects and me. Although I'd become a Savage through marriage, I was a Sherk at birth—not wholly of English heritage, as my acquired last name suggests, but not French either. The Blondins, by contrast, were French root and branch, and their history is marked by the struggle to survive with dignity on a continent dominated by an aggressive Anglo majority. My ancestors didn't experience the shock of the British Conquest or of *la guerre des Patriotes*. They didn't suffer through the economic collapse that sent nearly a million Québécois into the mill towns of nineteenth-century New England. Simply because they were French Canadians, the Blondins were implicated in these crises in ways that my own people were not. And yet, I do have a stake in these traumas, which left their mark on an entire continent, including the nation that I call home. They are among our foundational stories and belong to us all.

As my engagement with the Blondins deepened, I found myself swept up in a multigenerational saga that reached from the hill country of western France to the plains of Saskatchewan, and from the days of wooden sailing ships to the present. In its details, this narrative was unique, studded with individuals and enlivened by personal decisions. In its broad outline, however, the family's experiences read like a case study in the process of North American settlement. Along with millions of others, the ancestral Blondins were human motes caught in the flood of European colonial expansion. By the early twentieth century, that impulse had carried one branch of the family to the Last Best West of the Canadian prairies, where they unwittingly crossed paths with my own venturing grandparents. Dispersed onto square plots of land, the Blondins, the Sherks, and millions more like them struggled to put down roots, to gain a sense of inclusion and belonging.

Before I embarked on this research, I had no idea how fraught that settling-in effort had been. During my sixteen years of schooling, no one had ever told me about the obnoxious and ubiquitous presence of the Orange Order in English Canada. No one had mentioned the brief but revelatory flowering of the Ku Klux Klan in Saskatchewan or its mission to assert the ascendancy of white, Anglo-Saxon Protestants. Although that outburst of bigotry had waxed and waned by the 1930s, the smoke of burning crosses hung in the air for years. Half a century later, I would succumb to the temptation of adopting an Anglo surname to escape the lingering embarrassment of being "ethnic."

Do I have skin in this game? Yes, and I'm willing to guess that you do, too. The story of the Blondin family is fascinating and intensely human; it is valuable in itself. But it also opens up a window, a new perspective on the past, revealing truths that lie, half-forgotten, in the darkness.

1

— LITTLE HOUSE —

*Toute saison embellit
la maison de nous amours.*

Each season embellishes
the house of our love.

JEAN-GUY PILON, *Comme eau retenue: Poèmes 1954–1963*

FOR ALMOST HALF a lifetime, going on thirty years, I have lived with my family in an unassuming wood-framed house in a quiet city on the northern edge of the Great Plains. Five minutes' walk to the west lies the shining, low-slung valley of the South Saskatchewan River, with a view, across the water, of downtown Saskatoon and the fairy-tale silhouette of the Bessborough Hotel. My young daughter and I were lucky enough to arrive here in springtime, on a big, blue, blustery day when the trees were juicy with new-leaf green. I can still remember the sappy joy we felt the first time we walked down our street, amazed by the extravagance of this welcome.

That was in 1990. We had landed in Saskatoon following a five-year stopover in Yellowknife, Northwest Territories, an

6   excellent place in its own way but not exactly a garden city. In Saskatoon, we found ourselves ten degrees of latitude farther south, though still technically in the subarctic climate zone. To us, however, our new surroundings were exuberantly tropical. What's more, our surge of elation reassured us that we were truly *home*. Diana had begun life in Saskatoon, and now she was back on the cusp of her eleventh birthday. I was a stubble jumper, too, though that is a longer story.

Diana and I had left town when she was a toddler, following the sudden death of my husband, her dad. Despite the best of medical intervention, he had succumbed to a runaway infection at the age of thirty-two, the kind of thing that almost never happens these days but happened to him. Ever since, I had been reeling, spinning Diana along in my wake, and now, finally, we were ready to settle, to find our way back again.

This time around, home was to be the ordinary bungalow that anchored the corner of the block. Like most of the dwellings on the street, our house qualified as what is known in real-estate jargon as a "character home." In other words, it was old. It was drab, as well—sided in white-painted boards accented with gloomy brown trim—and, although I didn't see it that way at the time, in obvious need of care and attention. The carpets were worn and dingy; the ancient clawfoot tub in the bathroom scarred and stained with rust. The cupboards in the kitchen had been repurposed from somewhere else and might have appeared, to other eyes, as makeshift. But to me, these notional deficiencies were all selling points. The last thing I wanted was a jewel box that had to be protected from a child with a soldering iron in her hand or rollerblades on her feet. We needed a place that could cope with the rough-and-tumble of real living.

But, of course, that wasn't the whole story. I didn't fall in love with the house just because it was comfortably worn in. There was something else, a *je ne sais quoi*, that instantly made me feel welcome here. Perhaps it was the light that fell, trembling, on the sidewalk that led to the front door. The light that spilled into all the rooms through the large, well-proportioned windows. The prismatic glint that was caught by the old glass knobs on the bedroom doors. Modest as it was, the house had been built with pride, perhaps even with love. Its wide baseboards and solid fir doorjambs spoke of generosity and connection. Like the trees along the boulevard, the house was rooted in place.

As I longed to be.

In the days I'd spent packing all our worldly belongings into boxes in preparation for the leap south, I had been surprised, time and again, by a wordless daydream in which a gigantic spruce tree plummeted out of the sky, crash-landed out on the prairies, and hurried to push down roots. A spruce tree on the prairie? That doesn't make any sense. Why couldn't I be a clump of blue grama grass or a wild sunflower instead? After all, prairie plants are famous for their strong, deep systems of roots. "I'm a little prairie flower," went an old song that my mom used to sing to me, "growing wilder by the hour." That was more like it. Yet, incongruous as the image was, there was no mistaking its meaning. I had come home to stay. And what would those roots do, as they pressed fiercely into the earth? For roots are not mere holdfasts. They are seekers, and there is no way of foretelling how deeply they will reach.

8   WE'D BEEN LIVING in our house happily, uneventfully, for
two or three years before a stranger popped up in our midst.
It was Diana who first made the connection. One afternoon,
as part of a school project, she and her classmates caught the
bus from Greystone Heights School (now home of the Saskatoon Islamic Association) to the downtown library. In my
mind's eye, I can see them clattering up the broad, zigzag
stairway to the second floor and elbowing through the doors
of the Local History Room. That evening, she returned home
bearing a scrap of paper on which she had written, in a careful, penciled hand, a list of all the "heads of household" ever
to have lived at our address, with the dates they'd first moved
in. This information she had extracted, year by year, from the
library's comprehensive collection of civic directories. With a
disregard for privacy that makes the digital present look prim,
these volumes provide a permanent, publicly accessible record
of names, addresses, occupations, and affiliations, extending
back, in the case of Saskatoon, to the early 1900s. The series
ceased publication around the turn of the millennium, overtaken by concerns about our see-through online identities.

The final entry on the list, the most recent, was the first
to catch my eye. "1990," it read, "Savage, Candace." Look at
that: just by showing up, I had earned a place in the history
books. Above that momentous entry, eight other occupancies
stepped back through the decades, with two in the 1980s, one
in the 1970s, and then a single long tenancy that stretched all
the way back to the 1940s. ("Savage, Candace" will have to
hang on until the end of her days to break the previous record
for continuous residency.) Another three notations rewound
the tape through World War II and the Depression of the
1930s. Apart from my own, the names were all male—a fact

that was irritating but unsurprising, given the overall invis-
ibility of women in the historical record—and completely
inscrutable. Who knew who these guys might have been, and
who cared, really?

But there was one entry that gave us pause: the very first
one on the list. "BUILT 1928," it read. "Blondin, Napoleon S."

"Nothing before that, kidlet?"

"No, really, Mom, I checked. There wasn't anything here,
not even an address, until 1928."

"So, the first family here was *French*?"

TO UNDERSTAND WHY this possibility was so startling—
why Napoleon S. Blondin was the one name on the roster
to lodge in our memories—you have to know a little about
the origins of Saskatoon. The idea for a permanent settlement on this bend in the river was conceived late in the
nineteenth century by a Methodist-preacher-turned-colonizing-
entrepreneur from Ontario, the Reverend John Neilson Lake.
A heavy-browed man with a patriarchal beard and a Bible
verse to suit every occasion, Lake journeyed west in June of
1882 as the leader of an expedition organized by the Temperance Colonization Society of Toronto. His mission was to
examine the immense block of windswept prairie—almost
500,000 acres straddling a 40-mile-long stretch of the South
Saskatchewan River, or over 700 square miles in all—that
had recently been granted to the Temperance Society by the
Canadian government, at the come-and-get-it price of a buck
or two per acre. Having purchased the oceanic expanse of the
"great lone land" from the Hudson's Bay Company little more

10 than a decade before, Canada's inaugural prime minister, Sir John A. Macdonald, had staked his political future on filling the prairies—that no-man's-land at the heart of his National Dream—with a prosperous, agrarian society.

To satisfy this ambition, settlers would be called for by the thousands, but not everyone need apply. As one of Macdonald's supporters explained, the goal was to flood the prairies with members of "an energetic and civilised race, able to improve [the land's] vast capabilities and appreciate its marvelous beauties."[1] In taking up this challenge, the Temperance Colonization Society aimed to go the government one better by achieving not mere "civilisation" but absolute rectitude. Through the simple expedient of banning intoxicating beverages from the colony, the temperance advocates believed that they could liberate society from all manner of strife, perversity, and sin. The Reverend Mr. Lake was commissioned to choose the location for a town in which this "glorious resurrection" (as he once termed it) could be initiated. He was seconded in this task by several other members of the Society—Messrs. Black, Grant, Hill, Goodwin, and Tait, by name—together, according to his account, with "a Frenchman for cook, and a half-breed to look after the horses."[2]

In recalling this expedition several years later, Lake failed to acknowledge either cook or hostler by name. Presumably they were local hires, recruited from the long-established Francophone and Métis settlements that, even then, were dotted across that part of the country, at places like Talle-de-Saules (Willow Bunch), Montagne de Bois (Wood Mountain), Montagne de Cyprès (Cypress Hills), and Vallée de la Qu'Appelle (Qu'Appelle Valley). From 1865 onward, these communities had been served by French-speaking Roman Catholic fathers based at the Mission de Saint-Florent at Lebret. Although Lake must have passed through the mission, his diary does not acknowledge this "Papist" presence.

By the end of July, the little party of self-confessed tenderfoots finally reached their promised land. Once on site, they wasted no time in choosing a location for their new settlement. They were assisted in this decision by the Dakota chief Wapaha Ska, or Whitecap, who had recently settled, with his community, on a small reserve within the borders of the Society's grand domain. There was no better place than this, Chief Whitecap assured the new arrivals, for a future river crossing.

With that practicality out of the way, Lake hurried back to Ontario and returned the following spring, 1883, with a sturdy band of "earnest, determined" Methodists from Toronto, who were to get the colony up and running. By mid-August, a townsite had been surveyed on the east bank of the river, with a main street (christened Broadway because it was wide enough to accommodate a U-turn by a team of horses) that ran north toward the river and then northeast along an already established trail leading to the Métis community of Batoche. Lake named his new settlement Saskatoon, after a local berry. By September, a number of houses were poking out of the ground, straight-backed as prairie gophers keeping watch by their holes. "Had a general jubilation," Lake reported, "all the settlers around... to the number of 30 or 40 people."[3]

By then, one catastrophe had already been averted through Lake's quick and decisive action. He had discovered, to his consternation, that the surveyors whom the government had hired to demarcate the Society's estate were laying it out in long, narrow strips with river frontage, "like the [Métis] lands at Red River," following a pattern borrowed from the

12 seigneuries along the Saint Lawrence River in New France. What kind of backward, Frenchified thinking was that? Lake immediately rushed off to Ottawa for urgent consultations with the prime minister and other top-ranking officials. Soon, the telegraph lines were buzzing with orders to lay out the land in the officially approved American-style square sections.

But not even the ardent and well-connected Reverend Lake could prevent the successive disasters that were about to smite his godly initiative. Through an unholy confabulation of poor planning, inadequate infrastructure, ill-conceived government policy, internal discord, and uncooperative weather (on the prairies you can pretty much count on that), the project quickly foundered, and by 1885, even Lake was out, leaving, by his accounting, "about $8,000 of hard cash in the wreck."[4] When violence ignited at Batoche that year, provoked in large part by the government's prolonged refusal to acknowledge the right of Métis settlers to their riverfront lots, the Temperance Colony was essentially done for. Attracting incomers would prove extremely difficult for many years to come.

Nonetheless, the fledgling settlement carried on bravely as it had begun, as an outpost of strict and particular Protestantism. Even after the railway arrived in 1890, change was glacially slow. When a cluster of stores and houses sprang up on the west bank of the river (near the new railway roundhouse) and took over the name "Saskatoon," the east-bank community shuffled the syllables, more or less back to front, and rechristened their settlement "Nutana." (As city archivist Jeff O'Brien notes, the phonemes were "scrambled, no doubt, because of the small likelihood that anyone would ever want to live in a place called 'Nootaksas.'")[5] The place was a backwater, caught in a listless eddy.

Then, in 1903, a trainload of settlers from England, recruited under the slogan "Canada for the British," steamed into the station on the way to their own promised land, a tract farther west known—lest anyone mistake their intentions—as *Britannia*. Many of them stepped off the train, gazed at the dizzying horizons around the platform, and decided they'd come far enough. With these new additions, Saskatoon and Nutana were well on their way to becoming an enclave of white Anglo-Saxon Protestantism. A WASP nest.

Three years later, when the two municipalities came together with an adjoining hamlet to form the City of Saskatoon, the event was marked with patriotic speeches and a flurry of Union Jacks. A parade wound through the muddy streets to the stirring beat of an anthem of British supremacy, "The Maple Leaf Forever":

In days of yore, from Britain's shore,
Wolfe, the dauntless hero, came
And planted firm Britannia's flag
On Canada's fair domain.[6]

A few years later, in the 1910s and 1920s, the city would open its doors to a flood of immigrants from other parts of Europe, including the "men in sheepskin coats" from the Austro-Hungarian Empire: Galicians, Ruthenians, Poles. The self-appointed WASP elite made no secret of their disdain for these "aliens" and "non-preferred Europeans."[7] Soon, the population of the city began to segregate, with most "ethnics" residing in the working-class neighborhoods on the west side of the river, where they enjoyed ready access to purveyors of strong drink, and citizens of British ancestry, upright and

14 proper, ensconced on the gracious streets to the east. And yet, a man with a frankly French name had managed to gain a toehold inside this ultra-respectable domain. Who was this Napoleon S. Blondin, and how had he crossed the divides that marked, and in some ways still mark, this city?

ALTHOUGH I HAD tucked Diana's list away for safekeeping, there was no immediate way of answering the questions it had aroused. We set our curiosity aside and continued with our lives. It was then, as we settled more deeply into our house, that we began to sense something about it that we hadn't noticed at first. Something downright peculiar. Most houses are designed to provide clearly separated spaces, each with a designated use. But our house had been built to an unusual, flow-through plan, in which every room provides access to adjoining spaces. For instance, the back porch opens into the kitchen, which opens into the dining room, which opens to the living room, which, in turn, leads to a small front hall. From there, you can loop through the master bedroom, via a mini-corridor, back to the dining room or, alternatively, continue straight on to the den. A doorway on the far side of the den provides access to a steep set of stairs leading up to the second floor, where three more spaces are laid out end to end, like train cars. Except for the bathroom, every room in the house has two or three doorways, each of which leads in a different direction.

On a practical level, this design has a few, readily apparent disadvantages. If you're the kind of person who likes to go into your room and shut out the world, it wouldn't work for you.

But for us, the flexibility of this layout has turned out to be surprisingly accommodating. Opening the spaces to one another has also freed them up, to an unusual degree, for reinterpretation. Thus, the "master bedroom" was once Diana's room, then a guest room, and is now my office. And the fact that every room is designed to make connections and to take you somewhere you need to go—isn't that exactly what stories are for? Every episode leads you on to the next and the next, so that it is never quite clear where one ends and another begins, or which door to choose, or when it's the right time to loop back to the beginning. This house isn't just a house. It is a story.

IT MUST HAVE been around the time of Diana's memorable visit to the library, give or take a few months, that a new and unexpected happiness found us. Who knew that True Love could walk up to your door, ring the bell, and take a seat at the dining-room table? As it happens, it was the very table where a few weeks earlier I'd sat alone and clipped an ad from the Companions column of the *Saskatoon StarPhoenix*. "To enjoy travel, the arts, books and other pleasures," the ad promised. "For a relationship based on equality and love." Yes, please, I'll have one of those. And now, here he was, that "friendly, attractive professional man, mid-40s," in our dining room, serenaded by the splash of Diana's pet turtles, the rustle from her cage of white mice, the miasmic wheeze of our smelly old dog. If he'd made a run for it, who could have blamed him? But he didn't run; he lingered. In fact, when he headed home that evening (and wouldn't you know it, this being Saskatoon, he lived just down the block?), we'd been tête-à-tête, in conversation, for six entire hours. Where does the time go? Twenty-six years later, we are still at the same table, still talking nonstop, and Keith is father, by adoption, to Diana and an adored grandpa to her two little daughters.

Back in the 1990s, nothing spoke of love like moving in together and getting the kitchen done up. And so one day, after Keith's sleepovers had morphed imperceptibly into permanent occupancy and our search for a place to call our own had brought us back, again and again, to this very house, we realized that this was it. It was time to call in the contractors. Out went the battered old kitchen cabinets and down came the kitchen walls, choking the room with dust, splinters of lath, and a volcanic outpouring of wood-chip insulation.

As we gazed, aghast, at this scene of destruction, we were surprised to notice bits of flotsam poking out of the wreck, half-buried in crumbled plaster or caught between shards of wood. An old-fashioned button-on shirt collar, badly frayed along the crease. A grubby book cover emblazoned with the figure of a cowboy astride a bucking bronc. A cluster of tattered pages from a cookbook: Boiled Frosting, Brown Frosting, Milk Frosting, Chocolate Frostings I through III. Each item was torn and dirty and must have once been discarded. Why else would they all have ended up among the rubble inside our walls?

But soiled and damaged as these relics were, they were also eloquent. That collar had been abraded by some man's body. The book, with its cover once firmly affixed, had been held in a child's hand. The recipes had been fretted loose by a woman's repeated use. The connection these mementos offered was personal, intimate, filled with mystery. Which unknown young student had completed this painstaking page of calculations, every one of them correct? What woman had spent an

afternoon in a home-decorating store downtown and come
away with a tally card featuring an exotic lady playing an exotic
stringed instrument to an exotic bird? For whom could this
secretive valentine have been intended, if not, perhaps, for me?

> You cannot guess, I grieve to say,
> Who I am; though, come what may—
> Every day when you pass by,
> For your love, in vain, I sigh.

Indeed, that was the question. Who had left these traces—
these echoes of vanished lives—embedded in our house?
For the sake of romance, I wanted them to have belonged to
Napoleon Blondin, in company with his wife and a houseful of
happy kids, but there seemed no way to be sure who had left
them behind. After all, a lot of people had lived in this house
over a lot of years, and these oddments could have slipped
down the cracks in the floorboards or sifted through heating
ducts—or something—at any time. So I tucked these enig-
matic curiosities away for safekeeping along with Diana's list
and more or less forgot about them.

But every now and then, I'd come across my grubby stash
when I was looking for something else, at the back of a drawer
or under a pile of books. Once, overtaken by an uncharacter-
istic zeal for tidiness, I decided that several items, including
two photographic negatives, were too damaged and disgust-
ing to keep and rashly threw them away. ("If I'd known then
what I know now, I would never have parted with them": the
lament of the pack rat.) On the plus side, I had at least begun
to examine the items in my reliquary more attentively and
to notice things about them that I'd overlooked before. For

example: the books represented in the collection had all been published in the 1910s; an order form, never completed or submitted, had been issued in 1928. (It provided fill-in-the-blanks options for procuring "x" hundreds of feet of Equity Binder Twine from the United Farmers of Canada, Saskatchewan Section.) Even the homework bore a wobbly annotation that dated it precisely to January 15 of the following year. And who had lived in this house in those early days? Napoleon S. Blondin and family.

It would take me a decade to notice the final, confirming piece of evidence, though it had been staring me in the face all along. One of the pieces in my hoard was the lid of a small cardboard box, torn and flattened but still bright as new. Made to hold plasticine ("an educational amusement," the box proclaimed), it showed two fabulously talented children, both sporting pudding-bowl haircuts and floppy bows under their chins, engaged in fashioning remarkably detailed models, an elephant for him and a cow for her. I must have looked at the picture a dozen times before my eyes focused on the smudged inscription across the elephant-maker's ear. A round, childish hand had written "Ralph Blondin."

So it was true. The fragments in the walls had been deposited, however unknowingly, by the first people to live in the house, a family I was beginning to think of as adopted kin. More than a mere theory of storytelling, the house had turned out to be an abandoned archive, a midden of tantalizing clues. Binder twine: did that mean my Napoleon was a farmer? A cheesy detective novel about stock speculation: did he enjoy taking risks? The *Boston Cooking-School Cook Book*: perhaps the woman of the house had been ambitious, on a quest for finer things. The evidence was suggestive but insubstantial, murmured conversations just beyond the range of hearing, fleeting gestures caught by the corner of an eye.

And what was one to make of the ghostly figures who gazed out of the single brittle negative to survive my purge? Held to the light, it showed a group of adults arrayed in front of some kind of machine, a biplane, perhaps, or an old-fashioned automobile. In the center, three women, dressed in the long skirts of another era, stood clustered arm in arm. They were bracketed, to left and right, by two gentlemen, one in a flat cap and open-necked shirt, the other slouching stylishly in a fedora and necktie. Imprisoned in their impenetrable black-is-white world, their hair was bright, their faces dark; their eyes glowed eerily. "You cannot guess, I grieve to say, / Who I am ..."

And so the Blondins came to be acknowledged as a spectral presence in the house, like shadowy and undemanding guests. It was pleasant to imagine that all the walls we'd left undisturbed (everywhere but the kitchen, that is) still held traces of their time here. Yet it was also possible to ignore them entirely for weeks or months on end and focus on our own preoccupations. And then one day, this easy, come-and-go relationship was shaken by a chance encounter with another ghost, another Napoleon Blondin. This one had been dead even longer.

I WISH I could tell you precisely when this second Napoleon came into view. Until recently, I thought that all I had to do was reach for a certain book on a certain shelf in my office, turn to a left-hand page, and there he'd be, a few lines from the top. But book in hand, there's no trace of him, and so I

20 cannot say exactly how I first made his acquaintance. What I do know, however, is that my yearning for a settled existence—the desire for deep roots that had called me back to Saskatoon—has kept me on full alert for years. What does it mean to be *here*? What does it mean to live on the northernmost edge of the great North American plains, only the second generation in my lineage to be born here? What does it mean to be a prairie person?

If there's an organized course of studies dedicated to pondering these questions, some kind of Prairie Fundamentals 101, I haven't found it yet. And so my education has been self-directed, episodic, eccentric, and I've spent many happy hours rummaging in libraries and archives or consulting with other learners, in person and online. Like a shopper at a flea market, I'm not always sure what I'm looking for, but I sure do know a treasure when I see it.

The second Napoleon Blondin was one of those lucky finds. His name is featured on the Métis Museum website (in a left-hand column, toward the top, so at least I got that much right) among 114 signatories to a petition dated September 2, 1880, and addressed to the governor general of Canada, the very British Marquis of Lorne. The petitioners identified themselves as the "half-breeds of the Lakes Qu'Appelle and environs," and almost all had French surnames: Desjarlais, Poitras, LaPierre, Blondin. Maybe they'd heard rumors about the plan to hand over huge chunks of the North-West to private interests like John Lake and his determinedly unmerry band. Certainly, the petitioners were keenly aware of the Indian treaties the government had signed in the previous decade with their relatives and friends. "Hello," the petitioners interjected. "Remember us? We're still here."

In the politest possible language, with assurances of "profound respect" and "perfect submission" to the authorities, the members of the small Métis community laid out their concerns. They wanted recognition of their right to hunt, fish, and trade in their traditional territory. They were anxious about the status of their church, the Roman Catholic mission at Lebret, asking that it be allowed "the free and tranquil enjoyment of its possessions." They were alarmed by the lack of local government and the looming collapse of the buffalo herds. But amid all these urgent worries, one matter topped the list. Their very homes were at risk.

We the undersigned beseech you, the petition read: "1st, That the Government allow to the Half-breeds the right of keeping the lands they have taken or which they may take along the River Qu'Appelle."[8] These, of course, were the French-style riverfront lots that the Reverend Mr. Lake found so incongruous.

The people waited, but there was no answer, and soon their worst fears began to come true. Several families lost their land to the Ontario and Qu'Appelle Land Company, another private consortium with a vast acreage at its command. In 1882, when the petitioners renewed their appeal to the government, this same Napoleon, or Pollyon, Blondin again appeared among the signatories. But as before, there was no response, not even so much as a routine acknowledgment. Anxious and exhausted, many of the Qu'Appelle Métis packed up their households and left the district, hoping to find a sanctuary to the north and west.

If I'd known the whole story at the time, with its sequels of violence and loss, I would have been dismayed. But at the time, all I noticed was that thrilling name: Napoleon Blondin.

22 By now, I was used to thinking of my house as a box filled with stories about its first occupants. But what if it held more? What if it was a gateway to a larger landscape and a grander narrative, *une épopée des plus brillants exploits*, a deep story of French and Métis presence in the Canadian West? With the appearance of this second Napoleon Blondin, the walls of my office melted away to let the past come rushing in, and the room filled with dancing rivers and the songs of the voyageurs.

Auprès de ma blonde qu'il fait bon, fait bon, fait bon
Auprès de ma blonde qu'il fait bon dormir.

But this was no time for sleeping. A story was calling to be explored. Something told me this was going to be important.

2

— TANGLED ROOTS —

Car les racines, c'est aussi les morts.
For our roots are also the dead.

ANTONINE MAILLET, *Pélagie-la-Charrette,* 1979

WHEN I WAS a kid growing up in Alberta, a camping trip to the Rockies was always the most thrilling part of the summer holidays. There we'd be, packed into the family sedan, spooling across the seemingly endless expanse of nothing-much-to-see until, in a few breathtaking moments, a majestic wall of rock and forest and snow-capped peaks would rise before our eyes. Each time I experienced this transformation, my mind would flash to a lesson we'd been taught (and retaught) in school—how, in the 1700s, a French fur trader with the swashbuckling name of Pierre Gaultier de Varennes et de La Vérendrye had ridden across this same country on horseback, not knowing what lay ahead, and become the first European to see what, in his awe, he called the Shining Mountains. I was awash with wonder.

So it was disappointing to learn, many years later, that the story was not true. Historians are now convinced that

24   neither Pierre nor his sons and successors ever saw the Rockies, either in Canada or farther south, having reached the
limit of their travels in the Bighorn Mountains of present-
day Wyoming. And if what I thought I knew about the La
Vérendryes was not to be trusted, what did that leave me
with? What did I really know about the French presence
in the Canadian West? A few other oddments of dubious
information were kicking around in my mind. Wasn't there
something about a rascally team called Pierre-Esprit Radis-
son and Médard des Groseilliers, better known to the wits in
elementary school (of which I admit I was one) as Radishes
and Gooseberries? But that was almost the beginning and
the end of my knowledge. I would be starting my research
with an empty cupboard.

The obvious place to begin was with that enticing name,
Napoleon S. Blondin. A little poking around on the internet
immediately began to turn up clues. My Napoleon S. Blondin might have been a Napoléon Sureau dit Blondin. "First
& Middle Name(s)," the search page on the Ancestry website
prompted. "Napoléon Sureau dit," I ventured. Is that how it
should go?

"Last Name." That was easy: "Blondin."

I clicked the red button at the bottom of the page, and
bingo, there he was. It appeared that my guy had been born
around 1880, which sounded reasonable, and was the son of
either a Martha E. (birth name unknown) or a Georgina Trottier, and a man named Cleophas Sureau dit Surcan Blondin or
perhaps C. S. Hut Blondin. In a world where English reigns as
the default language, other tongues merge into an unintelli-
gible parley-voo, even in a nominally bilingual country like
Canada. This orthographic whimsy—Sureau or Surcan, dit

versus Hut—added an extra degree of bewilderment. I could
see that I was in for a challenge.

And so day after day, I posed as a Sureau dit Blondin descendant, searching for my roots. "Place where your ancestor might
have lived," the website queried. Day after day, I pretended.
It did not occur to me to worry that the fathers and grand-
fathers, the mothers and stepmothers, the aunties and uncles
and cousins—the legions of cousins—whose births and deaths
I was tracing were not of my own flesh and blood. The walls
around me were filled with their descendants; it was tempting to imagine them listening as I worked. The more I learned
about their story, the stronger the connection grew, and the
more honored I felt to be in their presence.

RESEARCHING FAMILY HISTORY on Ancestry is like poking
around an abandoned house, filled with cobwebs of wishful
thinking and littered with errors. Anyone can post whatever
he or she likes, with or without proof, and the contributions
do not always meet the loftiest standards of historical scholar-
ship. By contrast, clicking onto *Le programme de recherche en
démographie historique* (the PRDH, or Research Program in
Historical Demography) at the Université de Montréal is the
digital equivalent of entering a clean and well-lighted room.
Inspired by the upwelling of national pride that swept Québec
in the late 1960s, the PRDH was established with the modest
aim of creating a registry of all the original European families
of French Canada, including every person who arrived or was
born there in the 1600s and 1700s. Anyone whose ancestors
are included in this database is definitively *Québécois de souche*,

26 an expression that means something like "Quebecer from the ground up." In English, it might be "old stock" or "100 percent" or "dyed in the wool." In Québec's darkest moments, people who lack these deep roots are sometimes dismissed as outsiders, part of the "ethnic vote" on which *indépendantiste* Jacques Parizeau blamed his 1995 referendum defeat.

And sure enough, here in the PRDH is *la famille Sureau dit Blondin*, bedecked with fleurs-de-lys. Though really, I discover, that should read *la famille Sureau*. The rest of the family's elegant handle turns out to be a kind of nickname that was all the rage in New France. "Dit *Blondin*" simply means "called Blondin." (Ah, so it should have been First & Middle Name(s): "Napoléon." Last Name: "Sureau dit Blondin.") Just to keep things interesting, the "dit Blondin" tag was also attached to several other lineages, including people carrying the surnames Avon, Berneche, Lapierre, and Leclerc, among others. Thus, there are several lines of Blondins, all early settlers in New France but otherwise unrelated.

> **Blondin,** from the *Dictionnaire universel français et latin*, 1743
> Qui a les cheveux blonds, ou une perruque blonde; & figurément les gens qui font les beaux. Les coquettes aiment fort les blondins; ce sont de vrais séducteurs de femme.

> Someone with blond hair or a blond wig; & figuratively people who strut their stuff. Flirtatious women really love blondins; they are real seducers of women.

From this it is tempting to conclude that the first member of the Sureau tribe to attract the "blondin" nickname may have been a charmer, perhaps even a bit of a ladies' man.

His name was Hilaire Sureau, and we know that he was born in the 1650s, near Poitiers, in west-central France, the fifth child and second son of a vintner. We also know that in 1683 he journeyed across the dark waters of the north Atlantic to live and work on the Island of Montréal, in the employ of a Roman Catholic missionary society called La Compagnie des Prêtres de Saint-Sulpice, or the Sulpicians.

The Compagnie had established itself in the Saint Lawrence Valley for the sole purpose of evangelizing the Indigenous people of the region and leading them from error and sin. The arrogance of this intrusion, which was territorial, spiritual, and economic, did not sit well with the people of the Iroquois Confederacy, and the conflict that ensued between the French and the Five Nations was protracted and bloody. It didn't help that each side allied itself with the other's worst enemy: the French with the Hurons and the Iroquois with the English. In 1687, not long after Hilaire's arrival, the French military descended on a number of Iroquois villages, leaving ruin in their wake. Two years later, the Iroquois set fire to the French settlement of Lachine.

Hilaire was no stranger to lethal risk. Although he had grown up in a time of relative tranquility, France had been ravaged for decades by a grotesque civil war, and the region around Poitiers had been a flash point for violence. Christians had taken up arms against Christians. On one side, in fierce defense of the status quo, stood the Roman Catholics; on the other, in armed resistance, were the Huguenots, Protestant followers of the fiery French theologian Jehan Cauvin, better known to many of us as John Calvin. Among the Huguenots burned at the stake as heretics was a woman named Radegonde Sureau (a relative perhaps), one of the millions who

28 lost their lives in the uproar. An uneasy peace was finally achieved early in the seventeenth century when the king's army crushed the Protestant rebels, and their inevitable English allies, in the Siege of La Rochelle.

Although the overt warfare had ended, the soft violence of repression continued for decades afterward through *les dragonnades*, a policy that forced Huguenots to billet government soldiers in their homes. That directive came into effect in 1681, and it was just two years later when our Hilaire stepped aboard a sailing ship heading for the Saint Lawrence. No sooner had he settled in than, in 1685, King Louis XIV issued the *Code Noir*, which, in addition to regulating slavery in French colonies and ordering the expulsion of Jews, outlawed the observance of any dissenting Christian practices. Thus, although we cannot know what beliefs Hilaire Sureau held in his heart, we know what he would have said. There was no legal option except Catholicism.

THESE WERE NOT the kind of stories I'd expected my house to tell. And yet I wasn't entirely surprised by what I was learning, because the terror of the European Wars of Religion had caused convulsions for my own ancestors. In 1711, my paternal great-great-great-great-great-great-grandparents Ulrich and Barbara Schürch were packed onto a ship and deported from their home in Canton Bern for the crime of being Mennonites, too radical for the leaders of the Swiss Reformed Church. Eventually, they found refuge in Pennsylvania and established themselves on a large plot of land (acquired through the displacement of the Lenape, or Delaware, people) near a village they named Schoeneck, in memory of the home-land they had been forced to leave.

That was my grandpa Sherk's side of the story. Although he and my grandma had met and married in northern Alberta, it turns out that she had Pennsylvania roots as well. Her foun-dational North American ancestors, William and Nancy Jack, are said to have been born in Ireland and to have arrived in Mercer County, Pennsylvania, around 1800. According to an annotation in an old family Bible, William hailed from County Cork. But there are unsubstantiated rumors, kept alive in the Google-sphere, that his people were originally French and had been among the tens of thousands of Hugue-nots who were harried into exile.

Scholars tell us that, yes, it is true that some French Cal-vinists found their way to County Cork and, yes, the surname "Jack," from Jacques, does appear in their midst. But then the record goes blank. Did one of these Huguenot descendants emigrate to Mercer County? The ocean looms between A and B, and there is no way to know for sure.

For "Jack" is also a British name, and the family might just as likely have numbered among the thousands of Scottish Protestants who were transplanted to Ireland by the English government in the sixteenth and seventeenth centuries, in an attempt to outnumber and overrule the Irish Catholic major-ity. (The devices of power, it seems, are endless.) But whether French Huguenot or Scots Irish, there is no doubt which side the Jacks were on. That foundational ancestor, William Jack, was named for the Protestant standard-bearer King William of Orange, who famously defeated the Catholics at the Battle of the Boyne.

THERE'S A CURIOUS sideline to this story of Jacks and Jacques. It involves a nineteenth-century con man who gloried in the Frenchified handle of Gustav or Gustave Anjou. (His birth name had been tarnished by certain unfortunate convictions for fraud in his native Sweden.) After immigrating to New York in the 1890s, he established himself as genealogist to the rich and famous and to anyone else who could afford his fees. Suitably fortified with greenbacks, Monsieur Anjou provided the Jacks of Pennsylvania with a line of descent that went back, with nary a question mark, through an unbroken chain of twenty-two generations. Since Huguenots had earned a reputation for skilled craftsmanship and stubborn integrity, they were considered an ornament to any pedigree. And so, ever eager to please his clients, Anjou fabricated a paper trail that wound through the "archives" of seventeenth-century Eure-et-Loir (a *département* of France that wouldn't actually be created for another hundred years) and endowed the family with a bevy of bogus French Protestant ancestors. His inventions continue to haunt dusty, ill-lit corners of the internet, giving hope to Jack descendants who yearn for a touch of l'*élégance française*.

FROM WHAT I'VE said so far, you may have formed the impression that Protestants were the only people to suffer during Europe's religious wars. But when an entire continent was tearing itself apart over doctrinal differences, no one escaped untouched. Winners oppressed losers, and the virtues of Christian charity were forgotten. In England, for example, King Henry VIII was so outraged by the Pope's refusal to annul his first marriage so he could wed again (and again) that he had himself appointed as head of the Church of England. Soon, Roman Catholicism was outlawed as a species of treason, an affront to the Crown. Monasteries were ransacked and looted; priests were tortured and killed. Ordinary adherents who declared their faith were sometimes imprisoned and, always, stripped of their liberties, leaving them unable to own land, receive bequests, graduate from university, or qualify for professions. In 1673, a new law required anyone who applied for governmental or military office to take an oath denying the Catholic doctrine of transubstantiation, the belief that the Eucharistic bread and wine become the body and blood of Christ. Not, one would think, an obvious prerequisite for public service.

The next year, a man named Peter Curricoe stepped aboard an English vessel bound for Maryland, a colony created by Catholics for Catholics and dedicated to religious freedom. He arrived as an indentured servant (essentially a slave), put in the required seven years of work, and received title to fifty acres of land, acquired through the displacement of the Piscataway and Yaocomaco people, as his reward.

Five generations later, when my mother's mother, Mary Catherine Carrico, was born, she remained as fiercely and irreducibly Catholic as her forebears. By choosing my grandfather Humphrey, she became the first member of her lineage to marry outside the faith, and together, they fed the flames of religious discord around their kitchen table on the Alberta plains.

32   BUT BACK TO Hilaire Sureau. When we left him, he was a
young man of about thirty, engaged by the Sulpicians as a
laborer in Montréal. It can't be mere coincidence that his
employers were just then embarking on a major construction project, the Séminaire de Saint-Sulpice, now one of the
oldest surviving heritage buildings in the city. Built between
1684 and 1687, it stands as a tribute to the men, likely including Hilaire, who carted the stone and burned the lime and
mixed the mortar. With his three-year contract completed,
he could have returned to France but instead decided to leave
Montréal and take his chances downriver, in the town of Québec. Less vulnerable than Montréal to attack by the Iroquois,
Québec had nonetheless recently been forced to repel an
attempted invasion by les maudits Anglais, launched from the
English Protestant stronghold on Massachusetts Bay. There
was no escaping the toxic winds of religion and politics.

Hilaire, meanwhile, had other pressing concerns. Marriage-
able women were in short supply—most girls wed in their
teens—and here he was, rapidly scrolling through his thirties.
So it must have been with considerable relief that, in June
of 1691, he married a thirty-year-old named Louise Paradis,
a mother of four, who had been widowed earlier that same
month. Through this fortunate liaison, he connected his lineage even more deeply with the history of New France, since
Louise's line went back to the very beginnings of French settlement. The couple never became wealthy—for a time, Hilaire
worked as a carter for the municipal government—and they
likely resided in a modest house. The experts tell us that the
average home in Québec at the time had a footprint of around
750 square feet, with a large room on the second floor shaped
by the pitch of the roof, not unlike the one in Saskatoon where

his great-great-great-great-great-grandson would one day live. Into these narrow confines, Hilaire and Louise would welcome four more children, two daughters and two sons, all of whom would survive to raise families of their own.

The Sureau dit Blondin line was now firmly established among the pioneers of New France. From those roots came a stream of *begats* that spanned the centuries, as Hilaire's son Charles (1695) fathered Pierre Simon (1727), who fathered Pierre Simon *fils* (1752), who fathered Simon (1799), who fathered Augustin (1821), who fathered Cléophas (1844), who fathered Napoléon (1879), who ended up on the northernmost edge of the Great Plains. Generation after generation, these men allied themselves with good *canadienne* women named Marie Anne, Marie Élisabeth, Marie Amable, or Rose Marie, each of whom bore ten or a dozen children, sometimes even more, and took them to the parish church for baptism or burial. The family was so exuberantly French Catholic that, in the course of time, it would even produce a saint, Esther Sureau dit Blondin, canonized in 2001 as the Blessed Mother Marie-Anne, a not-so-distant cousin of Napoléon. "*Plus un arbre enfonce profondément ses racines dans le sol,*" she once wrote, "*plus il a de chances de grandir et de porter de fruit.*"[1] The more deeply a tree sinks its roots into the soil, the greater are its chances of growing and bearing fruit. You could never accuse the Sureau dit Blondins of having shallow roots.

IN SASKATOON, THERE'S an unwritten rule that any house more than eighty years old ought to be torn down. I think of this dictum every time I sweep the floor in our crumbling

34 basement or watch frost crystals sprout from the electrical plug-ins beside the kitchen sink. Over the years, Keith and I have done what we could—replaced most of the rattly old windows, added insulation to attic and walls—but there's no getting around it. The place is old, approaching its tenth decade, and it embodies standards of efficiency and comfort that belong to another age. It's easy to understand why so many of our neighbors have opted for the newer, infill houses that punctuate our block, some of them tastefully harmonious with the street's period aesthetic, others frankly not. Recently we have lost two more "heritage" houses on our side of the street, a block distant in each direction. Every time a house is demolished it represents a kind of forgetting.

Knowing what I now know, I walk from room to room in my house and seem to see portraits of all those Sureau dit Blondin ancestors hanging on the walls. The images are painted with broad strokes, black and white with vague faces, posed singly or in couples or clustered in tight family groups. And in one of the frames—something suitably ornate and gilded, I'm thinking—there is a map of Canada, with Saskatchewan and Québec highlighted in full relief.

Despite what it says on my passport, I have never felt fully Canadian, not in the *a mari usque ad mare* sense of the word. When I was a child, my world was bounded by my limited experience, first of the Norwegian-speaking community in northern Alberta into which I was born (though we were in no way Norwegian), then of the succession of small, multiethnic, English-speaking prairie towns to which we subsequently moved. When I became an adult, my map stretched northward to include Yellowknife—still, by some definitions, within the geographical province of the North

American plains—and then homeward, to Saskatoon. With each move, my identity became more firmly rooted in the ragged gestalt of the Canadian prairies, "east of the Rockies and west of the rest," to borrow from a Corb Lund song. Although I had ancestors and presumably even relatives in Ontario, they belonged to another world. As for Québec, my stilted, schoolgirl French marked me indelibly as an outsider.

But now this unassuming little house had opened its doors to a story that transcended petty barriers and boundaries. Small as it was, it encompassed solitudes and centuries.

GENEALOGICAL RESEARCH IS addictive: every discovery, no matter how insignificant, induces a pleasure rush. Look here—this maternal great-great-grandmother was a genuine *Fille du Roi*, one of the women (orphans and adventurers) sent out from France in the seventeenth century as wives for the colonists. And this fellow, he was a soldier in the famous Carignan-Salières Regiment, French army regulars deployed to New France in the 1680s to impose an uneasy peace on the Iroquois. As long as the sugar hits of satisfaction kept coming, it was tempting to go on and on.

But there was a purpose to this research, two questions I had set out to resolve. First, taking them in reverse order of appearance, was the mystery of the two Napoléons. Was there, or was there not, a connection between the Blondins of Saskatoon and their Métis namesakes in the Qu'Appelle? Such a linkage is entirely plausible since, in the early days of New France, marriages between Indigenous women and French men were encouraged. "Our young men will marry your

36 daughters," Champlain told a gathering of Hurons in 1633, "and we will be one people."[2] A few years later, Marie de l'Incarnation and her Ursuline nuns established a school for girls in the town of Québec, and their graduates, many of whom were Indigenous, frequently went on to marry settlers. Intermarriage was also integral to the fur trade, especially as voyageurs began to venture farther into the country around the Great Lakes, *le pays d'en haut*. These men often learned Indigenous languages, married into Indigenous families, and adopted their wives' customs.

Although Hilaire does not seem to have been involved in the fur trade, several of his descendants certainly were, including his eldest son, Charles. We know this thanks to a database of voyageur contracts co-curated by a historian at the University of Saskatchewan. (Where else would this arcane knowledge reside but ten minutes' walk from this house?) But no matter where or how hard I looked, I could not find any Indigenous women in the Sureau dit Blondin line.

So what about coming at the problem from the other direction? What if I started with the Blondins in the Qu'Appelle Valley and searched for their *canadien* forefathers? At first, the hits came thick and fast. There were Métis Blondins written all over Western Canadian history—a Paul in the Edmonton district, a Julia at Cumberland House, an Édouard Pierre at Saint-Boniface, all in the nineteenth century—and each of them held the promise of linking back to ancestors in French Canada. But the documentation turned out to be spotty, pocked with disappointing gaps, and all too quickly, the trail petered out, leaving me stranded on the shores of Lesser Slave Lake in the 1790s with a Pierre Blondin, parentage unknown.

Fortunately, I did find an answer to my second question: How had the Sureau dit Blondins ended up on the prairies? It turned out to be quite easy to map the family's serial displacements. Perhaps succeeding generations had taken their cue from founding father Hilaire, who, having moved from Poitiers to Montréal to Québec, returned to Montréal. Whatever the reason, the entire line of Sureau dit Blondins had remarkably itchy feet. If you've ever read Louis Hémon's classic novel *Maria Chapdelaine*, you will remember the closing scene, in which the long-suffering heroine hears "*la voix du pays de Québec*" echoing through her thoughts like the tolling of a bell. This is a nation, the voice informs her, where "*rien ne doit mourir et rien ne doit changer*"—where nothing must die and nothing must change. "*Alors je vais rester ici ... de même*," Maria concludes, choosing to stay where she is, "patient and without bitterness," certain that this is the Québécois way.[3]

The Sureau dit Blondins clearly weren't buying it. As new agricultural frontiers opened up—and despite their passing involvement in the fur trade, the family were farmers first—Napoléon's forebears had opted for change and a chance at getting ahead. At first, they'd migrated from parish to parish in the vicinity of Montréal: Pointe-Claire, Pierrefonds, Laval. That's where they were in the autumn of 1759, when the French army fell to the English on the Plains of Abraham, and, a year later, when the entire colony of New France surrendered to the British. Then, in the 1800s, Hilaire Sureau's descendants made two surprising leaps: first, to the extreme west of the former French province (now known by its British overlords as Lower Canada) and, second, in a shocking breach, across the border into the laps of the English. It was from this toehold on Georgian Bay in Lake Huron that Napoléon and

38   other members of his family would set out for Saskatchewan in 1904, to establish themselves in the wide-open spaces west of Saskatoon.

Some twenty-five years later, Napoléon, by now accompanied by his wife, Clarissa Marie née Parent, and four young children, would finally touch down in this house. Around them spread a grid of streets, laid out by the Temperance Colonization Society fifty years before, that paid tribute to the glories of the British Empire, with streets named Albert, Victoria, Lorne. How had the family coped with being planted in this "foreign" soil? What kind of a welcome had they found in the Last Best West of the Canadian prairies?

As I was wondering how to clothe the bones of fact with flesh and feeling, a promise of help materialized out of thin air. An email message appeared in my inbox offering to put me in touch with an actual, living descendant of Napoléon Sureau dit Blondin. "Howdy," it began invitingly, "I just turned up your query for information about my wife's grandfather via a Google search." Imagine: a granddaughter. Apparently, by poking around on the internet, I'd left a trail of digital footprints that led directly to my inbox. And it seemed that Napoléon's granddaughter—her name was Lorena—had also been working on her family tree and was willing to share what she had learned. But would we get to the heart of things? Would she be willing to share family secrets with an inquisitive stranger?

3

— MAKING CONNECTIONS —

Je n'aime pas les maisons neuves:
Leur visage est indifférent;
Les anciennes ont l'air de veuves
Qui se souviennent en pleurant.

I don't like new houses:
Their face is uncaring;
Old ones have the air of widows
Who remember through tears.

SULLY PRUDHOMME, "Les vieilles maisons," *Les solitudes,* 1869

A N EXCHANGE OF messages ensues. When I learn that Lorena and her husband live in Regina, a few hours' drive to the south, my first impulse is to pack my bag of questions, hop in the car, and turn up in time for tea. In my mind's eye, I can already see myself ringing the bell, waiting eagerly on the front step—but, no, that would be pushing it. It's one thing to stalk someone else's ancestors from a decorous distance and quite another to intrude, uninvited, into her day-to-day routine. Better to phone ahead.

The voice on the other end of the line is low-pitched and restrained. No, Lorena hadn't really known her grandfather

40   Napoléon Sureau dit Blondin. "I was born a month before he died," she says. "They carried me into the hospital so he could see me. That was all." Mentally, I rifle through my knowledge of Blondin vital stats. Napoléon died in Saskatoon in the fall of 1946. That would make Lorena a couple of years older than me.

But she'd heard about him growing up?

"Yes, of course. My dad talked about him. He was 'Paul' in the family, but I always call him N. S. My dad said N. S., my grandfather, was proud of his ancestors. Proud to be French Canadian."

"And you? Do you speak French?"

The line goes dead for an instant. Have I insulted her already? How would I feel if someone I'd never met called me out of the blue and started asking personal questions about what I could and couldn't do? But instead of the click of a cut-off connection, there's an exhalation of breath.

"No French. Not a word," she says. "Couldn't get it through my thick head. I remember the French teacher at my high school, meeting him one day in the hall. 'You should be a natural for this,' he said. 'Blondin. You're French.' But we only spoke English at home. I couldn't get it." Another pause. "Just couldn't."

I think of my very different experience: how my school-teacher father, whose own lost, ancestral language would have been Plattdeutsch, or Mennonite Low German, fell in love with the vision of a bilingual Canada (and possibly, innocently and briefly, with a fellow teacher who was similarly inclined, adding fuel to the flame). We're talking about the early 1960s, around the time Lorena would have been struggling with French in school. As for me, I was a kid in small-town Alberta, with no opportunity to test myself against the challenge of a second language and no awareness of the storm of

French–English tension brewing in the country during those years. The Royal Commission on Bilingualism and Biculturalism was always top of the news, but its findings were wasted on me. All I heard was a static hiss of meaningless, grown-up verbiage.

And yet the vision of a country in which the English and French languages enjoyed equal status in national affairs touched me personally. Every morning when I came downstairs for breakfast, I'd find my patriotic, and usually very dignified, father reading *L'actualité*, the French edition of *Maclean's* newsmagazine, as he pedaled away furiously on his exercise bike. Here was the unexpected, and slightly flushed, face of Canadian bilingualism.

For my dad, putting some muscle into improving his French had become a pleasure of citizenship. And when it was finally my turn to start learning a second language, at the age of fifteen, I was *très heureuse*. Swotty to my father's sweaty, I spent my weekends reviewing French grammar and conjugating irregular verbs. (Some people really know how to enjoy themselves.) But if it hadn't been for that chance to start learning French, or if the language had, for some reason, felt beyond my reach—as it had for Lorena Blondin—I would have grieved the loss. And, as far as I could tell, it wasn't even the language of my ancestors.

I cast around for something to say, but everything I think of sounds lame. "High school can be so miserable," I mumble, but fortunately, Lorena isn't listening. Instead, she's telling me about a conversation she had with her own dad.

"He told me my grandfather didn't speak real French. 'Métis French,' he said. I said, 'Yeah, sure. Quebec French.' But he insisted. 'No, Métis French.'"

42 "What do you make of that?" No meandering through my own thoughts now: I'm all attention.

"I've always wondered, I guess. I have dark skin and brown eyes, kind of Indian looking. I got teased at school. You know." A beat of silence. "When I told my dad, he said, 'You just tell them you're not Native. You're *French*.' So maybe the dark skin comes from my mother's side, people from Eastern Europe. We haven't found Métis connections on our family tree. Have you?"

I tell her about the second Napoléon Blondin and my inconclusive research. "But something could still turn up. I'll let you know if I find out anything, for sure."

"Okay," she says. "You know, it's about your house, that's why you're doing this, right? My grandfather *built* a house in Saskatoon, a new house, and he lost it. That's the story I've heard."

My heart skips a beat.

"It was on—I'd better check." She breaks off, and I hear a rustling of pages, as if she is leafing through a file. Please let it be this house. Please. I hold my breath.

"Crestwood," she says, "it was on Crestwood." Wrong address.

THE MINUTE I put down the phone, with a promise to talk again, I am on a quest to locate Napoléon Blondin's mystery building site. I've never heard of a Crestwood in Saskatoon, though that doesn't prove anything. Still, it's odd that I can't find any trace of it online, no Crestwood Blvd. or Cresc., not even a cul-de-sac. Odder yet, when I consult the listings in the civic directories—the year-by-year inventories in which

Diana had first encountered "Blondin, Napoleon S."—there's no sign of it there, either. So it's not a street name that was used in the past and has since been forgotten. As I'm running through other possible explanations (maybe he built a house in some other town?), an email from Lorena's husband arrives and saves the day again. It reads:

"Lorena says, 'I have spoken to my Uncle Charles and [your place] is indeed the house that N. S. built.' So there you go."

So there you go, indeed. My unlikely hero, Napoléon Sureau dit Blondin, had not only lived here with his family; he had built the place with his own hands. Every nail hammered into place. Every windowsill leveled and planed. Maybe his wife and kids had moved in partway through construction, allowing those bits and pieces of intimate memorabilia, the shed skin of everyday living, to be absorbed inside the walls. ("I'm sorry, Teacher," young Ralph might have said. "The house ate my homework.") From my phone conversation with Lorena, I know that Ralph was her father and that I'd missed my chance to meet him. He had died just over a year earlier, in the spring of 2013, aged ninety-three. Later, I will look up his obituary: "It is with heavy hearts that we have to say goodbye to Ralph Ernest Blondin." Of Napoléon and Clarissa's six children, only two are still alive. One, their eldest daughter, has closed the door on the past.

"I've tried, but she won't answer any questions about the family," Lorena tells me. "She says, 'It's over, my childhood is over.' She says, 'Why would you want to go back there?'"

But the other, her uncle Charles, is different. Although he lives near Calgary, six hours' drive to the west, and although the Blondin clan has never been especially close, he has always

44   been approachable, always been ready to help. "He's a good guy," Lorena says. What's more, even as an octogenarian, he has a prodigious memory, with perfect recall of every phone number and street address from his youth. If Uncle Charles says this is the place, there's no doubt about it. It is.

When Lorena and I pick up the phone again, there is only one subject to discuss. When would she like to come for a visit? Having pestered her with my intrusive questions, I am gratified to have something of value to offer in return. Come and see this lovely little house that your very own grandfather built. And you'd like to bring your sister? Yes, of course. And so, the next thing I know, not one but two of Napoléon and Clarissa's granddaughters are wheeling under the leafy canopy of the gracious street their grandfather chose for his home. Admittedly, the house that stands before them is no longer exactly as he intended it to be. For instance, Keith and I know, from scraping away at the siding, that the building was originally painted white with pale "heritage"-green trim. We have done it up in a soft turquoise, with white window frames and a cherry-blossom-pink front door. We hoped it would look like a place where happy people lived, and if it ended up resembling an ice cream parlor, well, we'd have to take that risk.

The other change we've made to the facade is the addition of a small window in the wall of the former-master-bedroom-that-is-now-my-office so that I can look outside as I work. As a result, by craning my neck ever so slightly, I am able to watch as two petite women—one with dark hair piled on top of her head, the other wearing multicolored leggings and sporting locks of reddish gold—climb out of their car, glance around

to get their bearings, and step toward the front door. Their
shoes ring on the painted boards as they climb the front steps,
almost as solid today as they were more than eighty years ago,
when their grandfather put them in place.

Once the introductions are over—the dark-haired one is
Lorena, as I'd guessed; the redhead, her sister, Fran—we make
a looping tour through the house, kitchen to dining room
to living room to office to den and then up the steep back
stairs. I can't remember if I mentioned the possible connection between the flow-through layout of the upper floor and
the houses of New France. But I do remember how relaxed
and at home the sisters seemed to be, as if they were walking
through a space that was already familiar to them.

"This must have been where the children slept," one of
them says, considering the connected rooms upstairs. "There
were four of them then, weren't there? The two girls, Don, and
Dad."

"And, remember how Dad used to say he'd sit on the
stairs—"

These stairs.

"—and listen to the adults talking in the kitchen?"

"Not just talking. Arguing. There was a lot of shouting.
That's what Dad always said."

A small figure slumps in the narrow stairway, his ear
pressed against the wall. The house rings with angry words:
Crisse! Ostie! He is eight years old in 1928, the year the family
moves in. He will turn twelve in 1932, the year they leave for a
house across the river, a shack with no indoor toilet. Napoléon
Sureau dit Blondin built a home for his family, and he lost it.
No wonder there was shouting.

46 THROUGH THE INTERMEDIARY of Lorena's husband's emails ("I just leave the computer to him," she tells me with a wry grin), she has offered to share what she knows about her family's story. Now, true to her word, and having seen all there is to see of this little house, she produces an ordinary-looking three-ring binder, the kind you can buy in any stationery store. But there is nothing at all ordinary about what it holds. This is Lorena's collection of family treasures. Look, here is a photo of this very house when it was being built. The earth around the site is bare and trampled, and the structure lacks windows and doors, but from the line of the foundations to the curve of the eaves, the place is unmistakable. If there were any doubt about the authorship of the house—which there isn't, since Uncle Charles has spoken—this picture would lay it to rest. Napoléon must have downed tools for a moment to document his work-in-progress.

In the background, across the side street, the photo also catches a glancing view of the house where, as I know from perusing those invaluable civic directories, one of his brothers lived for a while. That dwelling was torn down a couple of years ago (a handsome clawfoot tub on the second floor dangling, suspended in midair, before plunging into a cloud of dust and debris) to be replaced by a modernist fortress.

If there was strife and shouting in the Blondin household, it is not evident in the family photos that Lorena is handing around. One snapshot shows three of the Blondin children, aged perhaps eight to twelve, standing up to their knees in a luxuriant patch of potatoes. From the houses in the background, it is clear that the picture was taken on the boulevard outside our back door. "That's Dad in the middle," one of the sisters says, pointing to a boy with slicked-back hair and hands stuffed into his trouser pockets. The children are neat and well-dressed and look healthy; their smiles are sweet. And the same sweetness infuses the portraits of their parents, Napoléon and Clarissa, captured (I'm told) on their wedding day, in 1916. The bridegroom is appropriately dark and handsome, with a broad forehead, aquiline nose, and laughing eyes. A faint smile plays around his mouth, as if he cannot quite believe his good fortune. The bride is cherubic, with a glowing complexion, soft curls, and a clear, direct gaze.

"My grandmother was beautiful," Lorena says, reading my thoughts. "So tiny. Blue eyes. Fair skin." Her voice softens. "We all loved her. And how she loved to dance."

"Remember how she'd just show up, unannounced, for a visit?" Fran interposes. "Wouldn't tell you she was coming. Wouldn't even let you pick her up from the bus. She was a real free spirit."

There are lots of pictures of Clarissa in the album. "Clara," Fran corrects me. "She was always Clara."

Okay; there are lots of pictures of Clara. Head held high, on a dock, gazing into the distance. Looking adorable in a bicorne hat, a baby in her arms. Squinting into the sun, a hand wrapped protectively around one of her daughters' shoulders. I recall what I've learned about her from my research, in all those weeks when I've been pursuing phantoms. Like the Sureau dit Blondins, the Parents are certifiably *Québécois de souche*. The family's foundational male ancestor, Pierre, was a master butcher, recruited in the 1650s to serve at Boucherville, the first organized community in New France, where he gave rise to an immense lineage. He and his wife, the astonishing Jeanne Badeau, got things off to a rousing start by acquiring

48 farmland, establishing a successful stone quarry, and engaging in endless litigations with their business associates. Jeanne took a leading role in all these endeavors while at the same time producing a brood of eighteen children. Apart from one who died as an infant, all the others (even the bonus set of triplets) survived to adulthood and produced a grand total of 195 grandchildren. That's a lot of birthdays to remember. And so things continued through successive generations of Pierres and Simons, Marie-Annes and Marie-Jeannes.

By the early 1800s, Clara's branch of the family had made its way to the westernmost reaches of French Canada, to settle in the very same parish as the Sureau dit Blondins. It was there that Clara's great-grandmother Josette Parent gained such a reputation for clairvoyance that people began to seek her out to have their fortunes told. Perhaps she alone foresaw the way in which the two families were fated to become intertwined, for when the push came to expand from Québec into northern Ontario in the 1850s, both families answered the call. In this new setting, Josette offered her prognostications to a broader clientele with the assistance of a niece, who provided translation from French to English.

More to the point of our story, Ontario was also the place where the connection between the Blondins and Parents was first sanctified, through the marriage of Napoléon Sureau dit Blondin's cousin Rose Anna to Josette Parent's grandson George. The wedding took place in Tiny Township, Simcoe County, Ontario, in 1897. Rose Anna and George's eldest daughter, Clarissa Marie, was born there the following year.

"N. S. and Clara were related, you know," Lorena says, as I hand the photos to her and watch as she snaps the pages back into place. "But I expect you already know that. Second cousins."

I nod—yes, I did know they were related. I'm not surprised, because marriages between relatives were common among people who lived in close communities; my Sherk great-grandparents had been "kissing cousins," too. But I don't let on that Lorena is mistaken about her grandparents' degree of kinship. Napoléon and Clara weren't second cousins; they were first cousins once removed.

Still, it's not my place to sour the moment with my superior expertise. So instead of trying to score a point, I spread out my own small stash of treasures for Lorena and Fran to peruse: the torn pages, the ragged collar (not entirely unlike the one constricting Napoléon's neck in his portrait), the flattened box inscribed with their father, Ralph's, childish script. As soiled and broken as these objects are, the sisters pick them up one by one, turn them over, pass them from hand to hand. It's no small thing to be in touch with the cherished dead.

And there's also my one surviving photograph to consider, the crumpled negative. By now, I've realized that, given the miracles of modern technology, I can scan and print the image without difficulty. As a result, the figures that previously looked like a troupe of zombies have resolved into a line of five normal human beings dressed in old-fashioned clothes (ankle-length dresses for the ladies, wide lapels and hats for the gents), standing in front of a turn-of-the-century car (acetylene-gas headlights, cloth top held up by struts). In the background, beyond the automobile, screened by scrubby trees, a body of water catches the glint of midsummer sunshine.

My gaze sweeps across the line of faces, some of which are too blurred and damaged to read, and settles on the two figures on the right-hand side of the image, a round-faced woman with a steady gaze and a man with a strong nose, his hands plunged deep into the pockets of his trousers. "What do you think?" I ask my guests. "See anyone you know?"

The sisters take their time studying the photograph, but in the end, they both shake their heads. "I'm not sure," Lorena says. "Maybe try Uncle Chick? He might be able to help."

"Uncle Chick?"

She laughs. "Sorry. Uncle Charles. I don't know why we've always called him that." (What a family for pseudonyms these Blondins are turning out to be.)

"Do you think, maybe, he'd—"

"I can ask." The man is in his eighties, I remind myself, and there is absolutely no reason for him to let me in. Napoléon and Clara's youngest son. Someone who grew up in their inner circle, a person who'd heard their stories from their own lips. As unlikely as it seems that he will say yes, I can't help hoping.

TOO SOON, IT is time for the sisters to pack up and head for home. As we say our goodbyes, Fran reaches into her purse and pulls out a small cloth bag. Inside are two porcelain medallions, which, she tells me, are of her own design and making. Would I like one of them?

"She's the artist in the family," Lorena says. "We're very proud of her."

How could I refuse, not that I want to, of course. As I consider the offerings in Fran's outstretched palms, the choice makes itself, and my eyes settle on a white disc over-written with flourishes of black. Three women are dancing a wild fandango across the face of the moon. It's only much later that I will realize what I have been given. More than a hostess gift. More than a token of acceptance, nosy parker that I am. More than an expression of Fran's own redheaded persona. What I have in my hand is a memento of Clara, great-granddaughter of Josette, descendant of Jeanne Badeau, a spirited woman with a mind of her own.

AS MUCH AS I've enjoyed meeting the Blondin sisters, I have to admit that the visit has left me a little bruised. Before they arrived, I'd felt quite smug about how much I knew, all the precious scraps of information that I'd pulled out of the wood-work, both figurative and literal. (And of course, I was also the go-to person on "first cousins once removed.") But Lorena, in particular, has made me see how much I still had to learn. The characters I'd been pursuing through my research were as two-dimensional as stickmen, mere names and dates on the page. And even at that beginners' level of understanding, I hadn't always succeeded in getting things straight. Unless I wanted to embarrass myself in front of Uncle Chick, I was going to have to do a lot more homework.

For instance, one of the pictures in Lorena's album was an almost unreadable portrait of a bearded man with a bee-keeper's veil drawn over his head, manhandling a large wooden hive. "Cléophas," she'd said. "He was N. S.'s father. You know that, right?"

"Yes."

"This is the only photo we have of him, but I think he must have been quite a character. You saw where he'd listed himself on the census as a 'free-thinker'?"

Um, no, I'd missed that. Just as I'd missed any and all mention of his third wife, Philomène, who died after the family came west and was buried in the cemetery at the small town of Harris, Saskatchewan. And while I knew that the Blondins had homesteaded in that district and that later Napoléon had run a store in town, I didn't know anything about the time his business had burned down. No, I hadn't observed the shocking omission on his marriage certificate—the gaping blank space where his mother's name should have appeared. No, I hadn't noticed the almost-twenty-year difference in ages that separated him from Clara.

The lesson was painfully clear. If I hoped to come close to understanding what had befallen this deeply rooted French-Canadian family when it was transplanted to the west, I was going to have to dial up my attention to detail. And even then, even on full alert, I could easily misread the clues. I'd always assumed, for example, that people like the Blondins who have a coherent ethnic identity would be proud of who they were. This is partly because my own mixed European background makes me something of a mutt. (As a child, when I'd ask my mom about our ethnicity, she'd reply casually, "You're a little bit of this and that, dear. Heinz 57, really.") So it seemed to me that the Blondins, who had spoken and sung and, yes, shouted at each other in French since the beginning of time, would be proud of their heritage and on guard to defend it. Whether Québec French or Métis French, they would have loved their language. But no. This had not been the case, not for Clara.

"That's what my dad said," Lorena had told me. "If my grandfather spoke to her in French, she refused to answer him. Even at home. No French. Only English."

I was stunned by this revelation. Why would anyone ever think of imposing such a grotesque rule? No French? Not even in the privacy of your own four walls? This isn't what I had expected from my sprightly dancing girl. Yet, come to think of it, there was not a single word of French on the pages that had tumbled out of the walls. *Pas de recettes de glaçage*, just recipes for frosting from the Boston Cooking-School. Desensitized by the normalcy of an English-only world, I hadn't even noticed that the Blondins had parted company with their ancestors.

"I think my grandmother was lonely," Lorena said, when she saw how shocked I was. "She just wanted to make friends. The other women, I don't think they ever let her in. It twists my heart to think of it."

How lonely would you have to be to give up your mother tongue?

4

─ AN AGITATION ─
OF GHOSTS

*La tristesse vient
de la solitude du coeur.*

Sadness comes from
the loneliness of the heart.

MONTESQUIEU, *Arsace et Isménie,* 1730

WALKED THE SISTERS to their car and watched them
drive down the block. What was I to make of Lorena's
revelation? Yes, it was disappointing to think that Clara
Blondin might have been unhappy here. But to give up your
natal language? Really, that was too much. I stomped back to
the house and pulled the door shut with a thump.

There had to be more to the story, some deep ache, something I didn't yet understand. The more I reflected on Clara's
unaccountable decision, the more I began to suspect that it
needed to be seen with a wider lens, as part of a bigger story.
What if the isolation that she had suffered hadn't been hers
alone? What if her loneliness, like her Frenchness, had passed
down through her family tree, from generation to generation?

After all, there had been a moment when, for the people of New France, eternity had stopped, when roots that spanned centuries and continents had been abruptly cut off.[1] In my mind's eye, I can still almost see the paragraphs in my high school history text (right-hand column, black type on a glossy page) recounting the defeat of the French by the British on the Plains of Abraham in 1759. I remember the twist in my heart when I learned that France had deliberately abandoned its own children, the sixty thousand French colonists who were settled along the Saint Lawrence, preferring instead to retain a cluster of sugar-producing islands in the Caribbean. In the end, the French Catholic people of New France had been ceded to the Protestant British not by the sword but at the conference table, with a flourish of a quill pen. And my Napoléon and Clara's great-great-grandparents had been among them.

"DO YOU THINK things that happened in the past, way back, a century or two ago—" I begin haltingly, stop, and start again. "I mean, do you think that the big events of history sometimes echo down through people's lives for generations afterward?"

I'm putting my questions to Keith. (With Diana long since grown up and launched into a life of her own, he is the person I naturally turn to for wise counsel.) Now he is looking at me askance, as if surprised by what I've just said.

"Yes, of course," he answers. "Isn't that obvious?"

"Even if the people all those years later, the descendants, don't know the details about what happened in the past?"

56   "Yes, I think so," he says. "You don't have to know *why* your parents and grandparents do what they do to be shaped by them."

Right, on with the story, then.

FOR THE POPULATION of New France, the Conquest and the long war that preceded it were disastrous. "*Le Canada est écrasé,*" the historians tell us. "*La Nouvelle France s'efface de la carte.*"[2] Many people were left homeless, farms and settlements lay in ruins, the economy lurched to a halt. To make matters worse, a gang of obnoxious new arrivals had burst onto the scene, intent on turning the crisis to their own advantage. They were English-speaking entrepreneurs from England and Massachusetts, looking to make a quick buck. Boisterous and entitled, they encouraged the incoming authorities to rule with an iron hand, by subjecting their new French subjects to the full force of British law and tradition. If that meant barring the entire Papist population of the colony from medicine, the military, and most other professions, so be it. Roman Catholics were denied civil rights in Britain: making an exception for mere colonists, the incomers said, would violate "our most sacred Laws and Libertys" and tend to "the utter subversion of the protestant Religion."[3]

The new colonial governor, however, was unmoved by this argument. His first priority was to ensure a peaceful transition. The last thing anyone wanted was an armed insurrection like the one already brewing in the Thirteen Colonies. If all it took to win the loyalty of the king's new Francophone subjects were a few minor concessions, then the way forward was clear.

In due course, legislation was passed to recognize the French land-tenure system—thereby protecting the riverfront holdings of *habitant* farmers like the Blondins and Parents— and to remove the legal restrictions that were imposed on Roman Catholics in other parts of the British Empire. In Québec alone, a Catholic male could serve on a jury or train as a pharmacist without denying the teachings of his church. As for the Anglo business lobby, they were, in the governor's candid opinion, a bunch of "Licentious Fanaticks"[4]—bigots and schemers—whose secret purpose was the complete subordination of the *Canadiens*. But they wouldn't get away with it on his watch.

Still, even this kinder, gentler takeover came as a shock. A cabal of English-speaking interests was swaggering around the colony, accusing the population of disloyalty and casting scorn on the Catholic Church. Freedoms that had previously been taken for granted now had to be bargained for. The heart-connection with France—the ties of family, custom, and language—had been broken, once and for all. A troubadour of the day expressed the mood in verse.

> *Amant, que j't'ai donc fait*
> *Qui puiss' tant te déplaire?*
> *Est-c'que j'tai pas aimé*
> *Comm'tu l'as mérité?*[5]

> Lover, what have I done
> That so displeased you?
> Did I not love you
> As you deserved?

58 "I'M STILL A little mad at her, you know," I admit to Keith over supper that night. We are at home, seated in our dining room, with the kitchen to the west and the living room to the east, midway between the Rockies and the Laurentians.

"Which her would that be?" he asks, mildly. After all our years together, he is no longer alarmed when I break out of a private reverie with a seemingly random remark. For better or worse, however, he has not learned to read my mind and occasionally requires clarification.

"Clara. Clara Blondin. And I'm not actually mad at her. More disappointed, really." A sigh. "I mean, I know that we all live in context. As much as we might like to go into our little houses and shut all the windows and doors, we can't seal ourselves off. We live in history. You know what I mean?"

He nods encouragingly.

"Things that are beyond our control can make or break any of us."

"The four horsemen of the apocalypse," he says. "Death, famine, war, and conquest. There's a famous painting by a Russian artist—what's his name?—Vasnetsov." Keith is an art historian and knows this kind of thing.

"Yes," I say, "that's exactly it. Conquest. French Canada was conquered. And I get it that being under the boot of an enemy causes damage, even if the boot was, I don't know, the satin slippers that English gentlemen wore in the eighteenth century."

"And you're angry with Clara Blondin because—?"

I pick up my fork and put it down, reach for my glass of wine.

"It's just that I've been reading about what happened after the Conquest, trying to see the big picture. What would make a person refuse to speak, or even be spoken to, in her own language?"

Another nod of agreement. "That's pretty extreme."

"I've been trying to convince myself that it goes way back, that the despair set in a long time ago. But, you know, lots of people never gave up. Think of the people who started my choir, for example. I want Clara to have been like them."

The choir in question, my choir, is Le Choeur des plaines, a community choral society dedicated to performing "*les plus belles chansons du répertoire francophone*," the most beautiful songs of the French repertoire. *Choeur* translates as choir, but it happily invites confusion with *coeur*, or heart, and the ensemble is proud to identify itself as an important element in maintaining Francophone culture in this English-speaking stronghold. Curiously, I first learned about it thanks to a performance of a musical masterpiece that comes to us direct from eighteenth-century Britain, from the very decades when the English military was making mincemeat of the French. On this particular evening, however, an amateur choir was making mincemeat of the *Messiah*. Seldom had the yoke of Handel's allegros been less easy, or the footfall of his trills and runs more burthensome. In fact, the whole thing quickly became so unbearable that Keith and I walked out at intermission, something unheard of for us, but not before we'd taken note of the tenor soloist, whose clear, pure voice had provided the evening's one saving grace. The program identified him as the conductor of Le Choeur des plaines.

Fortunately for me, Le Choeur turned out to take an open-door approach to new admissions. "I've never known us to

60 turn anyone away," a voice on the other end of the line told me when I called to inquire. And so ever since, I've spent one happy evening a week in the music room of l'École canadienne-française, a few blocks from my house, practicing *les plus belles chansons* of the likes of Gabriel Fauré, Claude-Michel Schönberg, and Gilles Vigneault.

"The people who started the choir treasured their language. Napoléon and Clara, their ancestors had spoken French forever. Then *pfft*, they throw it away as if it doesn't matter."

Keith raises an eyebrow and fixes me with a skeptical gaze. "When exactly was the choir founded? Twenty-five years ago, isn't that what you said? And when did the Blondins live here? The 1920s versus the 1990s: you're talking about two different worlds."

He has a point. I shrug in acquiescence.

"You wouldn't do that for no reason," he continues, "give up your mother tongue. Maybe your Blondins were just trying to survive. I don't think you've drilled down far enough to find the answers yet."

Right, then. It's time to keep opening cupboard doors and see what tumbles out.

THE ENTENTE BETWEEN the government and *les Canadiens* would turn out to be short-lived. When the Thirteen Colonies declared their independence from Great Britain in 1776, they upended the game board of colonial power, sending pawns and rooks flying in every direction. Among the players displaced by this crisis were thousands of American colonists who were opposed to independence and who fled en masse. Many of these ultra-conservative, ultra-monarchist, ultra-Protestant refugees resettled in the British colony of Nova Scotia, but about six thousand of them ended up near present-day Kingston, then within the boundaries of the Province of Québec. A decade or so later, my own Sherk ancestors (pacifists during the revolutionary war but pro-British nonetheless) would pull up stakes in Pennsylvania and make the trek north, adding to the incursion of English-speaking settlers.

Shaken by what they saw as the dismembering of Empire, the loyalists arrived in Québec with the intention, as one of their leaders put it, of creating "a perfect image and exact copy of the British government and constitution."[6] Imagine their distress when they found themselves instead governed by French civil law, impeded by a feudal system of land tenure, and surrounded by people who submitted to the Pope and spoke "foreign." Worse yet, they were ruled by an appointed despot, based in distant Montréal, without any sign of government by and for the people. Although a tiny minority of the population, the newcomers were mighty in their influence, and London was quick to respond to their demands. In 1791, the sprawling colony of Québec was divided into two side-by-side jurisdictions: Upper Canada to the west, with British civil law and freehold land tenure, and Lower Canada to the east, still a homeland for the French.

Although the loyalist newcomers were satisfied with this arrangement, the commercial class of Montréal, by now in complete control of the economy, were indignant about what they saw as more weak-kneed pandering to the French. In their view, it was high time for the "old settlers," the Francophones, to recognize the superiority of British institutions, give up their alien ways, and become ordinary British subjects. Faced

62 with this hostility, the *habitants* of Québec rallied to defend their distinctive heritage. "There are 120,000 of us," they dared to remind the king. As a majority of the population, they felt their interests should "carry the balance."[7] Still smarting from the loss of its Thirteen Colonies, rattled by rising sectarian tensions in Ireland, and freshly alarmed by news of the revolution in France, London decided to take the hint. Best to keep on the right side of as many people as you could.

But behind that cloak of smiling benevolence, there now lurked a sneer. The new constitution granted each of the Canadas a democratically elected assembly but was careful to deny those bodies any real power. Authority was vested in officials appointed by the Crown and answerable only to the colonial office in London. This setup left the administration open to cronyism, self-aggrandizement, and backroom shenanigans, tactics that fit neatly within the skill set of the colonial elite. Nepotism and corruption were endemic. Decisions were made in secret and imposed without consideration for the harm they caused. Meanwhile, the people's elected representatives could do little but mutter, obstruct, and fume. And so the tension continued to mount through the 1810s, the 1820s, the 1830s.

The final insult—the spark that would set off a violent explosion—came midway through that decade. In 1834, the legislature of Lower Canada confronted the British government with ninety-two demands for reform. Top of the list, not surprisingly, was a call for democracy and an end to the excesses of the governing clique. In this, they spoke in unison with their neighbors in Upper Canada, who were advancing similar claims. But the French-speaking colonists also had grievances that were uniquely their own.

Item: The British Parliament had passed a law to reform the seigneurial system in Lower Canada that was so badly worded it threatened to deprive farmers of their land.

Item: The British government had granted vast tracts of the province to London-based colonization companies and other speculators, thereby depriving the French-speaking residents an opportunity to expand. What was to become of the ever-increasing population of sons and daughters?

Item: The colonial administrators systematically discriminated against people of French ancestry. Why else, in a jurisdiction where French speakers still held a considerable majority, would Anglophones hold two-thirds of government jobs, including all those with the greatest responsibility and the highest pay?

Three years would pass without an official response from London. When the answer finally came, in the spring of 1837, it was a slap in the face. Apart from a small concession (an offer to reconsider the land-tenure issues), the British government either ignored the requests entirely or dismissed them with a single haughty word: any such change would be "inadvisable." As tempers rose in the months that followed— there was an armed clash between English loyalists and Francophone *patriotes* in the streets of Montréal that fall—the British authorities called up military reinforcements, and the population steeled itself for trouble.

No conflict is lonelier than a civil war. Communities tear apart along all the usual shear lines—class, ethnicity, religion—and new rifts open up. Even among the *patriotes*, there were disagreements over tactics, as some adherents sharpened their arguments to continue the war of words, while others organized militias and began sharpening their scythes

64   and pitchforks for battle. But perhaps the most painful break of all occurred between the *patriotes* and their church. In the decades since the Conquest, Roman Catholicism had become almost synonymous with French Canada, woven into every birth and death, every hope and fear. But now this guardian of the people had chosen to ally itself with the enemy, by standing on the side of constituted authority. In the parish of Saint-Polycarpe, in the southwestern corner of the colony, parishioners were so enraged when their priest instructed them to sing a *Te Deum* to honor Britain's newly crowned queen that they sealed him in a barrel, delivered him to the quay, and put him on a ship bound for the United States.

Clara Parent's ancestors lived in that parish; her great-grandmother Josette was married in that church. Wherever their loyalties fell, whatever their political stance, it hurts one's heart just to think of it.

AS FOR THE Blondin side of the family, the *guerre des Patriotes* found them in the parish of Sainte-Rose-de-Lima, just north of Montréal, in the epicenter of the trouble. Napoléon's grandfather Augustin turned sixteen that year, 1837, and it is easy to imagine him as a fresh, unshaven face in the crowd, a thousand strong, that shouldered into the local inn that autumn. Perhaps he climbed onto a bench at the back of the smoky hall to catch a glimpse of the orators, including the cousin of the famous leader of the Parti Patriote, Louis-Joseph Papineau. "The church has fomented the trouble," someone shouted, and the gathering roared its approval. The laws governing land tenure were "*partiale, secrète et vicieuse."* Agreed. France had contributed to the rise of civilization, sciences, literature, and the arts, and had never taken second place to the British. "Forward," everyone shouted. When the crowd dispersed that night, it was clear that trouble was coming.[8]

A few miles from Sainte-Rose, on the other side of the Rivière du Chêne, sat the village of Saint-Eustache. In normal times, people moved freely back and forth between the two settlements; as an infant, Augustin had been taken to this neighboring village for baptism. But in these terrible new days, Saint-Eustache had become known as a hotbed of *patriote* agitation, and the British army, stung by a humiliating defeat in its first engagement with the rebels, was on the march north. The villagers tried to deflect the attack by destroying a strategic bridge, but the army sent out a party of artillery to test the river ice. Then came the ordinary weekday morning when two thousand redcoats marched on Saint-Eustache, their field guns and rocket launcher rumbling behind them, their bayonets glinting in the sun.

The might of Empire had been deployed against two hundred ill-equipped villagers, and the outcome was never in serious doubt. A few hours into the battle, soldiers breached the church where the last of the defenders had taken refuge and set fire to the altar cloths. As the conflagration rose through the building, the *patriotes* leaped from the window casements and were met by gunfire as they fell. Three soldiers and seventy villagers died in Saint-Eustache on that dreadful afternoon. Jubilant in victory, the loyalist forces ransacked the entire district, reducing houses and farm buildings to smoldering ruins. This was the price of advancing the cause of freedom. This was the price of being French.

66   By the time the resistance was fully suppressed a year later, a total of three hundred *patriotes* had fallen in battle, fourteen hundred more were imprisoned, and three thousand had been forced into exile in the United States. Twelve men, convicted of high treason, were taken to the grim, stone-walled Prison Au-Pied-du-Courant in Montréal, marched onto a high scaffold, and hung by the neck until dead.

WHILE I WAS piecing together the details of this calamity, a friend from choir named Jean posted a comment on his Facebook feed. He is the mainstay of our tenor section, and though he has lived in Saskatoon for many years, he grew up in Québec. It seems that a radio station in Québec City had recently decided to test the general knowledge of CEGEP (freshman university) students by challenging them to name the capital city of Manitoba. "Their answers?" Jean lamented. "Yellowknife, Régina, Victoria, Saskatchewan (!), Saskatoon, Alberta (!)." Not one of the students questioned had given the correct response. "Décourageant," he wrote. "Québec–Canada, *encore les deux solitudes apparemment*," still two solitudes apparently.

Yes, disheartening. But what about the gaping holes in my own knowledge? Sure, I could rhyme off the provincial capitals; but if you'd asked me, even a month ago, to map the historical landscape of Québec–Canada, to describe the shaky foundations on which our national house is built, I wouldn't have known where to start. Of course, I'd heard of the Rebellions of 1837; we'd learned about them in school. William Lyon Mackenzie versus the Family Compact, Louis-Joseph Papineau versus the Château Clique. But the conflict had always been presented in brightly optimistic trappings, as a stage in the inevitable March Toward Democracy and Responsible Government. There was no place in this sanitized telling for villages left in ruins, for gunshots and gallows. For defeat.

Three hundred dead in battle. Fourteen hundred imprisoned. Three thousand forced to flee. Twelve men marched to the scaffold and executed.

Those harrowing events must have left their mark on everyone, including the ancestral Blondins and Parents. Generations later, a small boy will sit in the stairwell of a house in the middle of the prairies, hearing voices raised in distress. "No French," a woman will plead. "No French in this house."

5

— TOWNSHIP OF TINY —

*Les souvenirs, c'est ce qui reste
quand l'oubli vous a guéri d'un malheur.*

Memories are what's left
when forgetting has cured you of a misfortune.

FRÉDÉRIC DARD, *Les pensées de San-Antonio,* 1996

ALL I HAD wanted were a few "home truths," an understanding of what it means to be rooted here, on this street corner, in this city, on the banks of the South Saskatchewan River. Now I was being told that my house of stories was larger, more complex, and much bloodier than I had ever guessed. Although my life went on as if nothing had changed, I was anxious and disoriented. Then one day when I was walking across town to do some errands, I had the good fortune to meet a friend whom I hadn't seen for several years. Emma Lind grew up around the corner from us, on Temperance Street, and I've known her since she was a kid. These days, however, she is based in Ottawa, where she is completing a PhD in Canadian cultural studies. Just the person who could help me.

Over lunch at our crowded corner café, Emma introduces me to the concept of a "usable past." It's the idea that the stories historians choose to tell—or to silence—are not pre-ordained. They are "curated," or chosen, Emma says, and then "consolidated to form a heroic narrative."

"The omissions are designed to look like nothing is missing," she explains, when she sees me looking confused. "The silences don't sound like silences."

"And so, when we start to notice gaps in the story—" I begin.

She nods. "When we critique official histories, it's like pointing a finger and saying, 'Look over there. See that empty corner? It's really a screen. Someone would rather you didn't know what's going on behind it.'"

I walk home slowly, wondering what else might be lurking in the shadows.

THE GUERRE DES PATRIOTES was over, but for the Blondins, there was no peace. Soon, Augustin had drifted a day's travel upriver to the parish of Saint-Polycarpe, the very place, as it happens, where the Parents had settled. There, together with his young wife, Adéline Trottier, and a baby son named Cléophas (our Napoléon's father-to-be), Augustin took land on the outskirts of the community. But the family must still have felt unsettled because, after only a couple of decades, Augustin and Adéline packed up the entire family, by now a brood of eight, and headed west, to settle in the territory formerly known as Upper Canada and now—on the eve of Canadian Confederation—readying itself to become the Province of Ontario. "Ut incepit Fidelis sic permanet," the

70 new jurisdiction's motto read. "Loyal she began, loyal she remains."

"Loyal," of course, meant "British." White, Anglo-Saxon, Protestant. English-speaking.

And yet, to the loyalists' loud displeasure, there existed within the new province enclaves where the population was stubbornly Roman Catholic and even more stubbornly French. One of those places was a knobby finger of land that juts north into Lake Huron's Georgian Bay. That's where the Blondins were headed, to the community of Lafontaine, near the farthermost end of the Penetanguishene Peninsula. Here, in the Township of Tiny, the French presence ran deep. In the early 1600s, Samuel de Champlain had paddled the waters around the peninsula and had spent the winter in a Huron settlement. It was there that a member of his entourage, a priest named Father Joseph Le Caron, had celebrated the first mass in what would one day become Ontario. A few decades later, in the 1640s, the Jesuit missionaries Jean de Brébeuf and Gabriel Lalemant were tortured and killed nearby, long afterward to be venerated by Catholics, including the devout of Lafontaine, as *les saints martyrs canadiens*, the sainted Canadian martyrs.

But that was in the distant past, and the glory and terror of those early times had long since faded away. The year was 1866. What did this remote spit of land have to offer to incomers like the Blondins? On the plus side, the settlement was proudly French and Catholic, offering the reassurance of a home away from home. The community was named in tribute to Louis-Hippolyte Ménard dit La Fontaine, the *patriote* orator and political operative who had guided French Canada through the decades of repression that followed the rebellion. When the use of French was prohibited in the Canadian legislature in the 1840s, La Fontaine had fought to bring it back. When an ugly row broke out about providing compensation to people in Lower Canada for losses suffered during the war—a benefit that had been extended to Upper Canadians without a second thought—La Fontaine had stood firm for justice.

"The end has come," an English-language newspaper in Montréal brayed the day the compensation was approved. "Anglo-Saxons, you must live for your future; your race and your blood shall be your supreme law, if you are true to yourselves."[1]

In response to this call to action, a mob of loyalist thugs took to the streets, fired shots through La Fontaine's office window, and burned the parliament building in Montréal to the ground. And yet, even in the face of this violence, La Fontaine did not flinch. His memory alone was enough to give a person courage.

On the minus side, however, the community to which La Fontaine had given his name was miserably remote. The railroad ended at the town of Barrie, fifty miles to the south. From there, goods could be shipped onward by steamship, if you happened to have the cash; otherwise, it was a bone-jarring journey by stagecoach or oxcart on a sand-bogged track. And there were other challenges that wouldn't become apparent until after you'd settled in. Although nominally united by language and religion, the community around Lafontaine was riven by cliques, defined by where your family had come from and when they'd moved in. The first arrivals, in the 1820s, had been Métis families from nearby Drummond Island, who, as a reward for supporting the British in one of the endless colonial wars, had been granted land on the steep, heavily forested slopes around Penetang Harbour.

72 Next to come, in succeeding decades, were two waves of settlers from different parts of Lower Canada, followed, in due course, by the belated arrivals from Saint-Polycarpe.

Naturally, the early arrivals on the peninsula (including the Métis who had assimilated into settler families) had secured the best land for themselves. As latecomers, the Blondins had no choice but to make the best of what was left. A map from 1871 shows Augustin and Cléophas, father and son, established on either side of a concession-line road. Although inconveniently distant from Lafontaine and on the outer margins of the French settlement, they had an impressive four hundred acres between them. A few minutes' walk down the road, the shining waters of Lake Huron lapped onto a glittering shore. But even this stunning natural beauty would prove to be poor compensation for the fragile, sandy soil. Today, the Blondins' former holdings have reverted to stands of spindly trees, and the glittering shore at the end of the road is a resort called Balm Beach.

THE RESORT WAS half-deserted the afternoon I stopped by for a visit. In the glow of a setting sun, picnickers were folding up beach umbrellas and calling their children out of the waves. Haze ghosted the far horizon across the infinity of the lake. Augustin Sureau dit Blondin, the head of the family, had died not long after they arrived here, still in his fifties, leaving his widow and several dependent children without any means of support. It had fallen to Cléophas, as eldest son, to pick up the burden. By then, he had a family of his own to care for, through his marriage to a girl named

Georgina Trottier (a cousin of his mother, Adéline, though many times removed). Births had followed in quick succession: two daughters, Antoinette and Allelina, and a troupe of sons: Alexandre, Hercules, Télémaque, and Ulysse. Michel-Napoléon, my Napoléon, had arrived on September 11, 1879, the middle child in the family.

It felt good to imagine the Blondin children here in this dazzle of light and wind-on-water, running and shrieking like the modern-day kids who were now being led to waiting cars and taken home to bed. And yet I knew that the Blondins' childhood had been marred by sadness. Their mother, Georgina, had died, at the tender age of thirty-one, when Napoléon was only eight. His eldest sister, Antoinette, succumbed to tuberculosis two years later. An English-speaking stepmother named Martha had come and gone in a matter of years, presumably another premature death. Through it all, Cléophas had somehow managed to keep his household afloat. One year, for instance, he made a few dollars selling oats and straw to the reformatory in the town of Penetanguishene, and there was often work to be had in the local sawmills. But Cléophas was a farmer; what he wanted was productive land. By the mid-1800s, he had acquired a nice little property just outside of Lafontaine, only sixty-five acres but still, a step ahead.

And yet, he was profoundly discontented. If the ties that bind had become frayed in his father's time, for Cléophas something had snapped. Despite the anti-clericalism that lingered after la guerre des Patriotes, he had been brought up Catholic, and even as an adult, he had honored the rituals of the church. He and Georgina were married in the magnificent stone cathedral l'Église de la Sainte-Croix, which dominated the village of Lafontaine. As his children were born, he carried them to the priests for baptism. When his parents died, and then Georgina, he laid them to rest in the church's peaceful graveyard, with its broad views of rolling hills.

But though he had gone through these motions, his heart was in revolt. Asked to declare his religion for the census of 1881, he replied with such vehemence that the census taker ground his pencil hard against the form. *Rationalist.* The rest of the entries have faded away with the years, but that forceful declaration still stands out, bold and emphatic in its defiance. The rest of the family, including his then-wife, Martha, were listed as Methodist, this at a time when "mixed marriages" between Protestants and Catholics were a shocking affront to community standards.

And so it was, several years later, that Mr. C. S. Blondin of Tiny Township, Simcoe County, sent a blistering letter to the *Toronto Mail*, complaining about the quality of education provided by his local public school. Although supposedly non-sectarian, the school was, in his fervent opinion, tainted by Catholicism. Just look at the book his little daughter had been given as a prize: it was all about the Mass!

"I assert that the education the children get with us is worse than no education at all," he declared, "for their minds are warped, filled with prejudice and wrong views of life generally. The man is killed within the scholar, to be substituted by a pigmy."

When this indictment landed on the minister of education's desk, he ordered an immediate investigation. Cléophas's surviving daughter, Allelina, aged twelve, was brought in, peppered with questions, and made to refute her father's claims. Several respected community members came forward voluntarily to add their denunciations. There was no religious

teaching in the school, the ministry concluded (the prize-book
had been an isolated error that wouldn't happen again), and
French was "rapidly giving place to English" among the pupils
as, of course, it should.[2] In sum: Mr. C. S. dit Blondin was a
crackpot and a troublemaker.

A story made the rounds in the district about a woman
who had dared to speak out against the Church. The Sunday
after she'd made her heretical remarks, the priest stood in his
pulpit and predicted that when she died—and it wouldn't be
long—her corpse would be eaten by dogs. And, the whispers
said, that is exactly what happened.

Cléophas now found himself at odds with everyone for
miles around, from the Department of Education in Toronto
to his neighbors down the road. What he needed were wide-
open spaces where a man could think and act for himself. But
where in the world could you find that kind of freedom and
tolerance?

A MAN COULD grumble and a man could rage, but still life
went trundling along. Every now and then, it even brought
a moment of pleasure. Take the day in the fall of 1897, for
example, when Cléophas's niece Rose Anna married a local
farmer named George Parent. Like the Blondins, the Parents
had left Saint-Polycarpe in the mid-1800s and headed west,
into the land of the English. Restless, rootless, unable to get
ahead, they had shuffled around northern Ontario for a generation or two before finally coming to rest alongside their old
friends and neighbors in Tiny Township. As the latest of late
arrivals, they had been relegated to the outermost margins

76   of the community and to the least arable land. Not the most auspicious of circumstances—or, as it turned out, of marriages—but still a reason to raise a glass.

Unlike her uncle Cléophas, Rose and her new husband identified as solidly French and Catholic. Their first child, Clarissa Marie Parent, was born on March 5, 1898 (just five months after the wedding, a fact that must have made tongues cluck), but no one could accuse her parents of neglecting their religious duties. When the infant was only a few days old, they took her to the monumental church in Penetanguishene townsite—more imposing by far than even Sainte-Croix in Lafontaine—and placed her in the arms of the priest, to be baptized into the Catholic faith.

Sadly, however, there was no earthly salvation for Rose or her babe-in-arms. George Parent turned out to be a boozer. "They were poor," Lorena tells me when I call to ask her about her grandmother's early life. "They went on to have ten kids, you know."

Ten. Just like my mother's family: I knew how rough that had been. Ten kids on a hand-to-mouth farm had been too many.

"There was no food," Lorena says, and her voice hardens. "'We were starving.' That's what my grandmother said."

When Clarissa finished grade four, she and her sister Mabel, aged about ten and nine, respectively, were sent out to neighbors to do housework, in return for room and board. And "housework" didn't mean running around with a duster. In the winter, you'd wake in the morning to find the water in the kettle frozen into a clanking lump. Run out for an armload of wood and build a fire. Hurry, before the family gets up. Clean the chimneys of the coal-oil lamps—careful that nothing

breaks—trim the wicks; refill the reservoirs. Bake bread, make
soap, gather eggs, slop the pigs, weed gardens, do the laundry.
Heating flat irons on the stove in midsummer could be the
worst job of all. As a woman who grew up on a nearby farm
later recalled, childhood on the Penetang Peninsula could
be "very happy, despite the poverty and lack of comfort." But
"sometimes," she acknowledged laconically, "it wasn't funny."[3]

A few decades later, my teenaged mother would also be
hired out to do housework, as a way of earning her keep.
Many years after her death, I can still hear her voice bristling
with resentment when she remembered ironing, and re-
ironing, Mrs. Howard's sheets.

WHEN I SAID that Clarissa and Mabel had gone to work for
neighbors, I should admit that's not exactly what Lorena said.
What she told me was that the two little girls had been sent
down the road to work for their somewhat better-off relatives,
the Blondins. "That must have been where he"—meaning her
grandfather—"first saw her," his wife-to-be, as a pretty little
girl. But now, in retelling the story, I realize that this version
of events (like so many of our most cherished family legends)
cannot be entirely true. By the time Clarissa was put to work
at the age of ten, her much-older cousin, Napoléon, would
have been long gone out west.

But that still lay ahead. The year Clarissa was born,
Napoléon turned nineteen. There he was, marooned in back-
of-beyond Ontario, preparing to face the future with six years
of formal schooling. To his credit, he could speak two languages: the local Francophone dialect that included a number

of Cree or Anishinaabe words and that his son would later classify as "Métis French," plus the classroom English mandated by the provincial department of education. Apparently, the local school hadn't been a total waste. As historian and author Daniel Marchildon points out in his study of the region in which he, too, was born, "parents who had been handicapped all their life in an anglophone labour market because they didn't speak English well enough didn't want their children to suffer from the same problem, and they encouraged them in an exaggerated fashion to learn English."[4] Cléophas would have seconded this attitude with enthusiasm.

But if Napoléon entered adulthood with certain advantages, his path forward was far from clear. The only place he had ever known was the Penetang Peninsula, a narrow world hemmed in by water and trees. It was called Township of Tiny, and tiny it was, a place of constant limitation where it was wise to nurture small thoughts and modest ambitions. As his father knew only too well, life was constrained in many dimensions—spiritual, intellectual, social—but the limitation that hit hardest of all was measured in dollars and cents. Through much of the nineteenth century, the district of Lafontaine was a cripplingly hard place to get ahead. Although some people were more successful than others, and the Blondins seem to have managed as well as anyone could, neither they nor any of their neighbors were getting rich fast. The least fortunate among them went to bed hungry, and little kids like Clarissa Parent were shoved out of the nest early to fend for themselves.

As the new century approached, Cléophas and his now grown-up children must have paused to take stock. The old man, head of the family and still its driving force, was in his mid-fifties, having surpassed his own father in longevity and outlived two wives. But who knew how long he had left? Time was running out to achieve a secure future for the family, yet none of the options that presented themselves promised a quick fix. Moving into town—Barrie, Orillia, or Toronto— wouldn't accomplish much. As unskilled workers with "foreign" names and a French tang to their speech, young men like Cléophas's sons would quickly fall to the bottom of the heap. Not even worth considering.

Another alternative, equally problematic, was to join the hundreds of thousands of French Canadians who were flooding across the border into the United States. Between 1860 and 1900, an estimated 410,000 Québécois (more than a quarter of the population) packed their belongings onto a southbound train, seduced by the allure of the Land of Opportunity. Although many of the emigrants disembarked in the lumbering centers of Michigan or Maine, by far the majority poured into the mill towns of New England, where they were promised reliable, if poorly paid, jobs in the textile factories. "Everyone was happy in the United States," one émigré smirked. "There was money, a livelihood. In Canada, nothing but poverty."[5]

Back home in Québec, the chattering classes, especially the clergy, writhed in rhetorical agony over this dismaying turn of events. How was French Canada to fulfill its sacred mission if its people dispersed? How could Québec stand as the rock of the one true religion, the Catholic faith, if its population was endlessly dissolving into the sea of Anglo Protestantism?

Don't leave home, they pleaded. We'll open new parishes up north, in Québec and even Ontario. You can farm there, stay close to the land, to your language, to your church.

But while some Québécois responded to this call—
including the first waves of families to settle at Lafontaine—
emigration to the northern states not only continued but
accelerated. (By 1930, the total out-migration would approach
a million.) Times were hard everywhere, and no amount of
pulpit-pounding could keep people from trying to improve
their lives. Unable to stem the flood, church leaders eventually decided to make the best of it. Wasn't it possible, they
suggested, that they'd been mistaken in seeing the exodus
to the United States as a mortal threat? What if, instead, it
was part of God's beneficent plan to extend the Catholic faith
across the continent? Energized by this cheering proposi-
tion, the church began funneling resources into establishing
Francophone parishes, or "*Petits Canadas*," in all the major
Franco-American towns, 147 of them in total.

In the long run, unsurprisingly, this investment was for
naught. Final score: divine providence 0, pessimists 147. Cast
as outsiders by their neighbors, beset with persistent demands
to "speak American," the newcomers eventually bowed to
the demands of assimilation. "I cannot write my native language," a second-generation immigrant would lament in the
mid-1900s, "have no native home anymore, and am amazed
by that horrible homelessness of all French-Canadians abroad
in America."[6] That lost soul was Jean-Louis Lebris de Kérouac,
the son of middle class French Canadians in Lowell, Massachusetts, better known to the world as Jack Kerouac, the
author of *On the Road*. And even in the short term, the move
to New England came with no guarantee of success. In the
summer of 1897, for instance, a mill worker named Napoleon
Blondin (no relation, so far as I can tell) was arrested in Lowell and hauled into court on the charge of skipping town and

failing to provide the necessities of life for his wife, Clara (ditto), and their two children. Betting the farm on the USA could end in disaster.

Cautionary stories like this must have circulated everywhere in French Canada, even in outposts like Lafontaine, brought home by people who crossed the border for seasonal work or by the thousands of returnees who, giving up on the tinsel dream of instant prosperity, had been drawn back to family and friends. Cléophas Sureau dit Blondin himself was almost certainly one of them. In immigration documents filed years later, he noted that he'd spent time in Vermont in the late 1860s, presumably as a loom-fixer or carder in a textile mill. I can't tell you how many times I'd glanced at that entry without grasping what it meant, but one day, there it was, suddenly obvious.

No one had to tell Cléophas that life in a grim industrial town was unforgiving—crowded tenements, twelve-hour work days, starvation wages, the infernal shriek of the machines—not at all what he had in mind for himself or his family. Despite his "advanced" views on religion, Cléophas was, in many other ways, cut from the same bolt as his ancestors. His calling, as theirs had been for generations, was agriculture. If he and his children were going to bet the farm on anything, it would be on attaining better and bigger farms. And the miracle was that the government of Canada was, just then, essentially *giving away* unimaginable acreages of the northwestern plains to anyone who wasn't afraid of a little work. Go west, old man, go west!

6

— PRAIRIE FIRE —

*Même sans espoir,
la lutte est encore un espoir.*

Even without hope,
resistance is still hope.

ROMAIN ROLLAND, *L'âme enchantée,* 1922

EACH NEW PULSE of narrative leaves me dazzled and amazed. To think that this epic tale had been sparked by the humblest of clues: a penciled name on a scrap of paper, a handful of grubby remnants tumbling out of the walls. As I'd followed the trail from event to event, doors had swung open before me to reveal rooms I didn't even know existed filled with movement and memory. Inside each successive frame, people were engaged in struggles that were unique to their circumstances and yet recognizably the same. From the European Wars of Religion and the clash of rival empires during the Conquest, to the civil strife of *la guerre des Patriotes* and on to the intimate ruptures between the Blondins and their neighbors, the same questions had hung over all of these troubles. What did French Canadians, as individuals, as a society, have to do to survive or even to flourish on a continent dominated by *les maudits Anglais*, the Protestant English?

Fractal: *noun and adjective.* In mathematics, a complex shape (say, a snowflake) in which the constituent parts that make up the shape (microscopic snow crystals) look much like the shape itself.

Was it possible that our lives, like snowflakes and shorelines and galaxies, are fractals, infinitely repetitive? In the case of the Blondins, it was clear that similar patterns had recurred at different times and on different scales, provoked by religious and social conflicts that stirred nations or neighborhoods or individual souls. Presumably, these spasms went on repeating endlessly until the underlying injuries were resolved, allowing persons and societies to move on. And theoretically, it should sometimes also be possible to leap out of these repetitive patterns by leaving one historical context and entering a radically different space.

That is exactly what Cléophas Blondin and so many others like him, including my own grandparents, were hoping for when they first thought about heading west. They yearned for a clean start. A great escape. A daring reboot of their fortunes. There's a name for this kind of strategy: it's called a "geographical cure." And this tactic just might have worked for the Blondins except for one unfortunate glitch. The "Licentious Fanaticks" of Anglo-Canadian bigotry were already one step ahead, intent on claiming the Last Best West of the Canadian prairies exclusively for themselves.

84   TO PICK UP the threads of our story, we have to loop back a
number of years, to 1867. That was a momentous juncture
for the Blondins, then recently arrived at Lafontaine and
awaiting their first harvest. Meanwhile, far away in London,
England, the British government was engaged in an even
more nerve-racking venture—the creation of an entirely new
country. When the British North America Act was passed
on July 1 of that year, it brought together four preexisting
British colonies to form the Dominion of Canada, an event
so consequential that it has been accorded its own Heritage
Minute—one of those sixty-second clips illustrating important moments in Canadian history.

"Separated, the colonies are isolated and weak," one of the
bearded, frock-coated Fathers of Confederation observes,
when I pull up the reenactment on my phone.

"But united, just imagine," a clean-cut John A. Macdonald
counters, with a sweeping wave of his hand. "In the east, the
Atlantic provinces. Then Upper and Lower Canada. Across the
prairies to the Rockies and beyond. A new country made one
by a railway from sea to sea.

"Gentlemen," the soon-to-be prime minister concludes
with a flourish, "the time for union is now. I ask you to take
the dare." [Cue applause and swelling music.][1]

There you have it in a nutshell, the story of Canada's origins, though one could quibble about a minor error of fact.
By the time of Confederation—or so the history books
remind me—Upper and Lower Canada were actually called
Canada West and Canada East and were notionally yoked
together in a "united" government. This arrangement had
been imposed after la guerre des Patriotes in the hope of curb-
ing dissent but with the result instead of endless wrangling

and bitterness. For despite the show of unity, the reality remained unchanged: the two populations were sharply divided by language and faith. Under the constitution of the new country, however, this problem would surely be resolved once and for all, through guarantees of mutual respect and tolerance.

With questions of language and religion thus set aside, the infant Dominion turned its attention to fulfilling its destiny, as a nation *a mari usque ad mare*, from sea to sea. To achieve this bold vision, Sir John A. made a deal to purchase the northern heartland of the continent—1.5 million square miles in all—including parts of present-day Québec, Ontario, Nunavut, the Northwest Territories, and the three Prairie Provinces. The nominal owner of this immense region was the Hudson's Bay Company, which based its claim on the decree of an English king. How a European monarch could grant rights to land that did not belong to him was a question that no one bothered to ask. Similarly, with the land transfer now in process, no one thought to consult with the people who were most directly affected by the change, the 75,000 people of Nehiyaw, Anishinaabe, Siksika, Kainai, Nakoda, Dakota, Lakota, Dene, Métis, and European descent who lived in the region.

Even Prime Minister Macdonald knew that this was a shoddy way to proceed. "No explanation it appears has been made of the arrangement by which the country is to be handed over," he confided in a letter to a friend. "All these poor people know is that Canada has bought the country from the Hudson's Bay Company and that they are handed over like a flock of sheep to us."[2]

It was a shame, but there was no standing in the way of progress. And progress was what Macdonald had in mind for the wide-open spaces of the prairies. He was so anxious to get the region surveyed, sold off, and densely populated by immigrants that he dispatched a party of surveyors to the forks of the Red and Assiniboine Rivers several months ahead of the agreed-upon transfer date. Once in place, this crew eagerly set to work staking out the prairie in square-mile plots, as if the entire country was up for grabs.

In fact, however, those river forks were already the site of the well-established Red River settlements. Of the roughly twelve thousand people who lived in the district, about a third were "country-born"—English-speaking and Protestant—while most of the rest, the majority, were "*bois brulé*," French-speaking and Catholic. Whether Anglo or Franco, all were Métis. Despite the divisions of language and religion, these people were bound together by kinship, a shared history, and a sense of identity as the "New Nation" of the prairies. Although the peace between English and French speakers was sometimes tested, the community was drawn together by their common concerns. Most important at the moment was their status as owners of the narrow riverfront holdings, *à la façon de la Nouvelle-France*, which were suddenly being menaced by the surveyors.

"The intentions of Canada soon became apparent," a Red River resident later recalled. "It wanted to introduce itself into the country as if to a deserted land with no regard for the people who lived there... [T]he surveyors... set about drawing lines all over the place, whether they were on private property or not."[3] In some cases, the survey ran directly through people's buildings or placed one family's home on another's lot.

To make matters worse, a gang of obnoxious new arriv- als had burst onto the scene, intent on turning this crisis to advantage. They were English-speaking entrepreneurs from Ontario, hoping to make a quick buck by buying the surveyed properties on speculation. Blatantly racist, pro-British and anti-Catholic, these operators saw themselves as the vanguard of the "energetic and civilised race" of white Anglo-Saxon Protestants to whom the future belonged. Even the prime minister had reservations about this clique, whom he judged to be "exceedingly cantankerous and ill-conditioned."[4] Other observers were even more unsparing in their assessment, focusing on qualities like "brute force," "selfishness," "greed," and "want of principle."[5]

"I JUST DIDN'T get it," I admit to Keith. "I mean, everybody knows that the government of Canada screwed up big time at Red River. There's nothing new about that."

"'The abuse of power comes as no surprise,'" he suggests with a crooked grin. "Isn't that one of Jenny Holzer's truisms?"

"Yes, I guess," I say, not really listening. "But the blatant bigotry of the Canadian party in the settlement—it takes my breath away. I've read about these guys before, of course, how they saw the prairies as the exclusive property of English Canada. But what I didn't see until now was how *full-on* they were."

I turn back toward my computer screen. "Look at this," I continue. "It's from the *Dictionary of Canadian Biography*, not exactly a hotbed of careless overstatement. It says here that

88 the worst of the Canadian party at Red River wanted the Métis to be 'exterminated.'"[6]

I look up at Keith, and he reaches over and gives my shoulder a squeeze. Neither of us can think of anything clever to say.

WITH TEMPERS RISING and the Canadian government still dithering over the transfer, the Métis established an interim government to keep the peace and represent their interests. The leadership of this daring initiative soon fell to an articulate twenty-five-year-old named Louis Riel. French-speaking and devoutly Catholic, educated in the seminaries of Québec, Riel was the descendant of old French-Canadian stock, with a proud claim to Métis identity through his grandmother. Now, determined to keep his diverse Nation together, he sought the support of his English-speaking neighbors. But the real muscle of the resistance would come from French parishes like Saint-Boniface and Saint-Norbert.

The Canadian government, still lacking a legal mandate for its actions, appointed an Ontario politician named William McDougall as governor of the territory and sent him west to take command. A veteran of the sulfurous politics of central Canada, McDougall had once characterized French Canadians as "a foreign people" and denounced them as "followers of a religion which is not the religion of the Empire."[7] And so the battle lines were drawn, in a sour, racialized version of the familiar discord. The Métis stopped the governor in his tracks and sent him back to his masters in the East: Canada would not be allowed to ride roughshod over the people of Red River.

It was much harder for Riel and his allies to restrain the bigots in their midst. Armed and dangerous, these "loyalists" were determined to bring down the provisional government. The most troublesome of the troublemakers was a young tough named Thomas Scott, whose credentials included a previous conviction for aggravated assault, an apprenticeship in the sectarian bloodshed of Ireland, and a paid-up membership in the militant Protestant brotherhood of the Orange Order. Taken captive by the provisional government, he was so belligerent and unruly—taunting his guards, threatening to murder Riel—that even his fellow prisoners wanted nothing to do with him. In the end, Scott was charged with insubordination, tried by an improvised court, and—on the afternoon of March 4, 1870—shot by a Métis firing squad.

As news of Scott's execution ricocheted across Ontario, all the old sectarian hatreds were reignited, and a cry went up for revenge. Although Scott's death sentence had been a collective decision, popular sentiment among English Canadians pinned the blame for the "murder" squarely on Louis Riel. In their eyes, he was simply another fractious Frenchman, another rebel against God and the Queen. Twice elected to represent Red River in the House of Commons, Riel was never able to take his seat because the Anglo-Protestant majority there voted to refuse him entry. "If Riel is such a fool as to poke his nose into that mess," the prime minister commented, "he must abide the consequences on his person. I have little doubt that the mob will soon dispose of him."[8] And so, Riel, like the "rebels" of la guerre des Patriotes before him, was forced into exile in the United States.

And yet, this time, despite the personal cost to Riel and against all odds, the people of Red River had won. Shortly after the shock of Scott's death—perhaps because of it—the Canadian government agreed to consider the residents' demands. The result was that when the Red River district was finally welcomed into Canada, in May of 1870, it was not as a mere territory, ruled from Ottawa, but as the tiny but fully fledged province of Manitoba, equipped with all the institutions of democratic self-government. Instead of the WASP's nest that Scott and the "Canada party" had envisaged, the new jurisdiction was officially bilingual, with equal status for English and French in the legislature and the courts. There was also a provincial senate to safeguard minority rights and guarantees for both Protestant and Catholic schools. In all of these respects, the arrangement echoed the agreements that had been reached through the BNA Act to foster a permanent linguistic peace. This hope was now extended into the western territory.

Everything was going to be fine. Riverfront lots? No worries. The "custom of the country" would be respected in full. What's more, the government of Canada promised to allocate an additional 1.4 million acres—2,200 square miles, or about one-sixth of the initial postage-stamp-sized province—"for the benefit of families of half-breed residents."[9] This gesture was intended to acknowledge and extinguish the Métis claim to Aboriginal title. Far from being handed over like a flock of sheep, the Métis had achieved an astonishing victory. But a flock encircled by wolves still has to be wary.

THE ROMAN CATHOLIC clergy in the new province were acutely aware how quickly their gains could be lost. Anglo settlers immediately began pouring into the country, imbued, as the local archbishop observed, with "*la force, l'énergie, le nombre et la haine au coeur*"—strength, energy, numbers, and hatred at heart.[10] The only possible solution would be to recruit thousands of Francophone Catholics and settle them in Francophone parishes, thereby establishing a new French-Catholic homeland on the prairies.

The initial step in this process should have been easy. Under the Manitoba Act, the Métis had been promised title to their existing holdings, plus efficient distribution of that additional 1.4 million acres of land. Once these claims were settled, the French Métis parishes would take on a new permanence and serve as a magnet to attract an influx of Francophone settlement. But this hope was quickly crushed. First, rules were imposed that made it almost impossible for the Métis to establish legal claim to their existing lots. Then, through a toxic combination of ineptitude, delay, and chicanery, the dispersal of the additional lands promised to the Métis was thoroughly bungled. As the Supreme Court of Canada concluded when it reconsidered this process six generations later, in 2013, "[a] government sincerely intent on fulfilling the duty that its honour demanded could and should have done better."[11]

Add to this the racism of the Canadian soldiers who were stationed in Red River after the resistance, some of whom chose to remain, and it is not difficult to understand why the Métis began to pull up stakes and move farther west, to places where they might still have a chance to live on their own terms. Slowly but inexorably, the grappling hooks of Anglo-Canadian settlement were being thrown across the northwest, putting the Métis's Catholic culture and

92 French-style riverfront holdings in jeopardy. The same old *déjà-vu* all over again.

IT IS DIFFICULT to describe what happened next without setting the page on fire. By now, we are west of everything: west of Montréal and Saint-Eustache and Saint-Polycarpe, west of Lafontaine, west even of the new province of Manitoba. Around us spread the tawny, sibilant expanses of the Saskatchewan country. On the banks of a beautiful river known locally as *la Fourche des Gros-Ventres* and newly inscribed on official maps as the South Saskatchewan, we find the Reverend John Lake and his band of teetotalers, hunkered down in scattered dwellings under an endless sky.

The year is 1885. The little settlement of Saskatoon is bisected by a trail that connects the Métis community of Prairie Ronde (Round Prairie), a short distance to the south, with the sister settlements of Saint-Louis and Batoche, a couple of days' ride to the north. A group of travelers is trekking northward along this route, and from the shrieking axles of their Red River carts, we know they must be Métis. Although fifteen years have passed since the resistance at Red River, the same trouble is afoot. Here, too, the surveyors are pushing in, extending their invisible lines of force across the Métis's riverfront claims. (The Reverend Mr. Lake, you'll remember, had rushed off to Ottawa to make sure the Métis lands were erased.) Now, with no response forthcoming to their petitions, the Métis from the district have invited Louis Riel to come out of exile and help them formulate a plan. He'd persuaded the authorities to bargain before. Why not try again?

It soon becomes apparent, however, that the government is in no mood for parley. Shots are fired—skirmishes escalate into battles—trainloads of soldiers are rushed west via the new Canadian Pacific Railway line—and the Métis find themselves engaged in a war against the Dominion of Canada. By the time the government has reestablished its authority, the "rebel" villages have been reduced to ruin—homes are looted by militiamen, out to avenge Thomas Scott's death—and hundreds of Métis fighters have been forced into exile in the United States. As for Louis Riel, he surrenders to the authorities and is taken to Regina for trial, on a charge of "wickedly, maliciously, and traitorously" making "war against our... Lady the Queen."[12] Despite his request to have the case heard in French, his fate is decided by an English-speaking jury and an English-speaking judge. On November 16, 1885, he is escorted to a grim clapboard barracks on the Regina plain and hung by the neck until dead. This is the price of advancing the cause of democracy and respect. This is the price of being French.

Except, of course, that Riel and the community he represents are not French or French Canadian. They are Métis, a new people born on the prairies. Seen from a distance, however—seen through the haze of centuries-old hatreds—this is a distinction that can too easily be smudged. When French Canada looks west, it sees yet another Anglo outrage. Considering the same events, English Canada sees the usual Papist defiance. The Métis are caught in the crossfire of an ancient blood feud.

Hundreds more dead in battle. Thousands more forced to flee. The number of men marched to the scaffold and hung has risen to thirteen.

94   "FOR THE LONGEST time, I didn't get it," my friend Maria Campbell says one day. We're having tea together amid the jukebox-era decor of Saskatoon's Broadway Café, but the questions that are troubling her lie in a deeper past. She looks past me through the café's smeared windows at a blur of passing cars, and I wonder if she is remembering the way her people used to travel along this very route. Broadway Avenue follows the old Métis trail from Round Prairie to Batoche, and Maria is Métis—Elder, scholar, storyteller, historian.

"I just didn't get it," she says again. "Why they hated us so much." By "us" she means her own Métis people; by "them," she means the Canadians who pillaged the Métis villages and killed Louis Riel. "But, you know, I've been doing a lot of reading, going way back, and what I've realized is"—she shifts her gaze back to me, her eyes wide with amazement—"it wasn't us they hated. It never was. All this time I wondered, but no, they hated the *French and the Catholics*."

🏠

I DON'T KNOW what Cléophas Blondin made of all the trouble, whose side he took when debates broke out on the station platform or the main street in Lafontaine. But I do know what he did. For the longest time, he stayed put on the Penetanguishene Peninsula, with his family around him. The anti-French fury that engulfed the West after the Métis resistance was far from welcoming, and the news that filtered back to Lafontaine from former neighbors who had taken the prairie gamble was even more worrying. One of them was moved to tell his "sad, sad tale" in verse:

If I ever made enough money
I'd go back to Lafontaine
To rejoin my extended family
And I'd stay, that's for sure…
The future of my children
Would be much less in doubt.[13]

But *le temps guérit toutes les blessures*, as the saying goes. Time heals all wounds. The years ticked by, and a new century rolled around. The Last Best West was still there for the taking, or so the government brochures promised. "*Le dernier mieux de l'Ouest: Le Canada au vingtième siècle, vastes ressources agricoles, résidences pour des millions.*"[14] Canada in the twentieth century, vast agricultural resources, homes for millions. And it was with these blandishments ringing in his ears that, on the cusp of his sixtieth birthday, Mr. C. S. Blondin of Tiny Township, Ontario, finally set aside his misgivings and booked passage on a westbound train. All aboard for Assiniboia, North-West Territories.

7

— LAND CLAIMS —

Aimez d'avance cette vie ignorée
qu'on appelle l'avenir,
travaillez pour lui, il naîtra.

Love in advance this unknown life
that we call the future.
Work for it, it will be born.

JULES MICHELET, *Du prêtre, de la femme, de la famille,* 1845

TWO HUNDRED AND twenty years, and six generations, had passed since Hilaire Sureau stepped on board a sailing ship at the port of La Rochelle, bound for what, to him, was a wild and unknown world. Now, Cléophas Sureau dit Blondin had embarked on his own reckless adventure. The West was a fresh page, a new start, a place where a man could shake off the burdens of the past. Hour by hour, as the steam engine jostled and belched its way across the country, the limitations of Cléophas's old life grew more distant.

The upset with Riel and the Métis twenty years earlier had already been relegated to a distant and misty past and could safely be forgotten now. The Indians, both the minority who had sided with the Métis and the majority who had not, had been brought under control and close supervision on designated reserves, and their children had been removed for reeducation in residential schools. The Métis, meanwhile, were living quietly, carefully, out of the public eye, and without the ambiguous benefits of official "assistance." In the grand scheme of Western settlement, they had been declared irrelevant.

The people who mattered now were fortune seekers, men with the future in their sights, men like Cléophas. For a fee of just ten dollars, about the cost of a lady's dress or an off-the-rack gentleman's suit, any male over the age of eighteen could obtain an "entry" on an unassigned quarter-section, or "homestead," of his choosing. The same opportunity was also available to women, again eighteen-plus, who were the heads of their own households, that is, widowed or divorced. At the end of three years, provided that the entrant met the prescribed conditions—built a modest home and took up seasonal residence, broke the required acreage and put some of it in crop—he or she became the legal owner of 160 acres. The prairies were open for business, and this deal was available on a come-and-get-it basis to anyone with a little ambition, except, "naturally," for most Métis and all Treaty Indians.

It is easy to imagine Cléophas reeling off the train in Regina, drinking in the scope of the place, the optimism, the dazzle of pure possibility. The country around the CPR line was already filling up, but a little farther north, the options were essentially infinite. Everyone was talking about a new frontier, the Goose Lake Country, west of a place called Saskatoon. The district was just being opened to settlers, and it

98 promised the best of everything, with enough quality land to satisfy not just Cléophas but also—it was almost beyond belief—to guarantee a future for all of his progeny.

His reconnaissance complete, Cléophas returned home and started to get his family into gear. By late in the spring of 1904, the family was packed and ready to move. The party included Napoléon, now aged twenty-four; his younger brothers, Hercules, twenty-three, Télémaque, twenty-one, and Ulysse, just nineteen; their older sister, Allelina, still unmarried at twenty-six; and Cléophas's third wife, Philomène, with a babe-in-arms, Alice. (At thirty-four, Philomène was almost thirty years younger than her new husband.) The only holdouts from the expedition were Cléophas's eldest son, Alexandre, twenty-eight, and his wife, Victoria, but they would follow in the family's footsteps a couple of years later.

And so the day came to bid farewell to the forests and fields and beaches of the Penetanguishene Peninsula. Whatever its constraints, this narrow world was the only home Napoléon and his siblings had ever known. Goodbye to the peaceful, rolling graveyard at Lafontaine where their grandparents, mother, and sister had been laid to rest. Goodbye to the daily comfort of speaking French, the language of memory. Goodbye to friends and neighbors; goodbye to rivals and enemies. Au revoir to a certain beguilingly cute little cousin. Goodbye.

The train from Toronto to Regina was crammed with trunks and parcels and people because, these days, it always was. The influx of settlers that the authorities had long hoped for—had been waiting for in vain from the 1870s onward—had finally materialized. Week after week, long trains made up mainly of day coaches, with hardly a sleeping car to be seen (no money to waste on mere comfort, not with the future calling) swayed westward across the rocky country north of Lake Superior. Inside each car were ranks of uncomfortable, straight-backed benches, and, at the rear, a flat-topped stove on which someone was always preparing a meal. Whenever the train pulled into a station, people rushed for the shops, hoping to replenish their supplies, only to discover that the shelves had been stripped bare by the hungry onrush that had gone before. Did you hear that just last year, in 1903, some twenty thousand people had taken up homesteads in the Districts of Assiniboia and Saskatchewan alone?

Already there was excited talk that the old administrative districts—Assiniboia and Saskatchewan on the central plains, with Alberta to the west and Athabasca to the north—were to be reconfigured into one or two or perhaps even four shiny new provinces, each with its own legislature. Power to the people and an end to bumbling administration by bureaucrats in Ottawa! And so the sun of British parliamentary democracy would rise over this far-flung outpost of the Empire.

Because the West was, and would always remain, British. That was beyond question. True, the federal government had recently stirred up a firestorm of protest by recruiting settlers from Eastern Europe, from places with unpronounceable names like Galicia and Bukovina. The federal minister responsible for this policy, a Manitoba-based politician named Clifford Sifton, would later speak boldly in its defense: "I think a stalwart peasant in a sheep-skin coat, born on the soil, whose forefathers have been farmers for ten generations, with a stout wife and a half-dozen children, is good quality... I am indifferent as to whether or not he is British-born."[1]

Indifferent as to whether or not he is British-born? In imperialist Ontario, that was heresy. Everyone knew that northern

Europeans, most notably Britons, constituted a superior race, surpassing all other peoples in vigor, intelligence, honor, and overall evolutionary accomplishment. By opening the door to "illiterate Slavs in overwhelming numbers," claimed Sifton's opponents, he was burdening the West with the lowest type of humanity—"physical and moral degenerates not fit to be classed as white men."[2] The next thing you knew, he'd be bringing in Negroes or Jews or Chinamen.

But even Sifton had his limits. Under his regime, non-Caucasians, together with supposedly loose-living southern Europeans like Italians and Greeks, continued to be categorized as "undesirable" immigrants. And though Sifton did succeed in attracting settlers from Eastern Europe—Doukhobors and Mennonites from Russia, farmers from Ukraine—most of his department's time and resources were devoted to recruiting the usual suspects: white Anglo-Saxon Protestants. Over the fiscal year 1902–03, for example, the government had spent a fortune—some $200,000 in all, over three times the amount they'd expended in all the rest of Europe—trying to persuade British farmers to take a chance on the West. Any Englishman or Scot with a demonstrated interest in farming would always be top of the list, the most desired of the "desirable" class of immigrants. After them came white Americans, followed at one remove by Germans, Scandinavians, and the Dutch, and then, somewhat grudgingly, by Belgians and Frenchmen.

The result was that if we'd been crammed into that stuffy, wheezing colonist train alongside the Blondins, we might have picked up snatches of conversation in Norwegian or Ukrainian or occasionally even French. But what we would have heard most was the language of Shakespeare. Of all the people who headed into the West in the early years of the twentieth century, around 80 percent were English speakers from Ontario, Britain, and the United States. Everyone else was expected to adopt British customs and "speak white"—the King's English.

Wittingly or not, these policies echoed a new trend in Western European thought. "Scientific racism"—the theory that race, and even ethnicity, are God-given and immutable distinctions—had first been formulated in the 1850s by an ultra-conservative French diplomat, Joseph Arthur, a commoner who preferred to style himself as the Comte de Gobineau. Little noticed at the time of its publication, his six-volume, 1,294-page *Essai sur l'inégalité des races humaines* (*The Inequality of Human Races*) eventually found its ideal reader in the composer Richard Wagner, who not only promoted Gobineau's white-supremacist doctrines but also infected them with his own anti-Semitism. Seen in the macabre light of this pseudoscience, all of "civilization" was said to have been inspired by an ancestral Aryan race, the whitest of white men, whose influence, it was claimed, persisted to a greater or lesser degree in contemporary European nations.

And where were the purest strains of Aryanism to be found? In England: Where else? *Je me trouverai amené à ne considérer comme vraiment civilisée, dans le passé et dans le présent, que la seule nation anglaise*, Gobineau declared.[3] "I am drawn to the conclusion that no nation, past or present, is truly civilized except England." And who could argue with science?

SOME EIGHTY YEARS later, the province of Saskatchewan would choose as its official motto *Multis e gentibus vires*: "from many peoples, strength." But in 1904, when the Blondins came west, that day was unforeseeably, impossibly, in the distance.

I KNOW SOMETHING about the men and women who crowded onto those colonist trains because my own people were among them. Great-grandparents who hailed from Hannibal, Missouri, or from Cincinnati, Ohio, or, like the Blondins, from small-town Ontario. Several, like Cléophas, were well into their fifties, old enough to have grown some sense, as my mother might have said. With them came the fresh-faced teens and young adults whom I would one day know as my grandmas and grandpas. Take, for instance, my grandma Humphrey, a clear-eyed girl of twenty, who for several years ran her own dressmaker's shop in the boomtown of Olds, Alberta, before making the mistake (a fortunate one for me) of marrying the dashing blue-eyed homesteader with big dreams of the future who came a-courting. Of all my prairie ancestors, she was the most overtly racist, and one of my cousins remembers how, when he was very little, she'd frighten him half to death by threatening to send the "darkies" after him, so much so that, when he eventually saw a black man on the streets of Calgary, his first response was terror—his second, shame. That grandma had grown up in Missouri, in a family that once owned slaves, and her prejudices were deeply ingrained.

My other grandparents were more moderate in their views or, at least, less inclined to outbursts of hate, and yet every one of them was quietly assured that he or she belonged to a superior race. White people were top of the pile, and Anglo-Saxons the best of the best. In particular, the incoming settlers knew with absolute certainty that they were more advanced than the "savages" who had been displaced to clear the way for them. As the Comte de Gobineau himself had put it, with barely concealed glee, the cerebellum of a Huron might look like it contained the germ of human intelligence. But if that were true, then why had the Indians not discovered the printing press or the steam engine? For the people rereading the government's seductive printed pamphlets while riding on steam-powered trains, this brutal argument passed as common sense. And so the settlers rolled west on a wave of entitlement, certain they were bringing civilization to a forsaken land.

And yet, in spite of everything I now understand about these people, I can't help loving them. One minute, they were ordinary men and women—laborers, failed farmers, housewives—but the second they took their seats on a colonist train, they became heroes, "pioneers," the makers of history. Imagine the weightless freedom, the giddiness, the exuberant folly of selling off everything you owned and taking a chance on the unknown. "We must have had rocks in our heads," my grandpa Sherk would say, looking back on it. At the time, however, the Sherks' westering journey in 1909 had been a splendid adventure. First, by train from Ontario to Edmonton. Then, together with a large party that included parents, siblings, and cousins, by oxcart—yes, really—north over a corduroy road through muskeg and forest to Lesser Slave Lake. There, a pause to cut cords of firewood, as payment for passage across the water by boat. And finally, a long trudge even farther north and west to take up land in the Peace River

Country. That's where I would be born, just forty years later, the air still ringing with echoes of this origin story.

BUT BACK TO the spring of 1904 and to the Blondins, last seen rumbling through the scrubby forests and shining lakes of the Canadian Shield, a terrain that bore a certain resemblance to the country they'd left behind. And then one day, after three or four nights of travel, they opened their eyes to a landscape of horizontals, to a boundless earth spread under a boundless sky. At first, the plains were broken by gnarled stands of burr oak—no challenge at all to a man who was used to claiming his fields with an axe—but soon even this minor impediment began to fade away. As the train clicked west from Winnipeg toward Regina, the horizon receded further into the distance, and the land that streaked past the train windows was reduced to a featureless blur. Not a rock. Not a tree. Surely God had made this land especially for the plow.

It was enough to make you believe that the stories you'd heard about instant success might be true. In your mind's eye, you could already see your furrows running straight and deep, cut into the dark prairie loam. *Your* wheat swaying in the wind, ripe and golden. *Your* house and barns and granaries standing snug against the onset of winter snows. The rumble of the train beat out a refrain: *Let's go, let's go, let's go.*

BUT THAT SPRING, as so often happens on the prairies, the weather had other plans. As temperatures warmed in late April, an ice jam formed on the South Saskatchewan River, sending torrents of water over the low divide into the Qu'Appelle Valley. Overnight, water levels rose six feet, then eight feet, and the operator of the train station at Lumsden, who stayed loyally at his post until the last minute, was forced to escape by boat. And so, after five weary days of traveling cross-country, the Blondins arrived in Regina to find that their journey had come to a halt. The Qu'Appelle, Long Lake and Saskatchewan Railroad—the only practical means of covering the next leg of their journey, the 160 miles from Regina north to Saskatoon—was partially underwater, and the rail bridge across the South Saskatchewan at Saskatoon had collapsed. No one was going anywhere until further notice.

By late May, a total of nine hundred northbound settlers were stranded in Regina, most of them Americans, Brits, or, like the Blondins, people from out East, along with sixty-one rail cars crammed with their possessions ("settlers' effects") and three hundred head of livestock that had to be fed, watered, exercised, and mucked out. According to a report in Saskatoon's new daily newspaper, the *Phenix*, a lucky few of the detained passengers had been put up in local hotels, but many others were bunking, uncomfortably, in idled rail cars. Days, then weeks, ticked past. "A great anxiety for those going farming," the *Phenix* observed, stating the obvious, "is that they are likely to be to[o] late for seeding and thus lose a year."[4]

It would be mid-June before, with service restored, Engine 466 puffed into Saskatoon over a hastily reconstructed trestle, bearing the first five coaches of passengers and the first dozen cars of settlers' effects. By then, the pressure of time was so intense that railway staff even worked on the Sabbath to unload the livestock and freight.

AND SO WE find ourselves back where we began, on the grace-ful bends of the South Saskatchewan River. Twenty-two years have passed since the Reverend Mr. Lake of the Temperance Colonization Society popped up out of nowhere, waved his rhetorical magic wand, and called for a town to spring up on the open plains where no town had sprung before. "Arise! Saskatoon," he had cried, "Queen of the Prairies."[5] (Or so he would later recall in the most lavish of his memoirs.) At first, little had come of this invocation—a huddle of low-slung shan-ties, a cluster of abstinent souls—but with the turn of the new century, everything was suddenly GO. In 1902, just two years back, the combined population of the hamlets that made up the settlement had finally struggled up to two hundred. Over the next eighteen months, that number had doubled, then quadrupled, so that by the time the Blondins arrived in the summer of 1904, they found themselves in a bustling com-munity of fifteen hundred and counting.

"One year ago, Saskatoon was a small hamlet scarcely worth noticing," a correspondent to the *Phenix* noted. "Now it is one of the leading cities of the North West."[6] Why, it even had wooden sidewalks and graded streets. The vast mud hole between the railway platform and these civic amenities was surely a minor impediment to an appreciation of the settle-ment's many promising achievements. The handsome new schoolhouse. The state-of-the-art telephone system, a first for the Territories. The ample provisions for Christian fellowship, whether among Catholics, Methodists, Presbyterians, Angli-cans, or Baptists. Newly fledged though it was, Saskatoon was also well endowed with fraternal societies, including groups like the Masons and the Loyal Orange Lodge. Everyone was welcome to join (except for females, Papists, and persons of color, of course). It was as if a little piece of Anglo-Ontario society had been set down on the prairies and was eagerly taking root.

For the Blondins, however, Saskatoon was just a frantic stopover, the jumping-off point for their final destination —the Goose Lake Country—another fifty miles to the southwest. In the handsome *Descriptive Atlas of Western Canada* ("issued by direction of the Hon. Clifford Sifton" a few years earlier), Goose Lake appears as a small, teardrop-shaped blob in a tantalizingly empty setting, the land on every side unmarked and ready for the taking. No towns out there, no railroads. To complete their journey, they'd need wagons and oxen or heavy horses. To start farming: a walking plow and seed drill. To build a shelter: hammers and saws, barrels of nails. Flour, sugar, lard. Pots, pans, bedrolls. Stoves for cooking and heating. Coal for fuel. So much to do, so little time: winter coming.

As incoming settlers, the family was entitled to a few nights' stay in the boxy, whitewashed Immigration Hall, which rose abruptly from the prairie on the edge of the small downtown or, failing that, in one of the white, government-issue tents that had sprouted along the riverbank. For all their many other requirements, the family had only to look to the "wide awake and progressive" merchants of this up-and-coming town. From haircuts (courtesy of the resident "tonsorial artist") to hardware, and from harness to haberdashery, the businesspeople of Saskatoon prided themselves on catering to all of the homesteaders' basic needs. And if one of those needs turned out to be thirst, that, too, could be satisfied. To the loud dismay of the righteous, the town was teetotal no longer (if it had ever truly been), and drunken men frequently overflowed from the saloons onto sidewalks and streets, causing "sensitively modest" women to blanch and beat a ladylike retreat.

The truth was that, for all of its aspirations and pretensions, turn-of-the-century Saskatoon was crude and provisional. Seen from the wrong angle, it could be a hellhole. Consider, for example, a picture taken by the settlement's premier purveyor of photographic services, a recent arrival from Ontario named Ralph Dill. ("Picture Postcards," his ad in the *Phenix* boasted. "Enlargements. Photo Jewelry. Prices Regulated by Size and Style. Our Motto: One quality only, and that the best.")[7] Dill's main preoccupation was documenting the go-ahead spirit of the place—bridges, buildings, streets—and, in keeping with his theme, the backdrop for this particular photo features the facade of a four-square, clapboard structure, probably a hotel. It's a fine day, and windows are propped open, curtains stirring in the breeze. On the grass out front, a large group of anonymous, somberly clad men is standing in uneven rows behind a hitching rail. As the fashion of the time requires, they wear neckties and hats—flat caps, bowlers, Stetsons— and are attired in rumpled three-piece suits. All are Caucasian, and most have the slightly dazed and travel-worn appearance of recent arrivals. Several of the figures in the front row clutch cigarettes between their fingers and slouch against the rail, the embodiment of cowboy cool.

In front of them, fenced off by the rail, a lone figure sits in the dirt. His arms and legs are bundled inside a blanket, his face half-hidden behind a tangled fall of hair. We can see just enough of his features to know that this is an Indigenous man. Arrayed behind him, three ranks of white gentlemen hold their heads high and gaze straight into the camera lens, not deigning to glance at him. The sole exceptions are two small boys on the left of the image (the only children in the group), who prop their elbows on the top of the rail, like spectators at a zoo, and look down on him, bemused. In their eyes, he represents everything the settlers have come west to improve.

THERE IS A lot that the Blondins cannot yet know about their adopted country and what it holds in store for them. They cannot know about the sweet little bungalow with curved trim and generous windows that Napoléon will one day build for a wife named Clarissa Marie and their houseful of young kids. They cannot know that his luck will run out, or that Clarissa will become Clara and spurn her mother tongue, or that crosses will be set ablaze in the new towns along the Goose Lake line. They cannot know that Napoléon, of all their number, will be the only one to die in Saskatoon, aged just sixty-eight, and that his bones will lie in the municipal cemetery, a short walk from the Immigration Hall that once welcomed them in.

Like all the incoming settlers, the Blondins are haunted by a future they cannot foresee, but they have no use for the past. In the noontide of their optimism, they cast no shadows. In their own eyes, they are pathfinders, the first settlers on the moon. Yet one of the things the Blondins do not know—and will never discover—is that they have deep roots in the West. The kinship doesn't come, as I had once suspected,

110 through the Blondins of the fur trade and the Qu'Appelle Valley. Instead, the affinity turns out to lie on the maternal side, through Napoléon Blondin's mother and grandmother, both Trottiers at birth. A couple of generations back, one of their cousins, an André Trottier, had left the Montréal area and reestablished himself in the Red River district; there he had married a Saulteaux woman named Louise. In 1904, some of André and Louise's descendants were living just upriver from Saskatoon at the settlement of Prairie Ronde.

If the Blondins had dropped by for a visit, they might have met their Métis cousin Charles "Wapass" Trottier, the leader of the community. He, in turn, would surely have reminded them about the struggles of his people in Manitoba and then here, on the South Saskatchewan, just twenty years earlier. Although the violence had ended, the Métis grievances had never been resolved. Even now he was having trouble with the bureaucrats in the Department of the Interior. At issue was a sliver of land on the east bank of the South Saskatchewan River that was known to the Department as SE ¼ 16-32-6 -w3 and to Charles Trottier as the place where, as a child, he had overwintered with his parents in the days when they were "hunting the buffaloes in the plains." According to a sworn statement of claim that he'd sent to the government in December of 1903, Charles and his family had returned to this same wintering spot for thirty successive years, from 1855 onward. Like their neighbors in Red River and their ancestors in New France, the Trottiers had occupied a long, narrow lot fronting onto the river. But as a result of John Lake's high-level intervention, survey crews working around Saskatoon had overwritten the existing river lots with the officially approved square plots, thereby rendering the Métis holdings invalid.

Still, memory cannot be effaced with a few quick strokes of the pen, and Charles Trottier was determined to press his claim. Surely it would count for something that, in 1884, he had broken a good fifteen acres of the quarter as cropland, "with the intention of sowing it the next year," and that he had erected both a house ("18 x 20 ft") and a stable. And while it was true that he had fled to the United States in 1885, "on account of the rebellion," as he quietly explained, he was back from exile now, living with his wife, Ursule Laframboise, in their old cabin.[8] Given that he had met and exceeded the government's homesteading requirements, and on the basis of his historic claim, he asked the department to give him title to his homesite.

Another Blondin cousin—there were lots of them at Prairie Ronde—had a similar story to tell. He was Norbert Trottier (Charles's nephew), and according to his affidavit, he, too, had been in residence along the river in the early 1880s, when the surveyors "passed over" his place. By then, he'd built a house and two stables, cultivated a plot of land, and fenced eighty acres of pasture. "I remained in residence upon this land from 1880 till 1886," he declared, but ultimately "had to leave as I had nothing left." Instead of the eight horses he'd once owned, he was down to zero, all of his animals "having been killed at the time of the rebellion."[9] Instead of a cabin and outbuildings, he had only their charred remains. In the aftermath of the rebellion, a jubilant Canadian militia had ransacked "French" "rebel" settlements, leaving ruin in their wake. (Shades of Saint-Eustache in the 1830s.) Like his uncle, Norbert didn't belabor these details. He just wanted his land back.

The all-powerful department was unmoved by this request. For one thing, the bureaucrats noted, Norbert

Trottier had not filled out the proper forms. For another, he had waited far too long before asserting his claim. To give him his land at this late date would set a "dangerous precedent."[10] As for Charles, an official explained that his homesite was "not at the disposal of the Department," since it was being held for possible selection by a private enterprise (the Saskatchewan Valley Land Company, backed by wealthy investors from the United States) in fulfillment of a million-acre grant to a railroad company (the Qu'Appelle, Long Lake and Saskatchewan Railroad, backed by wealthy investors in Ontario and England).

But Cléophas Blondin and his family knew nothing about these struggles, and like all the incoming settlers, they had problems enough of their own. They had land to select, land to register, land to break, crops to sow. Winter was pressing closer, and they didn't even have a home. It was mid-June, 1904, and they still had miles to go.

— PROVING UP —

Ses ancêtres furent des villains:
il sera un petit seigneur.
Vive la liberté dans la Saskatchewan.

His ancestors were peasants;
he will be a little lord.
Long live the freedom of Saskatchewan.

JEAN LIONNET, *Chez les français du Canada,* 1908

THERE IS NO place on earth more lovely than the prairie on a fine day in June. If it had been exciting for the incoming settlers to gaze through the train window at the wide, unspooling horizon, it was downright thrilling to find themselves, boots on the ground, moving into that blue-domed world. Everything new: a flash of feathered iridescence, the fat trill of an unseen bird, the sweet, heady scent of wild roses everywhere.

There were no roads anywhere in the country. To get to Goose Lake, the Blondins headed out of town on Avenue H and followed a rutted track that led south along the river and then west over the open plains. There, the trail gradually unraveled into a broad swath of more or less parallel pathways. This network was known collectively as the Old Bone Trail. During the previous decade, the route had been heavily used by Métis teamsters, likely including some of the Blondins' own cousins. When the railway arrived in Saskatoon in 1890, it had created a market for bison bone, whether to be ground as fertilizer, incorporated into fine china, or, weirdest of all, crushed for filtering sugar-cane juice. And where better to extract this multipurpose resource than from a region that, in the wake of a great slaughter, was strewn with thousands upon thousands of disarticulated skeletons? Suddenly, the sun-bleached relics of the bison herds achieved a cash value of between eight and fifteen dollars a ton, delivered to the rail yard. Thus incentivized, Métis families who had once been hunters of bison fanned out across the countryside as collectors of bison bones, which they loaded onto ox-drawn carts and hauled along these very trails into Saskatoon. In all, they brought in enough to fill three thousand boxcars.

By 1904, this macabre trade had gone quiet—an ecosystem and an economy erased—though anyone with a quick eye could still sometimes catch the glint of a vertebra or a femur lying beside the trail, where it had tumbled down from a load. Now, instead of the back-and-forth of Red River carts, the trail had been overtaken by a torrent of westward-bound settlers, burdened with everything they owned and driving every kind of rig imaginable. Up ahead on the trail, there might be a wagon drawn by oxen or heavy horses or even by a mismatched ox-and-horse team. Next in line, it'd be a hay rack laden with crates of squealing pigs and squawking chickens or a fancy go-to-church-on-Sunday buggy, with a milk cow tethered to the back and a dog running around wildly, chasing ground squirrels. Whenever the trail dipped into a low spot, these crazy, overloaded outfits were likely to bog down in the mud. Then they had to be unhitched and unloaded and re-hitched to yokes of oxen that were strong enough to pull them through, and then loaded up on the other side, ready to grind westward.

It was only fifty-odd miles cross-country from Saskatoon to Goose Lake, but what with one thing and another—the meandering trail, mishaps and delays—the trip wore on for days. Some people spent the nights out on the prairie, under a firmament huge with stars. Others checked into the "stopping places" that were situated at intervals along the trail. Although the Blondins were among the earliest settlers to venture into this country, they weren't the very first. The few homesteaders who were already established in the district opened their homes (often little more than hovels) as bed-and-breakfast accommodation for the incomers. Twenty-five cents would buy you a space on the floor for your blanket, followed, at break of day, by an all-you-can-eat spread of bacon, eggs, potatoes, bread, coffee, and pie.

Here, too, was a chance to meet some of the other people who were on the trail with you and who, likely as not, were about to become your new neighbors. They were farmers from Iowa and the Dakotas; farmers from England, Scotland, Ireland, and Wales; farmers from the Maritimes and the Eastern Townships of Québec. Most of all, they were farmers of British ancestry from rural Ontario, overwhelmingly white, Protestant, and loyal to King and country. Of the estimated ten thousand homesteaders who would flood down the Old Bone Trail between 1904 and 1906, by far the majority would fall into these same categories, thereby checking all the boxes of Clifford Sifton's top "desirability" ratings.

But in the spring and summer of 1904, an unexpected and somewhat "less-preferred" group of travelers was also on the move, heading toward Goose Lake. These families had names like Bézaire, Pajot, and Brisebois, and they came from places like Rivière-aux-Canards, Ontario, and Saginaw, Michigan. Somewhere along the way, the Sureau dit Blondins—who had come west on their own initiative, intending to leave the past behind—found themselves falling into step with this company of French-speaking, Roman Catholic settlers. After making a sweeping inventory of the countryside, the members of this group had decided to settle just south of the trail, right around the famous lake, in a district where everything a homesteader could possibly want was within easy reach. Waterfowl by the thousands. Fish in the nearby Rivière aux Aigles, or Eagle Creek. Wood for fuel and timber in the sand hills a few miles to the west. And, of course, all those endless miles of fertile land, flat as the top of a table, circled round by distant horizons, free for the taking.

AND SO, THE Blondins had come halfway across the continent to escape from the life they knew, only to find themselves on the fringes of a community very much like the one they were used to. A tiny island of home in a sea of strangeness.

It hadn't happened entirely by accident, this convergence of Francophones from different points of the compass on an unlikely destination. Most of the party (all but the Blondins) had been recruited for the colony by a *prêtre-colonisateur*, a colonizing priest, named Father Georges Bouillon. If the federal government had been halfhearted in its efforts to attract

French settlers—so lax, in fact, that French-Canadian nation-alists would rise in the House of Commons to accuse it of "genocide"[1]—the leadership of the Roman Catholic Church in Western Canada had been on the case from the start. In the 1870s, the archbishop of Saint-Boniface had foreseen the changes that, even then, were afoot. "*Le nombre va nous faire défaut*," Alexandre-Antonin Taché had observed. "We are going to be outnumbered, and since under our constitutional sys-tem strength lies in numbers, we are going to find ourselves at the mercy of those who do not like us."[2]

Us versus them. French versus English. Catholic versus Protestant.

Taché's predictions had begun to come true almost imme-diately. As settlers from Ontario poured into the infant province of Manitoba, the proportion of French speakers dwindled from a solid majority in 1871 to a scant minority a few years afterward. Empowered by force of numbers, the burgeoning Anglo ascendancy wasted no time in demolish-ing the linguistic and religious protections—the vision of mutual respect between peoples—that the Métis had suc-ceeded in enshrining in the province's constitution. First to go was the upper chamber, or provincial senate, that defender of minority rights. With this obstacle cleared away, the legisla-ture took aim at the use of French in government publications and the courts, through an act that recognized English as the province's only official language. Gone, too, was the sharing of public funding between Catholic and Protestant schools. Henceforth, the Anglo majority decreed, there was to be a single "national" system, avowedly neutral in faith but with a curriculum developed by Protestant educators and imbued with Protestant beliefs.

The Licentious Fanaticks of English Canada were up to their old tricks again. Their avowed purpose was to unify the country—to make Canada a British dominion in fact as well as in name—by extinguishing what they saw as the "acquired rights" of French speakers before they became more deeply entrenched. We don't know what Mr. C. S. Blondin, lately of Tiny Township, Simcoe County, would have made of this strategy. Perhaps he would have approved: there would clearly be no danger of finding books about the Catholic Mass in the new national schools. But for the French-Catholic residents of Manitoba, and for their supporters in Québec, the new laws were a betrayal, a stinging slap in the face.

And it didn't raise their spirits to know that a similar outrage was being perpetrated farther west across the prairies. When the government of the North-West Territories was set up in the mid-1870s, both languages and denominations—English and French, Protestant and Catholic—had been entitled to equal respect. But as the local council grew in confidence, the WASP majority had begun to flex its might. No French in the legislature. No French in the courts. Catholic schools held under centralized control.

IN HIS YOUTH, Louis Riel wrote a fable in verse about a group of mice—"*les pauvrettes*," poor little things—who were preyed on mercilessly by "*un chat de bonne race anglais*," a well-bred English cat.

Eh! *Toute une nation*
Qu'un barbare tyran dans son âme hautaine
Condamne de la sorte à la destruction!

Eh! An entire nation
Condemned in this way to destruction
By the haughty soul of a barbaric tyrant![3]

The only way out of this predicament, the poet counseled, was for the mice to stick together and to persevere in the face of disheartening odds. "Despair furnishes excellent resources," he noted. And it was despair, together with the conviction, as Riel put it, that *"Le bon droit est . . . toujours vengé"*—right always triumphs in the end—that impelled the leaders of the Catholic Church in Western Canada to keep on fighting. One thing was clear from the outset: to stand any chance of winning, they would need more mice. The task of bringing in reinforcements, of augmenting the French-Catholic population across the prairies, was delegated to the *prêtres-colonisateurs*, including *Pères* Lacombe, Gravel, Gaire, and Bouillon, among others. Fortified by the assurance that French Canada had been designated by God to spread the one true faith across the breadth of the continent, they embarked on their work with optimism. *Aux souris la victoire*. Victory to the mice!

On paper, the plan was simple. First, bolster the existing Métis parishes with an influx of French-Catholic settlers sourced from wherever they could be found. Second, encourage incomers to take up the lands that had been set aside for the Métis in Manitoba but that now were abandoned or unclaimed. And third, establish a chain of brand-new parishes extending west from Manitoba to the Rockies. With God's grace, these settlements would form the spinal cord of a second Québec, a French-Canadian homeland on the prairies. All that was lacking to make this dream come true was about, say, a hundred thousand true believers.

Some of the people who responded to this extravagant vision were a little high-strung. One of them was Countess Marthe Rosine Suchet d'Albuféra, an ultra-devout Catholic who lived in Paris. In the 1880s, she fell under the influence of a con-man-in-priest's-clothing, the *abbé* Rosenberg, who introduced her to her soul mate, a woman named Fanny Rives. When Fanny died unexpectedly, Marthe was so distraught that she continued to seek her advice from beyond the grave. Rosenberg, meanwhile, had heard of the need for French-Catholic settlers in Western Canada, and he persuaded the countess to underwrite a utopian community on the Manitoba plains as a memorial to her beloved friend. The new town, Fannystelle, or Fanny's Star, was to be dedicated to the highest moral standards, unlike l'*abbé* himself, who made sure that his contributions to the project were generously recompensed.

A location was chosen on the raw prairie, thirty miles west of Winnipeg, and the first recruits arrived, a ragtag assemblage of playboys, society ladies, poets, painters, musicians, and *bon vivants*, most of them direct from Paris. Observant Catholics but not exactly saintly, they whooped around the countryside for a few years—hunting, partying, racing fast horses—until their inheritances were spent, when, in most cases, they returned to France. A similar fate befell the contingent of French aristocrats who took up land along Pipestone Creek, in what is now eastern Saskatchewan. There, they built impressive houses with names like Richelieu and La Rolanderie, hosted soirées and balls, dressed up in Parisian finery, and hunted coyotes with horse and hound, all the while exhausting their fortunes on an inventive succession of ill-conceived business ventures. Then, like their compatriots at Fannystelle, they quietly drifted away, leaving the settlements in the much more capable hands of their ex-servants and social "underlings."

Here, at least, was a subject on which the Western bishops and the Canadian government were completely in accord: "quality" in the West meant people who knew how to farm. It meant "country mice" like Cléophas, Philomène, and their adult daughter and sons, lapsed Catholics though they were. Better yet, it meant people like their new neighbors Neré and Delphine Genest, Québécois who had already served an apprenticeship on a homestead in Manitoba—at Fannystelle, to be exact—before striking out for Goose Lake. But it would take thousands of additional recruits to flesh out the archbishop's plan, and where were all those good French-speaking, Catholic farmers going to come from?

Disappointed by their experience with loopy counts and countesses, the *prêtres-colonisateurs* set out to find the right stuff in rural Belgium and France. Here their meetings and pamphlets and sermons met with some success. Imagine the surprise of the Métis residents of Saint-Laurent, north of Saskatoon, when, one day in the early 1900s, several wagonloads of people from Brittany rolled into town, decked out in their traditional garb—lace caps, sabots, *pantalons à pont*— and speaking in Breton. ("They particularly excited the hilarity of the young snobs of the place," a witness reported, "who couldn't believe their eyes.")[4] But this influx, however captivating, was simply not enough. Francophones from Europe were trickling in, when what was needed was a flood.

Québec, then. But no, that door was barred and bolted. With the population already hemorrhaging into the northern states, the leaders of the Catholic Church in *la belle province* had no interest in opening another vein and watching even more of their precious parishioners bleed away to the West. The only option left was to search for recruits among the émigrés in the United States, in the Little Canadas of New England and around the Great Lakes. And that, in the end, was where the *prêtre-colonisateur* Father Bouillon had rounded up most of the takers for the Goose Lake colony, in the economically depressed lumber towns of Saginaw and Bay City, Michigan. The mice were heading home to the Western Canadian plains.

AND SO THE fates had granted the Blondins an unexpected amnesty. It would have been tempting to slip into the familiar pathways of everyday life and language within a new circle of friends, particularly since some of their fellow travelers appeared to be very agreeable. Take, for example, Dr. Wilfrid and Mrs. (Emma) Tessier, newly arrived from Saginaw, who settled immediately north of Goose Lake and opened up their home as a "stopping place" for subsequent arrivals. Leading members of the Francophone contingent, they were people of refinement and means, their lives sweetened by *joie de vivre*. Wilfrid would long be remembered for his fine singing voice and his occasional indulgence in drink. ("Don't mind the Doctor," Madame Tessier once counseled a patient on a particularly bibulous saint's day. "He has been celebrating and feels quite happy."[5] Even so, we are told, the patient recovered quickly.) Although the family had landed in the middle of nowhere, between a slough and a rutted track, they were equipped with all of life's basic necessities, including a piano, a violin, and the doctor's sax.

That very summer, a French-speaking community began to coalesce in a loose cluster within reach of the Tessiers' place, especially around the reedy margins of Goose Lake. And it was on the outskirts of that vaguely defined perimeter that one Napoléon S. Blondin decided to take his stand, by laying claim to 160 acres of flat, treeless land, the northeast quarter of Section 22, Township 32, Range 11, west of the third meridian (NE ¼ 22-32-11-w3). Although abutted on all sides by English-speaking settlers with names like Clarkson and Green, Napoléon's homestead was just two or three miles cross-country from the Tessiers and within easy reach of families like the Pajots and St. Pierres, French Catholics who had pulled in from Bay City and Winnipeg, respectively, that same summer.

When it came to Napoléon's father, though, that was a different story. Cléophas was proud of being French, proud of his ancestors, proud of his family name. "Sureau dit Blondin" he had been born, and so he would always remain. And, yes, it was a comfort (real, if scarcely to be admitted) to find oneself in the company of people who shared your tribal history and spoke your mother tongue. But he had not the slightest interest in getting deeply ensnared with them. He was finished with the Catholic Church and with being told what to think; he had come west to live large, in liberty. So, instead of squeezing himself into the French enclave near the Tessiers, he continued another eight miles down the trail to the next stopping place.

Here, hospitality was on offer from Richard ("Rich") and Mary Anne Harris, with their brood of tousle-haired little kids. Born and raised in Ontario, the Harrises had made the leap west to a homestead in southern Manitoba in 1891, so they were already hardened to the challenges ahead of them. There were no airs and graces about their establishment, no musical soirées in the parlor, no cheerful intemperance. The Harrises were Protestants, God-fearing Methodists, and Rich—his spiritual authority enhanced by a magnificently patriarchal beard—would go on to serve the district as lay preacher. Less prosperous than the Tessiers, who soon were welcoming their guests into a handsome two-story dwelling with a sweeping veranda out front, the Harrises lived in a soddie, an improvised shelter made from slabs of root-bound earth that had been sliced out of the prairie and piled around a crude framework of poles to form four walls and a roof. Although sod houses could be elegant and substantial, the Harrises' was not. It looked like a pile of dirt and had no windows.

But the search had to come to an end somewhere, and the district around the Harris stopping place offered everything a person could want. Rich Harris seemed to think it was a corner of paradise. Wood from the sand hills, he promised, enough to last for years. Fish in the creek. Waterfowl by the thousands from not one lake but two, the second, known as Devil's Lake, just a few miles away. And then there was the land itself, the soil black and substantial—deliciously crumbly in your hands—so different from the sand Cléophas and his sons had struggled with back at Lafontaine. By early fall, Cléophas had made his selection—NE ¼ 26-32-12-w3—a block of wonderfully level and unencumbered land, immediately adjacent to the Harrises'.

As part of the "proving-up" process, homesteaders were ordinarily expected to reside on their land for at least six months in each of three successive years, but this requirement was waived for fathers and sons who selected their holdings close to one another. Although Napoléon's claim was five miles away, he was granted this small reprieve. "I have no house," he reported to an approving homestead office, "as I live with my father." Where were you when absent from your claim? "I have been working with my father," he said.[6] Although Napoléon and two of his brothers claimed homesteads in the district, the old man's place was the hub for the entire clan, and home was the sod house the family erected there that first September. The structure measured twenty feet wide by twenty-four feet long (not bad, under the circumstances) and housed seven full-grown adults and an infant. It wouldn't be long before Cléophas's young wife, Philomène, was expecting another child.

THESE DAYS, IT'S absurdly easy to get from Saskatoon, via the hamlet of Tessier, to the village of Harris. A journey that took the Blondins two days of bone-jarring travel is now a forty-five-minute spin along the pavement of Highway 7. But finding your way from Harris to Cléophas's homestead still requires a measure of perseverance. As someone who grew up on the prairies, I expect all roads to be laid out with geometric precision, in a rigid network of straight lines and right-angle intersections. The highway that passes through Harris, however, has other ideas. Following the logic of the Old Bone Trail, it slices across the grid from northeast to southwest, a worthy gesture of remembrance but one that sends my inner compass into a tizzy.

That's why, the first time we go looking, I choose the wrong road out of the townsite, and Keith and I find ourselves scudding through a featureless landscape of fields. We count off the road crossings, mile by mile, but there are no clues out here. After a while, Keith points to the directional indicator on the dash—has to be that-a-way, he says—and so we bumble back into town to try again.

Now we're heading north, which should be correct, and thankfully, yes, here's the proof: a massive boulder, bearing a plaque, looms alongside the gravel road. The text informs us, with embossed solemnity, that we have reached the site of THE HARRIS STOPPING PLACE ON THE BONE TRAIL. "The sod home of Richard Harris," it reminds us, "provided food and shelter for the many travelers [along the route] and their animals."

Many travelers and animals then. Now: nothing but silence. Look around and all you see are more of those endless fields, indistinguishable in their bright-yellow sameness. A sky freighted with platoons of gray-bottomed clouds. A narrow gravel track dwindling into the distance. Cléophas's homestead is just half a mile ahead. Roll on.

More silence. More big, wide-open country running to the end of everything. On the rim of the earth, miles away, islands of trees are etched dark against the horizon, marking the sites of distant farms. These days, no one believes that it's possible to support a family on a single quarter-section, the vicious lie that was fed to the homesteaders. (According to the latest figures from Statistics Canada, the average farm in

Saskatchewan now encompasses ten times that much land.) Almost everyone has fled from the countryside, and it's lonely here. When I get out of the truck to take a look around, a breeze has risen, making the canola dance and hiss. No way I could go tromping through this midsummer crop. No way I'd find any trace of the Blondins even if I did.

One thing is clear, however. Cléophas must have chosen well, because his homestead is still in full-scale agricultural production after more than a century. And the same also turns out to be true of Napoléon: when we drive past his claim later in the day, we find the same lowering sky, the same unnerving quiet, the same glowing, productive fields. But if I had been hoping for more personal revelations—the footprint of a sod building, a buckle from a harness, a shard of kitchen crockery—I can see I won't find them here. This land has been worked and worried year after year for decades, and its memories have blown away like dust. If it was a little tricky to find our way to this location, it's even harder to find our way back to how it was.

"Wouldn't want to be out here in winter," Keith says, nodding into the wind.

"Six paces wide by eight paces long," I say. I scuff the outline into the road with my feet. "That's all the house they had."

Keith turns to look at the shape. "And I sometimes complain that *our* place is too small."

"Bet their soddie was better built than the Harrises', though. If it's anything like our house, I mean."

We stand in the center of the outline, fingertip to fingertip, trying to span the space with our outstretched arms. "Hardly enough room in here to swing a cat," one of us says.

Five men. Two women. The crying of an infant.

A FEW DAYS after the soddie was completed, Napoléon fell ill, an absence-from-duty that he would duly acknowledge on his homestead file. Although he didn't go into details, the problem must have been serious, since he went all the way to Winnipeg—two days by trail, two more by train—to seek medical attention. By late winter, he was well enough to take on jobs as a laborer, but it wasn't until spring, when he returned to the Goose Lake Country, that work would begin in earnest. In order to obtain title, a homesteader was required to break at least 30 of his 160 acres and put a portion of it in crop, goals that were supposed to be achieved within a timeframe of residency. In keeping with these requirements, Napoléon broke six acres that first summer; his brother Hercules (who had settled on land close to the family headquarters) managed about the same. This was a decent start, but they might have been farther ahead if they hadn't also been answerable to the demands of their old man.

Cléophas was a man on a mission that summer, on fire with ambition. There was something miraculous about this new country, the way it yielded itself to a farmer with a team and a walking plow. Not a stone to stop you, not a stump or a root. Those were your hands on the handles, guiding the blade; your feet pursuing the ribbon of sod that curled away from the mold board in a continuous twisted strand. A half mile out to the end of the field, a half mile back again. The creak of leather on sweaty flanks, the soft huff of effortful breathing, the steady fall of hooves. And over and around it all, a fanfare of ululating white birds, like a celestial benediction for work well done. By the end of their first full season, Cléophas and his sons had broken 120 acres of his

homestead and fenced the remaining 40 as pasture for his
teams. That done, they had proceeded to "backset" and
cross-plow half of their new breaking and planted Red Fife
wheat. It was an amazing achievement. There seemed to be
no limit to what muscle and willpower could accomplish.

It can't have been long before the Blondins (or my homesteading grandparents or thousands of others) began to think
of themselves as "locals," as true Westerners. Every morning,
they emerged into the sunlight from a dwelling that they
had constructed out of the land itself. Day after day, trudg-
ing behind the plow or seed drill, they breathed dirt, ate dirt,
thought dirt—dirt in their hair, their eyes, their dreams. How
much of the prairie did you have to get under your skin before
you became a part of it, before you became, in your own mind
at least, native to this place? Meanwhile, most of the actual
Indigenous peoples—the Nehiyawak, Siksika, Kainai, and
others who had relied on this rich part of the country for
food and medicine for generations beyond counting—were
incarcerated on distant reserves, forbidden to travel without
official permission from government agents. Only the Métis
had freedom of movement, and occasionally, they'd still come
rattling and squealing down the Old Bone with their carts and
wagons, livestock and dogs, full of color and life, creating a
moment of spectacle for the homesteaders. But the onlookers
watched the Métis families move past with incomprehen-
sion—they are gypsies, come to steal you, some of the Goose
Lake settlers told their kids—as if they were figures of fantasy
from a storybook.

Some people mattered more than others out here; some
people not at all. Cléophas Blondin and his sons had busted

a gut to win a place in the vanguard of those who mattered most, to be the most desirable of desirable settlers. But, as they were about to be reminded, membership in that exclusive club depended on your ancestry. *Les chats de bonne race anglais* were on the prowl again.

― CRYSTAL BEACH ―

Une certaine qualité de gentillesse
est toujours signe de trahison.

A certain quality of kindness
is always a sign of betrayal.

FRANÇOIS MAURIAC, *Le noeud de vipères,* 1932

I N EARLY MARCH of 1905, while Napoléon was still
recuperating in Winnipeg and the rest of the Blondin
family were holed up on their new homestead—feeding
their horses, tending the woodstove, biding their time until
spring—a group of white male settlers took time out from
their regular duties to meet in solemn conclave in Regina. As
delegates to the Fourteenth Annual Session of the Right Worshipful Provincial Grand Orange Lodge of the North-West
Territories (Eastern Division), these gentlemen represented
local associations in fifty-two communities across the central plains, in areas where settlement was already established,
places like Nutana, Saskatoon, and Moose Jaw. In their everyday lives, they were farmers and small-town businessmen,

132 with the occasional reverend in their midst, but today they were brushed and polished for the occasion, dressed in their dark Sunday best with shimmering sashes of scarlet or purple or orange draped over their midriffs. The meeting space in Regina's Orange Hall where they were gathered was bright, as well, bedecked with the red, white, and blue of the Union Jack. A handsome silk banner hung from a stand beside the lectern, fringed with shiny tassels and emblazoned with mystic symbols: a runic book, a temple, a five-pointed star. Clearly, something out of the ordinary was about to happen here.

The most striking of the emblems that decorated the room, whether worked in embroidery or depicted in pen and ink, showed William of Orange, also known as King William III of England, astride a prancing white steed, his right hand raised in a gesture of command. More than two centuries earlier, he had led a victorious Protestant army against Britain's reigning monarch, the Catholic James I. To the undying satisfaction of the Orange Lodge, "King Billy" had freed England from the tyranny of the Pope, a triumph made all the more precious by the spilling of ancestral blood. When Irish Catholics dared to resist the abrogation of their civil and religious rights, William had crushed their resistance, on July 12, 1690, at the Battle of the Boyne, an event that lived on among Orangemen as the "Glorious Twelfth."

As for that hand raised in defiance, there was no doubt what it meant. The Pope was always scheming for unfair advantage, and Protestants must remain on full alert. The Orange watchword was "No Surrender."

Anyone who doubted that Catholics were full of treachery had only to consider recent developments in Ireland, where Papist republicans were now openly encouraging sedition against the Crown. And here in Canada, from the Battle of the Plains of Abraham to the *guerre des Patriotes*, and onward to the present through a never-ending war of words, French Catholics had never been anything but trouble. Seen through the lens of the Orange Order, Québec was an aberration: foreign, unassimilable, mutinous, insatiably demanding. It did not escape the notice of the delegates in Regina that they were gathered in the very city where "one who proved himself a rebel and traitor to the constitution and laws of this great Dominion"—Louis Riel—had been brought to justice twenty years earlier.[1]

It was presumably this unholy stew of ethnic, political, and religious resentments that made Orangeism so attractive to English Canadians in the early twentieth century. You didn't have to be Irish or even British to join the movement, just loyal to King and country and fiercely Protestant. Hot-tempered, sometimes to the point of violence, the Order had been banned throughout the Empire at various times in the past. Nonetheless, by 1905, there were more Orange lodges in Canada and Newfoundland than in Ulster (the Orange homeland), and English-Canadian membership would continue to increase for the next twenty years, eventually accounting for 60 percent of the international total. In parts of Ontario, essentially the entire adult male population consisted of Orange adherents. In the course of the meeting in Regina, the assembly would learn that their own numbers had leaped ahead by 30 percent over the previous year, not bad for a region on the farthest-flung margins of Empire.

With guards at the door to repel outsiders, the delegates got down to business. Days earlier, the federal government had finally introduced legislation to carve two new provinces out of the North-West Territories, Alberta to the west and Saskatchewan to the east. Most people agreed with the plan in general, although local politicians were already squawking about Ottawa's decision to retain control of the region's lands and natural resources. The Orangemen were content to let that issue slip past, but what they couldn't abide were the limitations imposed on the new provinces with regard to schools. In these provisions, they caught a whiff of French-Catholic interference.

At first glance, the clauses in question didn't seem like much to get in a twist about. They were constitutional boiler-plate that acknowledged the new provinces' absolute control over education, with a single exception. The preexisting right of sectarian minorities to maintain their distinctive schools had to be respected. This stipulation echoed guarantees made at the time of Confederation to safeguard the inter-ests of Anglo-Protestants in Québec and then extended, in a spirit of fairness, to Ontario's (mainly French-speaking) Catholics, through the British North America Act. By some interpretations, the ideal of tolerance and mutual consid-eration embodied in this article formed the bedrock of the Canadian state. This was the vision the Métis had fought for at Red River in 1870, the vision that was expressed in the foundational laws of Manitoba and across the prairie West. The Alberta and Saskatchewan Acts merely restated a principle that had been expressed many times before, in the interests of peaceful coexistence and neighborliness.

But the gentlemen gathered that day in Regina were not interested in making nice. Their goal, stated freely and without hesitation, was to promote the advancement of Protestants against the provocations of the Pope, and to do so amid pro-testations of respect and goodwill toward their Catholic neighbors. In their own eyes at least, Orangemen were the highest type of citizens, men with the national interest at heart. In fact, as one of the speakers reminded the meeting, the Orange Lodge was conducting its "grand work" not *against* but *for* its Papist brothers, selflessly seeking the moment when "the mantle of Roman intolerance [and] superstition" would fall away from them, and they would be admitted to the liberties of Protestantism.[2] Guaranteeing the right of the Catholic minority to maintain separate schools would only delay that happy outcome by keeping people in the dark, a prospect that the Orangemen could not tolerate in good conscience.

And it wasn't just individual souls who hung in the balance; the entire country was at risk. Who knew how many of the incoming settlers were Roman, or even Greek, Catholics? Who knew how many of them spoke heathen tongues instead of the King's English? "A very grave responsibility has fallen to [our] lot," the Lodge's grand secretary would declare in 1906, his voice sputtering with concern. In its efforts to develop the country, the federal government had gone to "the uttermost parts of the earth" and recruited "vast hordes of people" to come to the West, some of them "dressed in the skins of animals and professing strange and, in many cases, false religions." This "heterogeneous mass of humanity" had been shipped to the plains in their thousands and "dumped down in our midst."

"And this is our task," the speaker concluded. "With their strange dialects, their superstitions and gross ignorance and filth, we are supposed to build up a homogenous [race] of intelligent, industrious, honest, clean, civilized people."[3] Hiving the riffraff off in separate schools would just make the problem worse. The only solution was to ensure that every

136   young person in the country passed through the refining fire of a centrally controlled "national" school, to emerge as a worthy citizen of the British Empire.

And so the Right Worshipful Grand Orange Lodge of the North-West Territories had no choice but to take a stand. In a telegram sent directly to the prime minister, they took the federal government to task for its "unwarranted and tyrannical" attempt to intrude into the educational affairs of the new provinces.[4] At the same time, they sent a note of thanks to their strongest ally in Ottawa, the now former minister of the interior, Clifford Sifton. Back in the capital after a lengthy absence, Sifton had taken one look at the separate-school clause, thrown his hands up in disgust, and resigned from the cabinet. Although he had taken the risk of opening the country to immigration from Eastern Europe, he was in other respects a man of conventionally narrow views, with a reflexive respect for the Protestant cause (an ancestor had fought alongside King Billy) and for the British Empire; he was also a prominent advocate for national schools.

Still powerful despite his dramatic abdication, Sifton succeeded in having the generic clauses replaced with more specific provisions. Gone was the deliberately woolly phrasing of the initial draft, with its evocation of the foundational principles of equality and respect. In its place stood the chapter and verse of regulations passed by the Protestant-dominated Legislature of the North-West Territories in 1892, and refined in 1901, which imposed severe limitations on minority schools. Although separate schools were still permitted, they were placed under government control, no longer able to choose their own textbooks, set their own curriculum, certify their own teachers, or choose their own language of instruction.

But no need to worry, the Protestant majority promised their
Catholic neighbors. We are fair-minded men. Trust us.

In the end, the squabble over the Alberta and Saskatchewan
Acts was a tempest in a teapot, *une tempête dans un verre d'eau*.
When the storm subsided, everything was pretty much the
same as it had been before: the Anglo-Protestant elite remained
in charge, and the status quo was reinforced. The gentlemen
of the Right Worshipful Grand Orange Lodge could congratulate themselves on holding the line against the Papists, though
they still had one regret. While separate schools had been held
in check, they had not been eliminated. But Orangemen had
long memories and knew how to hold a grudge. They would be
back, in numbers: you could depend on it.

IT'S DOUBTFUL THAT news of this kerfuffle ever reached the
scattered homesteads of the Goose Lake Country. It was late
winter, after all, the weather potentially lethal, nobody going
in or out more than necessary. There was no railway in the
district, no post office, no newspaper. No radio or telegraph.
The nearest connection to the outside world was the ram-
shackle coupling of hamlets—Nutana and Saskatoon—two
hard days down the trail. And even if the Blondins and their
neighbors had somehow picked up rumors of these distant
squabbles, they might not have been deeply stirred. They had
other, more immediate concerns, things like the prospect of
break-up and spring seeding, fences and binder twine. Things
like their ever-dwindling financial resources.

Besides, the tussle over minority rights was not exactly
news. Ever since the Conquest, the English had been trying to

138   make French Canadians over in their own image. The rhetoric that was now being deployed to restrict Catholic education in the new province of Saskatchewan had seen service before, whether in the Petits Canadas of New England or the Little Québecs of Ontario and Manitoba. (Cléophas Blondin had become so accustomed to the Protestant position back in Lafontaine that he had gone rogue—breaking with his ancestors, his family, and his friends to add his voice to the clamor against Catholic influence in education.) So there was nothing unexpected or surprising about what was going on.

Was the government to be trusted in its promise of fairness? Of course not, the French-Catholic clergy said. Over the preceding decade, the authorities had made lofty declarations of "benevolence, impartiality and justice" and then ruled against Catholic interests. Under this regime, "schools in the North-West could be materialistic, infidel or atheistic," the Reverend Father H. Leduc lamented in a tract on the subject entitled Hostilité démasquée (Hostility Unmasked). "At best," he continued, "they are permitted to be Protestant. But Catholic schools must disappear; such is the decree of the Lodges and the Triangles [the Orange Order and Freemasons]."[5]

If the Catholic faith, la vraie foi, was under attack, so, by extension, was the French language, la belle langue. Language and faith had become almost inseparable, a connection forged in the long struggle against the one-two punch of Anglo-Protestant rule. "La langue gardienne de la foi," the saying went. "La foi gardienne de la langue." So it was doubly painful for the Catholic leadership to watch the devious ways in which the law could be deployed. Consider, for example, what happened to the Blondins' Métis cousins at Prairie Ronde. Drawn back to their roots along the South Saskatchewan River in the early

1900s, the Trottiers had settled with their close relatives, in a kinship network based on the ties among married sisters: Ursule, Angélique, and Philomène Laframboise. The cluster these families formed was definitely Catholic and probably multilingual, with fluency in Cree, Michif, and French.

So that same winter, in March of 1905, when community members petitioned the government for a school, they might have hoped for some recognition of their special requirements. What they got instead was a bare-walled shack, without even such basics as a blackboard, so badly located that many children had to walk for miles through brush and wetlands to get to class. Most dispiriting of all, the teacher spoke only English, one language the Métis students lacked. The community complained to the government, and complained again, but no improvements were made.

Sometimes, however, the system could be gamed to advantage. Although the law made English the compulsory language of instruction, it also created an opening for a primary course, *un cours primaire*, in French (as well as for supplementary classes in other languages, at the parents' expense). The meaning of that crucial term, "*primaire*," was not specified. Who knew how long it might take to master the basics of French language and literature? And, really, unless the school inspector came calling, how was anyone to know which textbooks were used in the classroom or what language the teacher spoke? With luck and a certain measure of political acumen, a community might be able to create the kind of school it desired, simply by staying under the government's radar.

It was this work-around that permitted Father Bouillon to continue attracting French-Catholic settlers to his

French-Catholic colony at Goose Lake—the Lalondes and Champagnes, Provosts and Comeaults, Beauchamps and Gagnons, among others. By 1907, there were enough communicants in the district to form a parish centered on a pretty, white-steepled church south of the hamlet of Tessier. They named it Notre-Dame du Bon Conseil, Our Lady of Good Counsel. A few years later, the community celebrated the establishment of Bouillon School nearby, with seventeen Francophone students under the supervision of Madame Antonia Brisette, a French-speaking teacher. Despite the rumbles of animosity from "*les Loges et les Triangles*," they had cleared a space for themselves in the middle of their Anglo neighbors.

MEANWHILE, A FEW miles down the trail at Harris, everything was full steam ahead. No time for controversy or politics here, just work from sunrise to sunset. In short order, Cléophas had doubled his horsepower, from four beasts to eight, and acquired a small herd of milk cows and a couple of hogs. If only his old neighbors in Penetang could see him now: his granaries, his sheds and stables, the wood-framed annex he'd added to the family's sod house. They'd needed the extra space, especially after the arrival of baby Antoinette, little Nettie, in the winter of 1906. Her mother, Philomène, was now thirty-six; her father, still vigorous and unstoppable, in his early sixties.

The younger men in the family were also getting ahead, and no one faster than Napoléon. Fully recovered from his illness and advancing through his mid-twenties, he took on the homestead requirements at a frantic pace, meeting and exceeding the annual targets by breaking fourteen, then forty, then sixty acres in successive years and seeding his expanding fields to crop. By the fall of 1907, three years into this venture, he had his own shack, his own stable and granary, his own team of draft horses. A man could curse at those sweaty, swaying backsides in English or French, whichever came naturally; the horses didn't care about your religion or your ancestry. What mattered out here was keeping your eyes on the far horizon, keeping your plowshare in the ground. Do that, and you were guaranteed a prosperous future. Before you knew it, this land, which had cost you a tenner, would have doubled or tripled in value, and you, who had started with nothing, would be worth a fortune.

Whatever hesitation settlers like the Blondins had felt about coming west quickly faded away in the sunshine of their early success. "*Quand on a bu de l'eau de la Saskatchewan,*" a satisfied homesteader noted, "*on ne peut plus se passer d'en boire.*"[6] Once you've drunk the water of Saskatchewan, you can't stop drinking it. In this same state of near-intoxication, one of the Blondins' new Scottish neighbors wrote to his family back home: "I am getting on fine and am liking the country very much and you can do anything you like out here and nobody says anything to you."[7] In this atmosphere of freedom and liberality, a descendant of impoverished crofters or *habitant* farmers could become a man of substance and means, entirely through the exercise of his own abilities.

On April 29, 1908, having fulfilled all the prescribed duties and filed the appropriate paperwork, Napoléon Sureau dit Blondin became the registered owner of his quarter-section homestead. Within months, his father and his brother Hercules had received their titles as well, with Alexandre following suit a few years afterward. The family, which had been land-hungry for generations, had suddenly amassed an estate of 640 acres in four separate plots, the equivalent of one square mile of farmland. And that was just a start. In one way and another, whether through government come-ons or private deals, Cléophas, Hercules, and Napoléon would each soon acquire an additional 160-acre farm. They were going to be big men in this new country: no one could stop them.

All around them, the district was advancing. Every spring, hundreds more fortune-seekers came jouncing down the trail to settle on vacant land, enticed by hype about the region's fabulous "chocolate clay loams" and risk-free prospects. "The Finest Land of a Fine Country," one promotional brochure boasted. "Do you want to slave all your life or does complete independence in ten years sound better?"[8] For a man like Napoléon Blondin, the choice was no choice at all. When opportunity beckoned, he was ready for the call. Over the past several years, twin rails of steel—the Goose Lake Line— had been striking west from Saskatoon, along a straight-line approximation of the Old Bone route. In the fall of 1908, the track reached Mile 52, two miles straight south of the Harris stopping place, until then the center of community life. (Mr. Harris ran the post office there and presided over services at the new Methodist Church.) With the arrival of the railway, however, everyone's focus shifted to the new site along the tracks. The church was skidded into town, and businesses immediately began springing up: a butcher, a general merchant, a grain buyer. With his first harvest as a landowner safely in the bin—on fire with confidence—N. S. Blondin dragged a building in from his homestead, fitted it with a counter and glass-fronted cabinets, and set himself up in business as the community of Harris's Pioneer Hardware Man.

Through the following summer, and the next, the streets rang with the clatter of hammers. By 1910, the settlement's amenities included a doctor and a druggist, a harness maker and a blacksmith, two lumberyards, two feed barns, four grain elevators, and a flour mill. Whether you were looking for a cup of coffee or a coffin, you could find it here. Soon you would even be able to have your Sunday shirt and collar done up by Jim Kee at his laundry on Main Street, secure in the knowledge that, under a 1912 Saskatchewan statute, he was not permitted to hire white women to work for him, thereby protecting them from his "undesirable" Oriental inclinations.

Although the place was still rough around the edges, with its unpainted buildings, hitching rails, and muddy streets, the village of Harris held itself to a high standard, worthy of its undoubted future importance as a commercial hub. The two-room schoolhouse was proudly constructed of brick and offered a full range of classes, in English, naturally. But the settlement's crowning glory was its new resort. Despite its forbidding name, Devil's Lake, just west of town, was a beautiful spot, an oasis in this endless expanse of open country, with swimmable water, sandy beaches, and a fringe of scrubby trees. It wasn't exactly Georgian Bay, but it was something. In the summer of 1910, a party of volunteers—almost certainly including Napoléon Blondin, now "Paul" to his new friends—cleaned up a stretch of shoreline and invited everyone from miles around to a community picnic. The day was such a success that Devil's Lake was transformed into Crystal Beach, a summer playground for the entire district.

There's a wonderfully odd old photo that captures the scene at Crystal Beach in those early days. In the absence of the piers and pavilions that would come later, someone has driven a team and wagon into the shallows, and half a dozen gents in fedoras and suit coats are lounging on the wagon bed, seated or standing, shoulders relaxed, momentarily at rest. A dozen others, bolder, are waist-deep in the water, men and boys—what a man's world this was!—and one guy, front and center, is submerged up to his shoulders, his head comically afloat on the glassy surface. According to the files at the museum in Harris (a mecca for anyone curious about the town's history), that swimming figure is "a Blondin," though which Blondin it does not say. But I remember seeing a print of the same photo in granddaughter Lorena's album, with an arrow and a handwritten label from an earlier generation that identify him as "Dad." Everything in the photo, even the team of horses, seems to be holding its breath. There is no wind, the lake shimmers in the sunshine, and Napoléon Blondin's face beams with contentment.

Come to think of it, there's another photo that catches a similar summery vibe: the one that came tumbling out of our walls in Saskatoon. When I bring the image up on my computer for a closer look, I am amazed by what I see. The photo was clearly taken at Crystal Beach. The sheen of the water, the reedy edge, the encircling shade of trees, all now familiar to me. Even the building in the background, a feature I hadn't really noticed when I'd considered the photo before, is recognizable from other views of the place that I've seen at the museum. And having established the location, I can fix the date as well. The women's ankle-length skirts and updos suggest a time before World War I; there is no trace of the flapper's sassiness about them. As for the vehicle they are leaning against, Dr. Google informs me it is a McLaughlin-Buick Model 8 touring car, circa 1910.

On the right side of the image, a man with Napoléon Blondin's strong features stands at ease, hands thrust in his pockets, shirt open at the neck, a flicker of contentment softening his gaze. If only I could step into the picture, introduce myself, and warn him about what is coming next. Has he heard that the Loyal Orange Lodge has set its sights on Harris and is heading for Crystal Beach?

ORANGEISM HAD ARRIVED in the Goose Lake Country with the earliest Anglo settlers, though at first it was more of a tendency than an organized force. That changed around 1910, when the Grand Orange Lodge of Saskatchewan hired a man named William Henry Grattan Armstrong, a native of County Armagh, as a full-time, professional organizer. As Armstrong would report to his brothers at their annual convention in Saskatoon the following spring, he was not one to spare himself. With true missionary zeal, in just twelve months, he had traveled 17,744 miles, initiated 172 new members, "advanced" many others ceremonially through Purple, Blue, and Scarlet degrees, delivered dozens of public lectures, written hundreds of letters, and founded thirty-six new local associations. All of this, as he explained, was "to further the great and glorious principles we [Orangemen] profess—the maintenance of Protestantism and the transmission to posterity of the priceless heritage of freedom purchased for us by the life blood of our ancestors at Derry, Aughrim,

146 Inniskillen and the Boyne."[9] As a result of his prodigious and patriotic efforts, the Orange Lodge was now established in 126 communities across the province (up from around 50 just five years before) with a total strength of some three thousand members.

As the Goose Lake Line pushed westward, it opened up new territory to Brother Armstrong's proselytizing zeal. Wherever he stepped off the train—at Delisle, Laura, or Tessier, at Harris or the nearby rural community of Valley Centre, down the line at Zealandia or Rosetown—a new lodge sprang up in his wake, with its own Right Worshipful Master and regular meeting date. Local 2014 in Harris chose the first Thursday of the month (later, portentously, "the first Saturday after the full of the moon"). Membership was only open to the highest type of men: no blasphemers, no drinkers, and, of course, no Papists. Anyone who was a Catholic, had ever been a Catholic, or had married a Catholic was explicitly banned, a rule that automatically excluded the entire Francophone community near Tessier and the free-thinking Blondins of Harris.

More than just a social snub, this hard line could have far-reaching, even disastrous, consequences for those outside the fold, since Orangemen were bound by oath to stick together. In Toronto, this solidarity resulted in a "dark network," complete with a secret handshake and mystic signals, that focused support behind a succession of candidates for mayor and allowed the Order to dominate civic politics until the middle of the twentieth century. In a little town like Harris, Orange preference meant favoring one neighbor over another and could spell the end of a small operator like a Pioneer Hardware Man.

Somehow, in the face of this divisive intrusion, Napoléon had to find a way to stay friends with everyone. And perhaps that is one reason he invited the local Anglican congregation, which lacked a sanctuary of its own, to hold services in the upper floor of his store. But this makeshift arrangement did not sit well with the members of the newly formed Harris Orange Lodge, who thought the Anglicans deserved the dignity of a proper church. On July 12, 1911, as a fund-raiser, they hosted a celebration of the Glorious Twelfth on the shores of Crystal Beach, an event that was remembered long thereafter as "one of the largest and best ever held in this part of the West."[10] A local farmer in a foppish hat stood in for King William, with a saddle horse for his white steed, and the Orangemen, bright and jaunty in their embroidered collars, marched behind him as God's victorious army.

By the end of the day, the Lodge, with an assist from its ladies, had raised four hundred dollars through the sale of refreshments (completely teetotal, of course), enough to cover most of the cost of building the English Church. People had come from miles around for a day of good, clean family fun. They'd eaten rhubarb pie and hand-churned ice cream, clapped in time with the marching songs. They'd sung the national anthem, "God Save the King," with gusto. Through it all, the Orangemen had entertained the crowd with their dazzling contradictions: they were straitlaced yet showy, judgmental yet generous, dictatorial yet unstinting in their appeals to fair play and justice. And so, the Loyal Orange Lodge insinuated itself into the normal round of community life, poisonous and seductive.

10

— BATTLE GROUNDS —

L'angoisse, au fond,
n'est qu'un dérivé de l'espoir.

Anxiety, at heart,
is nothing but an outgrowth of hope.

HUBERT AQUIN, *L'invention de la mort,* 1991

OR THE MEMBERS of the Loyal Orange Lodge at Harris, the Blondins would always be outsiders because of their ancestry, too tainted by their French-Catholic heritage to be admitted to the fraternity. For the parishioners of Notre-Dame du Bon Conseil at Goose Lake, by contrast, they were not French Catholic enough. Yet the differences that set the family apart, though sometimes awkward, were not calamitous. Misfits though they were, they were not pariahs: it's not as if they were Métis, after all, or Jews or Chinese or peasants from Eastern Europe. They were bona fide British subjects, by birth and always, as they pointed out on their homestead documents. Although their mother tongue was French, they were Ontarians (not Quebecers, as census takers sometimes assumed) and thus naturally, necessarily, fluent in English, too. Most important, they were just the kind of go-getters who were called for out West, men of ambition and purpose.

As both a landowning farmer and a merchant, Napoléon "Paul" S. Blondin quickly earned a place for himself as a player in the community. He was as busy as ever, as witness the reports of his comings and goings in the town's new weekly paper, the *Goose Lake Herald*. "What we hear, what we see, we gather up and give to thee," the editor promised,[1] and since the Pioneer Hardware was a few doors down from the newspaper's premises, he saw and heard a lot about his neighbor's activities. Alongside notices about an "odd two-headed onion on display at the newspaper office" and an "upper set of Artificial teeth" lost near Crystal Beach,[2] the *Herald* provided up-to-the-minute reports of N. S. Blondin's many forays into Saskatoon as a "business visitor"—two hours in by train in the morning, two hours back at night—to keep his shelves filled with an array of stoves, pipes, polishes, paints, and widgets. "Never in the history of Harris has our stock been so complete," one of his ads declared.[3]

When Harris decided to enter a team in the Goose Lake Hockey League—to do battle against "unbeatable" Zealandia and ultimately bring it to its knees—N. S. Blondin attended the start-up meeting. When it was time to organize a retail merchants' association, there he was again. He even got himself elected to town council for a term in 1913. Small wonder that a year later, when the paper put out a special supplement to celebrate the town's fifth birthday, N. S. Blondin was honored as one of the district's first settlers and entrepreneurs. "He is energetic in every way," the paper attested, "and has succeeded in building up a substantial business."[4]

It was unnerving to note, however, that he was facing new competitors. Two well-heeled local gentlemen, Messrs. Jones and Trapp, had recently gone into business against him, rivaling his stock of hardware and furniture. N. S. Blondin was a force of nature and had fought for all of his success. But hard work was no guarantee that you wouldn't lose everything in an instant.

TERRIBLE THINGS HAPPENED to people out here. Over the last several years, while his own star had been rising, Napoléon had looked on helplessly as one of his brothers had come undone. "Harry," as Hercules was now sometimes known, had been happy in 1908 when he proved up on his homestead and received the title to 160 acres of fertile prairie land. He'd still been laughing a year or so later when, at the age of twenty-six, he'd married an English-born girl named Mabel Martin, sweet sixteen. And he'd been on top of the world the following spring, when he'd signed the contract for a "purchased homestead" three or four miles from town and just west of Crystal Beach. It was light land, some of it downright sandy, and the work went rapidly. By 1912, two years into this venture, he had 120 acres in cultivation, with the remaining 40 acres of sand hills as pasture for a milk cow, a small herd of hogs, and his all-important team of draft horses.

By then, the young couple had two small children, Lucy (named for Mabel's mother) and baby Lloyd, with another on the way. What would the bygone generations of Simon-Pierres and Marie-Amables have made of those stunningly

Anglo names? But the past didn't count for anything here, only tomorrow mattered. One day soon, they'd build a fine house with dormer windows and curlicue trim to replace this tiny, cramped shack. One day, Hercules would be an established landowner with money in the bank. Just look at what he, with the help of his young wife, had already accomplished. In a few short years, the physical requirements of the "purchased homestead" agreement had been met and exceeded—residency established, land broken and seeded to crop. All that remained was three more or less trivial payments of sixty-four dollars per year. With the price of wheat hovering around a dollar a bushel, it was a sweet deal.

And it was with this expectation, buoyed by faith in himself and in the country, driven by a desire to get ahead, that Hercules took what would turn out to be a fatal misstep. He made a modest investment in some modern farming equipment, including several plows, a separator, and a 25-horsepower gasoline engine. Again, the terms were agreeable: a small down payment, with the rest to be paid after the next harvest. But there was no harvest that year, 1913—no rain when it was needed, too much when it was not—and Hercules quickly tumbled into default. Almost before he knew what was happening, he had fallen behind on both his equipment payments and his homestead installments.

The implement company, International Harvester, was the first to strike. A sheriff turned up at the farm one day with an order against Hercules for the unpaid bill. With no satisfaction forthcoming, the sheriff ordered his crew to gather up everything of value, not just the farm implements but also the family's horses, cattle, and hogs. Item after item was loaded up and driven away from the farm.

Without the means to continue farming, Hercules skidded his house onto a lot in Harris—his wife and kids would be better off in town—and took a job as a hired man, demoted from the status of "farmer" to "farm laborer." In quick succession, two more children, Lily and Norman, were added to the family, meaning two more mouths to feed, and soon he was forced to sell his original homestead to make ends meet. A fifth child, baby Olga, would arrive in the summer of 1916. By then, Hercules's only remaining material asset, his second, purchased homestead, was in jeopardy as well. In the corridors of power in distant Ottawa, some faceless bureaucrat had initiated an "application for cancellation" against him. Pay up, the government ordered, or accept the consequences.

By now Hercules had been in the Goose Lake Country for twelve long and laborious years. And yet here he was, faced with the likely prospect that he would end up with nothing to show for it. "I am trying to get together money enough to go back to farming again after losing all to the machine company," he told the authorities, hoping for a sympathetic ear. For once, he was in luck. The inspector who was sent out to assess the situation not only confirmed his story—"financial trouble," "creditors closed on him," "no longer able to work the land"—but even went so far as to put in a good word on his behalf. "This Entrant appears to be up against it Very hard," he explained sympathetically, "and has a family of five Small children and if I may be allowed I would recommend that he get another chance to make good to hold his Land for he Surely needs it."[5]

Fair enough, the government responded. We'll give him another year to make things good. After that, if he hasn't paid up, he's finished.

TROUBLE COULD POUNCE without warning, not only on individuals like Hercules, but also on entire countries, even continents. From the summer of 1914 onward, that tragic teaching was being written in blood on battlefields around the world. Who would have thought that the assassination of an obscure Austrian nobleman in a city in Bosnia could unleash the horrors of a savage, mechanized world war? When Great Britain declared war on Germany, Canada was automatically and instinctively drawn in the maelstrom. "There is in Canada but one mind and one heart," Sir Wilfrid Laurier declared, voicing the general mood. "All Canadians are behind the Mother Country."[6]

The price of this filial loyalty would be shocking. "People are blinded, absolutely blinded, as to what war means," the Winnipeg labor weekly, The Voice, observed. "Those of the great majority think that it is brass bands, braid and feathers, and the throwing out of the chest, but if you have ever seen the regiments of militia on parade you will notice the stretcher-bearer section is there."[7] By the time the fighting finally ended, four excruciating years after it had begun, 66,655 Canadian soldiers, sailors, airmen, and nurses had been slaughtered, mostly in the trenches of Belgium and France, with another 172,950 among the wounded. Every town along the Goose Lake line would mourn its losses.

In the midst of this calamity, everyday life on the prairies took on a kind of garish intensity. Suddenly, a farm was not just a dicey little family business; it was a vital link in the war effort, a site of national, even global, significance. The Allied forces had to be fed, and Canadian farmers were encouraged to dial up production to meet this urgent need. The demand for wheat was especially strong, and prices spurted ahead—double, triple what they had been prewar—creating opportunity and risk. What went up must come down; when would the bubble burst? Uncharacteristically concerned about the stress this volatility created down on the farm, the federal government established an agency to manage the marketing of wheat, creating a small zone of order in a world of uncertainty. All in all, it wasn't the worst of times to be a farmer on the prairies.

But not everyone was able to ride this upsurge of prosperity. Hercules Blondin, for one, was caught off balance, out of sync with the times. The homestead he had sold in desperation in January of 1915 would go on, a few months later, to produce a bumper crop, as Saskatchewan farmers enjoyed a record harvest. Yields of forty to sixty bushels an acre were not uncommon, and the price of wheat edged up toward the two-dollar mark. In a publication entitled the *Agriculture War Book*, the federal Department of Agriculture described the crops that year as "luxuriant" and likened the province to the Garden of Eden.[8] But Hercules was among the fallen. As a hired hand, he was in the galling position of helping his more successful neighbors fill their bins and their bank accounts.

Thankfully, other members of the family were better positioned to weather the storm. Napoléon's hardware store continued to flourish, despite his competitors. His brother Alex and wife, Victoria, were managing to produce enough from their quarter-section homestead to maintain themselves and a brood of five kids. Meanwhile, the old man, Cléophas, was almost frantic with the strain of getting ahead. In addition to farming his home quarter near Harris, he had picked up a second, purchased homestead a dozen miles northwest of town. It hadn't been easy—like Hercules, he had been threatened with cancellation; there were so many rules and regs—but eventually, his efforts had been crowned with success. By early 1915, he held the title to two quarters, or 320 acres, of productive Saskatchewan farmland.

What's more, Cléophas had unexpectedly launched himself in an entirely new direction. Ever alert to opportunity, he was now drawn to a region of mixed-wood forests and tamarack swamps in central Alberta, almost four hundred miles to the west. With a rail line already pushing north from Edmonton to Athabasca, this new frontier was certain to produce the next great bonanza. Cléophas had seen for himself the magic that a railway could work on the country, conjuring entire towns out of nothing and attracting an influx of settlers. Here was another chance to get in early and profit from the prosperity that was sure to follow the laying of steel.

By now, Cléophas had used up his personal entitlements to "free" homesteads, but there were still a couple of angles left. For a limited time only, it was possible to purchase "scrip," or vouchers, that had been issued as a reward to Canadians who'd volunteered for combat on the side of the British in the Boer War. By purchasing a pair of these certificates—good for two quarter-sections each—Cléophas was able to stake his claim to an entire square mile of brush along the Athabasca Trail.

The Athabasca Trail: it suddenly strikes me that my grandpa Sherk and the rest of the Bull Outfit would have trekked over that very trail just a couple of years before, on their way to seek their own futures in the Peace River Country, hundreds of miles farther to the west and north. And I know that the Sherks, too, upon reaching their destination, would use Boer War scrip to acquire additional land.

156   The country was swarming with people like them, gripped by the same fever.

Having established his entitlement to this massive new holding, Cléophas was faced with the challenge of fulfilling the usual homestead duties. But with his business now spanning two provinces, he was needed everywhere at once, so it fell to his wife, Philomène, and their children—little Nettie and a new baby named Eva—to maintain the required presence on the bush farm. Fortunately, they were not left out there alone. Living with them, packed in cheek by jowl as always, were four other members of the Blondin clan, including two of Cléophas's grown-up children, his son Télémaque and his daughter Allelina.

We know what Télémaque was doing there: he was looking for a second chance. Having failed to claim land in Saskatchewan, he had no intention of letting that opportunity slip through his hands again. But Allelina's role in the project is more mysterious. Now in her mid-thirties, she had spent her entire life under her father's roof, whether in Lafontaine or in Harris or in this small frame shack alongside a trail in the middle of nowhere. As nearly as I can tell, she never married. And yet, here is Cléophas applying for a homestead on her behalf (as he was apparently entitled to do) and identifying her as a widow. Listed as members of her household are a teenaged son, who has popped up out of nowhere and who will vanish just as fast, and a little girl named Alice. She's the baby we heard crying in the soddie, the one they used to say was Cléophas and Philomène's own and who would later be written down as their adopted daughter.

What if Alice had always been Allelina's? Could it be that one of the family's reasons for coming west had been to escape the shame—the snubs, the leers—that attended an "illegiti-mate" birth? (Eventually, granddaughter Lorena, in her role as keeper of the family secrets, will reveal a far bleaker truth: a path through the woods in Tiny Township, a marauding swarm of men, a rape. A woman who would never recover her peace of mind.) And yet out here, in this newest of new countries, nobody knew or cared what had happened a thousand miles away and half a dozen years before. If you said you were a widow, you were a widow. No longer "fallen," you could hold your head high, your respectability restored. What's more, as the head of your own household, you were eligible to apply for a homestead. Perhaps that is what Cléophas was thinking when he submitted the claim on his daughter's behalf. He would help her get a foothold in life, become independent. Or perhaps it was only a ploy to grab more land for himself. It didn't really matter because, by the time the deal was completed, Allelina would be dead, of pneumonia, at the age of thirty-five, and her quarter-section would pass to her executor, her father.

Whatever Cléophas's intention, the too-early death of a daughter had not been part of the plan. In fact, nothing had ended up going exactly the way he'd anticipated. Although the rail line from Edmonton to Athabasca was duly completed, nothing much came of it. The line north to Peace River would eventually follow its own eccentric logic. In the end, Cléophas held the title to an impressive portfolio of Western land, but the future stretched out before him as uncertain as ever.

AS A MAN of action, Cléophas had little time for recording his thoughts and feelings. There are no diaries, no carefully

158 tied bundles of personal correspondence. His voice has come down to us, when we hear it at all, in shattered fragments. There was the outburst, back in Ontario, about the failings of the local school. And now, in the mid-1910s, there's another volley, this one directed against the officials in the Edmonton Land Office. In handwritten postscripts attached to his homestead applications, Cléophas is in a characteristic state of irritation. He is annoyed by the soil on his bush farm—"light sandy loam and stony, with very little humus." Annoyed by the hired men whom he'd left in charge and who, "by their lazyness," had cost him an entire year's harvest.[9] Annoyed, most of all, by the bureaucrats in the office and their power to boss him around. Hadn't he already been in twice to see them, with sworn statements and witnesses? Hadn't he told them he needed to get back to his main site of business, in Saskatchewan? He was getting old and deserved some consideration.

But outside that narrow window of bureaucracy and frustration, Cléophas and his family must have run through the full range of human emotions. There they were, mere human beings "à peine visibles dans l'immense contrée vierge,"[10] barely visible in an immense virgin country. The man who wrote that poignant description of their situation was Georges Bugnet, writer, future breeder of gorgeous roses (one of which, as I write this, is blooming in my yard), and, like the Blondins, back-country homesteader. Everything they were experiencing in the 1910s, he and his young family had experienced in the same challenging country a decade before. Between 1904 and 1906, while the Blondins were establishing themselves at Harris, Georges and his wife, Julia, had given up the pleasures of Paris to settle on a square plot of mosquito-infested forest northwest of Edmonton, certain that the northbound rail line would head their way and make their fortune. They, like the Blondins, were wrong.

What the forest had to offer the Bugnets instead was challenge and exhilaration, astonishing beauty, unexpected kindness, brutalizing labor, marital discord, spiritual poverty, and, ultimately, unbearable grief. All of this Georges Bugnet poured into a semi-autobiographical novel entitled *La forêt*, or *The Forest*, which was published in French in the 1930s and in a belated English translation in the 1970s. (Why am I not surprised to note that the translator, David Carpenter, lives just around the corner from me, on Temperance Avenue?) Bugnet's protagonists, Louise and Roger Bourgouin, are a pair of babes in the woods, newly arrived from France, she fearful, he excited, both clueless. Fortunately, the family on the next homestead is French Canadian (people much like the Blondins) and has been on the land for generations. Yet even with their neighbors' generous assistance, the Bourgouins soon find themselves fighting a losing battle against the glowering *forêt*, which seems to resent their very presence. When their little boy drowns in the creek that crosses their holding, they sorrowfully admit defeat. As the novel ends, we watch them leave, their "*pathétiques silhouettes*" diminishing into the distance until they vanish from sight.[11]

What had happened to the Bugnets in real life was, if anything, worse. One evening, while Georges was outside working, Julia left their young children alone for two minutes. When she returned, she found the littlest one, a toddler, engulfed by flames. He must have stumbled into the hearth or knocked over a kerosene lamp. Alone, far from medical assistance, the parents did what they could—smothered the fire, watched over the crib—but the next morning, the child was dead. "*Nos larmes et nos efforts sont restés vains*," Georges Bugnet wrote in a letter to his brother, so far away in France. "Our tears and our efforts were in vain."[12] Trouble could pounce without warning. You never knew what would hit next.

MEANWHILE, BACK ON Main Street in the bustling little Village of Harris, things were still coming up roses for one member of the Blondin clan. Unlike Hercules and Cléophas, who spent the war years engaged in their separate struggles with the homestead bureaucracy, Napoléon and his Pioneer Hardware were thriving. Crops were good, prices were high, and the customers kept coming. Whether it was a new screen door to keep out the flies or a foot warmer for the bed, N. S. Blondin prided himself on stocking whatever was needed. "You will find our store the best in the history of Harris," his ads declared.[13] His business was so successful that, around Christmas in 1915, he decided to leave things in the care of his assistants and go out East on a two-month holiday.

Sadly, the *Herald* doesn't provide a detailed itinerary, for once not nosy enough, but it isn't hard to guess where he was headed—back to see friends and family on the Penetanguishene Peninsula. No longer the raw youth who had left twelve years earlier, Napoléon reappeared in their midst as a farmer and entrepreneur, a person who had made a success of everything he put his hand to.

And there she was, watching him watching her, his beautiful cousin. Clara had only been five or six years old the last time he'd seen her, but now she was almost a woman—she'd turn eighteen in a few months. She was quick as a bird. Always laughing. A hard worker: she could polish a floor till it shone. Did he ask her to marry him then and there? Did she say she'd think about it, talk about coming out in a few months? Did she stand on the platform waving goodbye when he headed back west alone? He had certain attractions for an ambitious young woman like her, but at thirty-five, he was twice her age, almost old enough to be her father. Common sense said, "Don't go."

And yet a few months later, Clara stepped down onto the station platform at Harris. She had traveled across the country with her sister but immediately asserted her independence by taking a job in a stranger's house as a domestic servant. By May, the genial busybodies at the *Herald* had noted her presence, in the company of N. S. Blondin, going back and forth to Saskatoon on a pleasure jaunt. But the paper missed the outing that really counted. On Wednesday, July 19, the couple again took the train into the city, together this time with a new acquaintance of Clara's (a nurse who was employed in the same household) and an old friend of the groom's (a guy from Prussia who farmed next door to Hercules). With these two to bear witness, Napoléon and Clara stood in front of a minister in Saskatoon's English Church and promised to be true to each other from that day forward, for better or for worse. Although Napoléon gave his religion as Presbyterian and Clara as Roman Catholic, they apparently found a small zone of tolerance in the Anglican sanctuary.

"Christian name of bridegroom's mother, unknown," a clerk noted in the space left for comments on the couple's marriage registration record.[14] And that surprising not-knowing suggests a reason why, rather than marry a nice English girl as

162 his brother Hercules had done, Napoléon had trekked all the way back to Penetang to woo his Clara. With his family in Saskatchewan starting to fray around the edges—everyone overwhelmed and going their separate ways—she must have helped him to pull the threads of his life together, simply by being who she was. If there were moments when he felt like a motherless child, she was there to root him in their shared ancestry, a spindly, dislocated branch on an ancient family tree.

Whatever the ties that bound them, the newlyweds immediately settled down to enjoying their first summer as husband and wife. A couple of weeks after the wedding, they returned to the city for several days to wander through the exhibition halls at the big summer fair. By mid-August, they were camped out at Crystal Beach. "The weather here is magnificent," the *Herald* reported, and the resort, with its docks and dance floor, was the place to be.[15] The Glorious Twelfth had not been marked at the beach that summer, though a special train was arranged to take celebrants to a gathering elsewhere in the district. (The Harris local of the Orange Lodge had temporarily fallen apart, its leaders distracted by the call to maximize production for the war effort, but the lodges in towns up and down the line had remained active.)

Even without the stir of fife and drum, Crystal Beach was alive with excitement and sociability. For example, there was that day late in the summer, while Mr. and Mrs. N. S. Blondin were still in residence at the resort, when hundreds of people turned out for a picnic, and a huge thunderstorm blew in, sending the rain down in sheets, and everyone ran for cover, darting this way and that, shouting and waving their arms and squealing with laughter. And afterward the sun came out, and the trees were glistening. The world might be going to hell in a handcart, but right here, just for the moment at least, life was good, and people were happy.

WHEN TROUBLE CAME hunting for the Blondins again, Napoléon and Clara did not bear the brunt of it. The worst thing to befall them was a fire in one of the outbuildings behind the hardware store. And while that incident could have been catastrophic—the flames had only to reach the main warehouse where the drums of gasoline and other flammable materials were kept—thankfully Mrs. Mundle across the way woke up in the middle of the night to see strange lights flickering across her bedroom window and roused her husband, who raised the alarm. "I wish to thank the boys of the Fire Brigade and all who helped to save my property from destruction," N. S. Blondin said, by way of a notice in the next issue of the *Herald*. "The Brigade did excellent work, and I deeply appreciate their efforts."[16]

Mr. Blondin's losses on stock were considerable, an accompanying write-up said, but fully covered by insurance. If only the losses suffered by other members of the Blondin clan could have been so easily recompensed. Not only had Allelina died, but Alex and Victoria lost a baby girl and less than two years later their next born, a son. Then Victoria herself succumbed to the killer flu epidemic that swept the world in the aftermath of the war.

While Alex and Victoria, and then Alex alone, were suffering from these shocks, Cléophas was also experiencing a series of cruel setbacks. Philomène had been unwell for some time: gallstones, the doctors said. Now back in Harris (their work in Alberta completed), husband and wife made the journey into Saskatoon together so that she could seek treatment. But things did not go well. Instead of the expected quick recovery, Philomène died on the operating table. Cléophas was left with the care of three little girls: his own Nettie and Eva, plus Alle-lina's Alice.

Indefatigable as ever, he wasted no time in getting his life back on track. Within eighteen months, he had found a new wife, an English-born woman named Rose, who, like the late Philomène, was almost thirty years his junior. Tragedy struck him a side blow when, not long after their marriage, Rose's sister-in-law committed suicide at her home in Saskatoon by drowning herself in a rainwater cistern in her basement. But an even darker day was in store for the family. In early September of 1918, nine-year-old Eva was playing in the barn on her father's farm north of Harris when she was accidentally kicked by a horse. According to the report in the *Herald*, "the child staggered to her brother, who was in the barn, and while asking him to carry her to the house, dropped at his feet."[17] *Nos larmes et nos efforts sont restés vains.* The little girl was dead.

AND THEN THERE was Hercules. Somehow, he and Mabel, with their children, had managed to keep body and soul together through these troubled years, though—as we know and they couldn't—painful losses were lying in wait for them as well. Two of their youngsters were fated to die over the next several years. For the moment, all the couple knew was that they would never gain title to their purchased homestead, because they could never get enough money ahead to cover the few outstanding payments. Although well over half of the people who applied for homesteads in Saskatchewan in the 1910s and 1920s failed in their attempts to "prove up," this rate of attrition was not featured in the government propaganda. The attitude was that if you didn't fulfill the requirements, it was your own tough luck. The Crown retained ownership of the land, and you owned the failure.

The sad truth was that the land Hercules had chosen was not really suitable for farming, surely nothing you could stake your future on. In the words of the inspector who was sent to close out his claim, the land was SAND with a subsoil of SAND and fit only for pasture. Meanwhile, the government was dunning Hercules for small loans he'd taken out over the years, plus interest at 5 percent. All Hercules had to show for his work and worry as a homesteader was an inextinguishable debt.

BY THE SUMMER of 1918, the members of the Blondin clan were immersed in their private grief. How consoling it would have been if the whole community had come together in mourning, remembering lives lost in the lurid glory of battle, lives lost in the humble struggles of daily life. How comforting simply to sit with other people, creatures of a common flesh and blood, and share their sorrows as they shared yours. But instead, there was a nasty new agitation in the air, the sizzle of high-voltage rhetoric. Rather than drawing everyone together, the war had heightened preexisting social divisions, reinforced old prejudices, and weaponized the Anglo-Protestant claim to ascendance.

166   And who should come hurrying down the track at this inopportune juncture but our old acquaintance Brother Armstrong, the Right Worshipful Grand Organizer of Saskatchewan's Grand Orange Lodge. He arrived in town sometime in early 1918 and immediately set to work reinvigorating the lapsed Harris lodge and bringing the membership up to speed on issues of national concern. For instance—perhaps they'd heard?—the other locals in Goose Lake County had recently made a recommendation about "unpreferred settlers" from Eastern Europe. As former citizens of the Austro-Hungarian Empire, these people were now under suspicion as potential traitors. Although eight thousand of them had been segregated for a time in internment camps, and thousands more had been stripped of their right to vote, even more stringent action was urgently needed. They should all be rounded up, the Orangemen said, and made to perform forced labor.

When it came to French Canadians, Brother Armstrong said, they were nothing but "slackers," resisting the call to service, evading conscription, and generally displaying disloyalty to the British Empire. But what else could one expect from Papists, in bondage to Rome and naturally filled with guile? The Catholic Church itself—so the orator continued, retailing his alternative truths—was solely responsible for this terrible war. Who could deny that the conflict had been "fomented by Jesuitical priestcraft" or that the Pope was greedily anticipating his share of the bloody spoils? "Rome has ever been the gainer," Brother Armstrong declared, "when nations are at war."[18]

That year, 1918, the Glorious Twelfth was again celebrated on the shores of Crystal Beach. "Goose Lake Orangemen Have Big Day," the Herald proclaimed.[19] One observer put the attendance at four thousand people, transported in six hundred cars. Another doubled this record-breaking turnout. The monster rally was attended not only by the newly reconstituted locals but also by Orangemen from up and down the line: the morning train brought in lodges from the east (Outlook, Laura, Milden, and Tessier) and the noon train those from the west (Rosetown, Herschel, and Brock). Bedecked in their jeweled collars, the brethren formed up on the Crystal Beach siding and advanced in solemn procession to the beat of a marching band, marking their century-old tradition of sectarian hatred or, as the *Herald* preferred, "the noble principles for which the Order stands." Among the dignitaries who addressed the crowd were various grandees of the Order, federal and provincial politicians, and an assortment of Protestant clergy. "The speakers were listened to with marked attention," the *Herald* reported, "and their addresses lustily applauded."

From early morning until late at night, the martial rattle of snare drums echoed around Devil's Lake. The war in Europe was finally grinding to a close—Mother Britain and her allies nearing victory at last—but for the "Fanaticks" of English Canada, there could be no rest. What was the sense of defending the glories of British freedom in the trenches of Europe, at such an appalling cost, and then allowing them to be tainted by foreign influences on the home front? There were cultural beachheads to be taken, foes to be vanquished, battles yet to be won. "Onward, Christian soldiers," the Orangemen sang, "marching as to war." One of the targets fixed in their crosshairs was the use of French in public schools. How could any right-thinking citizen stand idly by while "the evil of bilingualism" was still afoot in the land, menacing the very foundations of the nation?[20]

— HARD TIMES —

Speak white
il est si beau de vous entendre
parler de Paradise Lost

Speak white
it is so good to hear you
speak of Paradise Lost

MICHÈLE LALONDE, *"Speak White,"* 1968

IN 1919, CLÉOPHAS Sureau dit Blondin turned seventy-five, and the years were telling on him. He was tired of squabbling with homestead officials, tired of the hard back-and-forth journey between his distant holdings, tired and sick at heart. *Little Eva, dead in her brother's arms, not yet ten years old.* Although the *Goose Lake Herald* was edited by an Orangeman and filled its columns with Orange events, her death had been reported with touching poignancy on the front page, a sign that the community had gathered around the Blondins with support and sympathy. And yet, for Cléophas, there was no rest, no assurance that these were his people and that he was safely at home here. Born into the jangly aftermath of the *Patriotes* war, proud of his French ancestry but at odds with the Catholic Church, he remained at heart what he had always been. An outsider.

And so, that spring, he sold off all his hard-won prairie acreage and relocated his household to Saskatoon. A few weeks later, in a move that was characteristically bold and unexpected, he and his family were on the road again, to take up a new life near one of his sisters in Spokane, Washington. With him on this venture were his fourth wife, Rose, and his youngest daughter, Antoinette, then barely a teenager. His "adopted daughter," Alice, only a couple of years older than Nettie, did not go south with them. Presumably, she stayed behind in the Harris district and earned her keep by doing housework in someone else's home, another motherless child left to get by as best she could.

But even in her grandfather's absence, Alice wasn't entirely alone, since most of her extended family—cousins, uncles, and aunts—were still living where they had put down tentative roots, in and around Harris. Her uncle Alex, for example, was on his scrubby homestead a couple miles west of town. Two babes and his wife had been laid to rest under the lawns of the Harris cemetery. Yet thankfully, his eldest daughter, at fifteen, was able to keep the household running and look after the little kids. Better yet, her younger sister would soon be old enough to go out to work. When the census taker canvased the district a couple of years later, in 1921, he found Edith Blondin, aged fourteen, working as a servant for a well-to-do family in town. Whatever she earned, and it wouldn't have been much, she took home to her father.

I know that's the way it happened, because my own mother was very nearly caught in the same trap. "They wanted me to go work for a neighbor woman and bring my wages in," she liked to remind me, contrasting my comparatively luxurious childhood with her own dirt-farm upbringing. But she had been fierce and stubborn, and, when she did go into domestic service, she didn't take her wages home. Instead, she used the money to support herself through grade twelve and Normal School, to end up with her certification as a teacher. For hundreds of other young women, like Alex's little girl, there was no means of escape, except possibly by marrying the right man.

Life was always treacherous, and marriage a lethal game of chance. Hercules Blondin's wife, Mabel, for one, had learned that lesson through experience. On her wedding day, her future had seemed secure. Her man was a proven quantity, a hard worker and the proprietor of his own farm. Strong by name and disposition, he was so robust that even the other men in the community were amazed by what he could do. In amateur shooting competitions, he had held his aim without using a "rest," relying on pure muscle to track the target. And yet, a decade into their marriage, the family's finances were in ruins, and their lives were now stretched between Harris, where the children were occasionally enrolled in school, and Saskatoon, where Hercules periodically managed to find employment. For while, he had a job as a "tractor expert" for an implement company, a twist of fate that, under less trying conditions, might almost have been amusing.

If any of the Blondin clan could claim to have found the high road to prosperity, it was Napoléon and Clara. After that first, honeymoon summer spent at Crystal Beach and on jaunts to Saskatoon, their lives had settled into a quiet routine, for a time in the apartment above the hardware store and then in the little cottage, a few blocks away, that Napoléon had built for them with his own hands. The house is still standing after all these years, its windows now blank and boarded, its hedge of lilacs gone wild and overgrown. Were there days when Clara felt lonely and confined inside those narrow walls? She was a newcomer here, far from everything she knew, and a conspicuous oddity in Harris. As a professed (if non-practicing) Catholic, she was automatically excluded from the denominational Ladies' Aids that brought her neighbors together for gossip and good works. The same went, even more emphatically, for the female auxiliary of the Orange Order—the Ladies' Benevolent Orange Association—that had recently been organized in town. The French-Catholic parish of Notre-Dame du Bon Conseil, where Clara might have been made more welcome, was only ten miles distant, though it might as well have been on the moon. With the rutted tracks that passed for roads, it was unattainable. Besides, she had chosen to marry outside of the Catholic Church, a lapse that made her a sinner.

And yet Clara's new life must have held its satisfactions. When she turned twenty-one, in 1919, she found herself, for the first time in her life, the mistress of her own home, and the boards she scrubbed to a luster were her own floorboards. What's more, she had a two-year-old child to fill her days, a daughter whom they'd named Bernice. Among themselves, they called her Belle, because she was beautiful.

AS HIS OLD man planned his next steps in life, Napoléon decided to make a move of his own. That spring, he sold his store, his homestead, and pretty much everything else he

172   owned. His assets, all now surplus to his requirements and up for sale to the highest bidder, included two heifers and a fresh milk cow; ten horses—bay, brown, sorrel, gray, and black—one of them a driving mare; and an impressive array of farming equipment: neck yokes and doubletrees, gang plows and harrows, seed drills and wagons, plus a complete Stanley Jones Threshing Outfit, a Ford car, and many other items. "Positively No Reserve," the notice for the auction counseled, "as Mr. Blondin has sold the farm."[1] For a guy who had started out with a few bucks in his pocket, he had done extremely well for himself. Now, he was positioning himself for continued success by acquiring top-quality land. Flush with cash, he purchased the 320 acres of the Blondin "home place" from his father.

And so Clara found herself uprooted again and more isolated than before, three miles from town and a good half a mile in any given direction from her nearest neighbor. But loneliness would soon prove to be the least of her concerns. For once, Napoléon's instincts had misled him. Everybody had made money during the war, when the market for wheat was strong, and a government marketing board had helped to keep prices stable. But with the emergency over and federal oversight removed, the export price for wheat began to sag and then to tumble, decreasing from around $2.20 a bushel, on average, in 1919, to about half that much a few years later. With dockages for quality and fees for transportation, the price on offer at Harris bottomed out at less than a buck. Meanwhile, the cost of production had risen mightily due to inflation during the war, and farmers were caught in a squeeze that would become all too familiar and menacing.

To make matters worse, the weather had gone rogue. Through the spring and summer of 1919, the Goose Lake

Country, like much of the rest of the province, shriveled in
a severe drought. By August, local farmers were appealing
to the rural council for road work, as a relief measure, only
to be turned down. In September, the *Herald* reported that
there was scarcely enough wheat in the district to keep the
local flour mill in operation. The following spring, dozens of
carloads of hay from Québec and other points out East were
unloaded at Harris, as feed for starving livestock.

The next few years went a little better—in 1921, N. S.
Blondin rolled into the *Herald* office to boast about a bumper
crop—but prices remained depressed. Drought struck again in
1924, and this time it was disastrous. By the end of July that
year, farmers around Harris had given up any hope of a harvest and were plowing their failed crops under, trailing clouds
of dust. That year, both Alex and Hercules bowed to the inevitable and left the district, the former finding work as a
hired man a hundred miles farther west and the latter taking
up year-round residence in the city of Saskatoon.

NOBODY SUFFERED MORE from this crippling downturn
than the French-Canadian settlers around Goose Lake. The
land they had chosen was marginal for farming, easy to break
in the beginning but with little staying power, and the people, for all their pioneering struggles, had remained poor.
Now, year by year, they were getting poorer, and the heart
was slowly bleeding out of their communal life. Some of their
foundational personalities had left already, the jovial Doctor
Tessier among them. There were rumors that his medical credentials had been rejected by the province, thereby denying

him the opportunity to practice his profession. Whatever the reason, in 1911, he and his family had packed up all their belongings and their infectious *joie de vivre* and headed back to the United States.

An even greater blow was dealt to the colony a few years later by the closure of Bouillon School. From the outset, keeping the one-room facility going had been a challenge. Teachers came and went with alarming regularity, often leaving after a term or two. Thus, Madame Brisette had been followed in quick succession by Mesdames Kelly, Parenteau, Pleau, and Brochu, each of whom bade her fond adieu within a year. Fortunately, the provincial Department of Education had always been helpful, willing to grant accreditation to whomever the local trustees (a committee of Francophone farmers) were able to recruit. But that laissez-faire attitude had changed abruptly in 1919.

That summer, the board submitted its application to operate as usual, with a Madame Ducharme in charge. But instead of receiving the expected okay, the request was turned down hard. Although Mrs. Ducharme's qualifications had earned her a teaching license in the past, those lax old days were gone. "Your knowledge of English is not sufficient to warrant the Department's continuing certificate," the Department of Education ruled. Bouillon School did not open that year, or the next, or the year after that, and the community's children were sent to a nearby school, for instruction in English. And so matters rested until the late 1920s, when the trustees again hired a French-speaking teacher and again were shot down. (This time, the Department's critique of the teacher's professional inadequacies was so searing that when I asked to see the file, the comments were removed, to protect the reputation of the long departed.) Shortly thereafter, Bouillon School District #3067 was reconfigured as Elk Valley #4816, and the community's hope of ensuring the survival of their mother tongue crumbled to nothing.

As their hopes eroded, so did the settlement. When a school inspector visited the district in the mid-1920s, he reported that "the children [had] nearly all vanished."[2] The eighty or so French-Canadian families who had once lived in the district had quietly packed up and left.

FOR SASKATCHEWAN'S ORANGEMEN, the closure of any school in which French was spoken—even a one-room shack on the shores of a reedy slough—was a source of satisfaction, another victory in their tireless crusade against the Papists. "Keep Canada British" was now their watchword, a phrase that rang with the Order's unswerving purpose.[3] The slogan was itself a local source of pride, since it had been coined by one of Saskatchewan's own leading loyalists, a Dr. Ellis from Moosomin, then in his glory as the Right Worshipful Grand Master for all of British North America. Relentless and ambitious as ever, Saskatchewan's Orange membership was now one of the largest and most consequential in the nation, with locals in 230 communities and a cobwebby network of influence that extended into almost every niche and cranny of decision-making.

Not so very long ago, an ebullient Brother Armstrong told his fellows, "our influence was only slightly felt in the councils of the Province and the Dominion; now we have but to inaugurate movements for reforms and remedial changes in our laws, and others follow our lead."[4] By getting the right men into the right positions, whether as school-board members, political candidates, or farm-movement activists, the Order had made common cause with a wide range of other "patriotic and progressive" groups. Soon, powerful allies like the provincial School Trustees and the Saskatchewan Grain Growers Association were standing with them, all singing the same refrain: "One Flag, One Language, One School."[5]

"Public opinion is now as never before fully alive to... the necessity of a National Non-sectarian School System," the Orange leadership affirmed, "where the English language will be the sole medium of instruction, where British ideals will be upheld and where British loyalty will be inculcated."[6] In the overheated atmosphere of postwar patriotism, there could be no space between education and imperial indoctrination.

If the Saskatchewan government was in any doubt about the kind of changes the public wanted, it had only to look at recent initiatives in two other provinces. Ontario had taken the lead back in 1912 by banning the bilingual (French–English) program that was taught in its Catholic schools. One day, instruction in French had been permitted; the next day, it was against the law. The only exemption was a brief transitional course, *un cours primaire*, for the very youngest students. Teachers who refused to comply with these orders lost their certification, and funding was withheld from schools. Unsurprisingly, this decree aroused fury across French Canada, a fierce anger that would smolder for years, inciting civil disobedience, fueling opposition to the war effort, and eventually provoking a national crisis over conscription. So much for fair play and the much-vaunted British respect for equality and freedom. (Franco-Ontarians would finally receive an official apology for this injustice in 2016, only to lose ground again the following year when French-language services were targeted as a cost-cutting measure.)

The Orange Order, which had fought hard for the ban on French-language schooling, was jubilant at its success. And the members enjoyed a second cause for celebration in 1916, when Manitoba made an even more radical change to its educational practices. Over the previous decade, the province had experimented with a multilingual system that allowed instruction in English plus other specified languages. Thus, lessons might be taught in English and French, or English and German, or English and Ukrainian, depending on local needs. To the Orange Order, this system was outrageous. What were the province's leaders thinking, allowing children to be schooled in "enemy" languages? Had the politicians learned nothing from the biblical story of the Tower of Babel? According to the approved Orange interpretation, "When the Almighty would destroy the union of those who tried to build the Tower... He did it by a simple means. He sent confusion of tongues, which meant that at once these people... became barbarians to each other."[7]

Persuaded that the province's schools were out of control, Manitoba took matters in hand. Here, there would be no fooling around with an introductory course for small children or a provision for French as a second language. From 1916 forward, schooling would be available in English and English alone. It had taken almost half a century, but Riel's founding vision of a bilingual and bicultural society had finally been wiped out.

178   AT CHOIR PRACTICE one night, we separate into two groups, men on one side of the room, women facing them on the other, to rehearse a piece called "1916." The score is drawn from a sprightly work of musical theater with the resolutely unsprightly name of *L'Article 23/Section 23*, a reference to the guarantees of French–English equality in the Manitoba Act of 1870. In the piece we're rehearsing, a school inspector, voiced by the male singers, is writing a letter of reprimand to a Franco-phone teacher. "Dear Missus Dandenault," he begins,

> you know a law was passed
> forbidding French in schools.
> Take my advice, follow the rules.[8]

Francophones are just a minority, he advises her, and, in a democracy, the majority always has the upper hand. "Don't be misled," he gloats. "French will be dead!"

But Madame Dandenault (the female singers) is not about to admit defeat. "*Il parle de loi*," she mutters to herself. "*Jamais de justice ni de devoir.*" He always talks about law, never about justice or duty. The more sneeringly self-assured the inspector becomes, the more impassioned is her response, until she, too, is ready to put pen to paper.

> *Monsieur l'inspecteur, enfin j'vous réponds et c'est non!*
> *Vous n'arriverez pas même avec vos lois à gagner*
> *Comprenez. C'est ma langue, mon passé*
> *C'est ma vie.*

> Mr. Inspector, finally I am replying to you and it's no!
> Even with your laws, you are never going to win

Understand. It's my language, my past
It's my life.

But *Monsieur l'inspecteur* is unmoved by this *cri de coeur.*
"You and I know," he rhymes, "French has to go." And that
same hard line would prevail in the real world of Manitoba
education for the next thirty years. (French was not readmit-
ted to the curriculum until 1947, when it was acknowledged
as a "foreign language.") In the meantime, the French
teaching-training program in Saint-Boniface had to be shut-
tered, and any teacher who defied the law did so at his or her
own risk: "You cannot win this time," the inspector gibed.
"Your job is on the line."

WITH THE HOPEFUL precedents in Ontario and Manitoba to
light the way, Saskatchewan's Orangemen and their legions
of sympathizers entered the postwar era confident of success.
So it was disappointing—scandalous, really—when, instead of
outlawing separate schools and banning instruction in French,
the Saskatchewan government responded with conciliatory
murmurs and little substantial change. Separate schools had
been guaranteed by the Saskatchewan Act in 1905, the provincial government noted, and were essentially carved in
stone. And while the argument for English-only education
was compelling, the existing law was adequate and simply
needed to be strictly observed.

But here, if it makes you feel better, the government told
the Orange lobby late in 1918, we'll reduce the primary course
in French from the first two years of schooling to a single

180   grade. (The option of an hour-per-day course in French literature and grammar was quietly left unchanged.) Surely with
this mincing approach, the Francophones wouldn't get into
too much of a lather about the new provisions, and the Anglo
public would have something to show for its efforts.

The leaders of the Orange Order took what encourage-
ment they could from this temporizing response. "Progress
has been made," the provincial Grand Master assured his
brothers in 1921. "Greater care is being taken in Foreign districts and the law is being better enforced."[9] (So the trustees
of Bouillon School had discovered to their cost.) But the battle
to ensure Anglo-Protestant supremacy still had not been won.
Of the almost three thousand schools in the province, seventy-
six were still providing the optional hour-a-day course in the
French language, at the parents' private expense. This outrage
was being committed in places where the *prêtres-colonisateurs*
had achieved their most lasting success, settlements like
Saint-Brieux in the northeast and Ponteix and Gravelbourg in
the southwest. "The long, Smooth-Finger[ed] Arm of Rome is
still seeking privileges," the Grand Master warned, "and [it is]
still getting them. This is seen in the use of French and laxity
in these settlements."[10]

Every word of French spoken in a Saskatchewan school
strengthened the Church of Rome and doomed the entire
nation to "inevitable disaster."[11] If only a new political force—a
white knight on a charger—would appear out of nowhere and
sweep the Anglo-Protestant forces onward to victory. But
until that happy day arrived, the Orangemen and their legions
of sympathizers could only hold steadfast to their beliefs, true
to the rallying cry of "No Surrender."

MY MOTHER'S YOUNGEST sister, my aunt Lil, was born on the family homestead in west-central Alberta in 1924, when the Orange Order was in its ascendancy. Now in her early nineties, she is tiny and full of spark, with a wry tilt to one eyebrow and a smile that is constantly threatening to give way to laughter. But if you get her talking about her childhood, her voice goes low and sharp, especially when she mentions her father, my grandpa Humphrey. Like the Southern belle her own mother was, she calls him Daddy.

"Daddy had to convert to Catholicism to marry Katie," she reminds me. Katie is her mother, Mary Catherine Humphrey née Carrico, the descendant of a long line of defiant Catholics.

I nod. Yes, that makes sense. Her family would never have countenanced a marriage to a Protestant.

He was a serious convert, my aunt assures me, and taught the catechism to his four eldest kids: my aunts Esther and Leora, my uncle Tom, my own mom. But then he made friends with an Englishman—she spits out the word—a neighbor named Mr. Poole. "I can still see them there at the kitchen table, heads together, muttering to one another." Mr. Poole might very well have been a card-carrying member of the local Orange Lodge for, as I will later discover, there was a thriving local in the district. Or perhaps he was a freelancer, on his own personal crusade to defend Protestantism and British liberty. In any case, he managed to persuade Daddy, my grandpa, that the Roman Catholic Church was "a bunch of bunkum."

"That's when the fighting started," my aunt says, knotting her hands in her lap. "Daddy and Katie were always fighting. I couldn't stand it. When I was sixteen, I left." She raises her head to look at me, and I see my own mother staring back. She is alone at our kitchen table, wreathed in smoke from her cigarette, and I know she is listening to voices from her childhood. No rain, no crops, no money, new babies year by year. But Harry Humphrey is ragging on, raging at Katie about the wickedness of the Catholic Church.

BY THE MID-1920S, everyone's nerves were on edge. Thousands of traumatized young men had come home from the war, only to find themselves out of luck and out of work. The crews of disaffected laborers who flooded the West to help with the harvest each fall were excitable and raw, all too susceptible, some observers thought, to radical ideas. "IWW Members Busy in Tessier," the *Goose Lake Herald* noted with alarm, referring to the International Workers of the World.[12] If the men who had been distributing the offending pamphlets were caught, the editor promised, they would feel the full force of the law. When strikes did break out among the workers, they were always quickly suppressed, their leaders rushed before a magistrate for summary judgment. Thus, in the fall of 1923, a guy named Nick Staff was fined ten dollars, or three days' wages, for helping to foment a disturbance against the biggest farmer in the Goose Lake district, T. B. Wilson of Lake View Farm. Staff's partner-in-crime, Ole Hadev, was dinged fifteen dollars, plus court costs, as the ringleader.

And it wasn't just the hired help who were agitated. Conditions in the district were so shaky that the local grocery store was no longer able to give credit to its customers on trust. "Owing to the present state of the affairs, and the condition of the community financially," the proprietors announced, all future purchases would have to be cash on the barrelhead.[13]

Even a substantial operation like Lake View Farm—with its
three barns, eighty Clydesdale horses, and 5,600 acres—was
vulnerable to distress. A year after the strike, T. B. Wilson was
forced out of business by debt, and the operation passed into
the hands of a consortium of Mennonite families newly arrived
from Ukraine. When they couldn't make a go of the place either,
he ended up buying it back, but the thrust had gone out of the
business.

The only hope for the farm economy lay in collective
action, and the entire province was on fire with excited talk.
Hundreds might still turn up at Crystal Beach to mark the
Glorious Twelfth, but these days, farm-movement picnics
were a much bigger draw. In 1923 and again in '25 and '27, people turned out by the thousands—gents in cloth caps, ladies
in cloche hats trimmed with flowers—to hear the charismatic
American activist Aaron Sapiro explain the potential of farmer-
owned marketing cooperatives. Sign up here as a founding
member of the Saskatchewan Wheat Pool. Alone, individual
producers were helpless, he said, stating an all-too-obvious
truth, but by banding together, they could combat the powerful interests that were ranged against them. Over his head, a
banner proclaimed "United We Stand."

And it was true: farmers were standing together. By 1925,
the Pool had attracted enough pledges to go into full operation, and soon its name was emblazoned in sassy orange and
red on its new elevator at Harris. That same year, voters in the
local Rosetown constituency elected a farmer-first candidate,
a Progressive, as their representative, charged with voicing
their grievances in the House of Commons. Meanwhile, Saskatchewan's two rival farm organizations, the Grain Growers
and the Farmers' Union, were on the verge of burying the

184 hatchet and merging to become the United Farmers of Canada (Saskatchewan Section). Even Mother Nature was in a benevolent mood, and the harvest that autumn was one of the biggest and best the province had ever known.

ON THE HOME place north of town, Napoléon Blondin had been hanging on for six nerve-racking years. He was busting a gut as usual, working around the clock, but at least this year, he'd have something bankable to show for his labor. Of course, he'd thought about calling it quits, following his father to Spokane or his brother to Saskatoon. But he hadn't left when times were dire, and so why would he buckle under now, when the sun was shining and the bins were full? He'd give the place another chance.

There were four little kids in the family now: Bernice, aged eight and going to school in Harris, and the others at home with their mom, Ralph, five; Ruth, four; and a baby named Donald. As for Clara herself, the *Herald* occasionally clocked her taking the train into the city to spend a day or two with friends, but otherwise her life was unobserved, at a distance. If anything, female society in Harris was even more forbidding in the mid-1920s than it had been a decade earlier, when she'd first arrived in town. In the summer of '25, the Orange Lodge moved into a fancy little hall on Main Street—the "Orange Temple"—not overly large but nice, with the latest in hardwood flooring and a generator that powered miraculous, flip-of-the-switch electric lights. From the day the doors opened, the Temple became the hub of community life, the A-list venue for bazaars, dances, meetings, whist drives,

tractor displays, magic-lantern lectures, and fowl suppers.
There were even folding seats in the basement for showing
moving pictures. When local politicians came to town—the
Member of the Legislative Assembly John Wilson, say, or the
new Progressive Member of Parliament, John Evans—they
often selected the Orange Temple as the place to meet their
constituents. This choice came all the more naturally since
they were, of course, both Orangemen.

Although Orange issues had been temporarily sidelined
by the farm crisis, the Order remained quietly, invisibly at
the helm, not only in the Goose Lake Country but in many
other communities throughout the province. And in the
shadows, across the nation, a new force was welling up. In
1922, fires had been set in the cathedral in Québec City, in
the junior seminary of the Pères du Très-Saint-Sacrement
in Terrebonne, even in the Séminaire de Saint-Sulpice in
Montréal. That same year, threats were made against the
Collège de Saint-Boniface, and a few months later, its dormi-
tory went up in flames, a middle-of-the-night conflagration in
which ten students perished. The following year, a menacing
letter was sent to a convent in Calgary, signed by the Ku Klux
Klan. The Orange Order had hoped for a champion to propel
them over the top, and an army of white knights was coming
their way, whether they liked it or not.

12

— INVISIBLE EMPIRE —

Délivre-moi des malfaiteurs,
et sauve-moi des hommes de sang.

Deliver me from evildoers,
and save me from bloody men.

PSALM 59:2

B Y THE END of 1926, Napoléon had reached a decision point. After the record crop of '25, the year's results had again been disappointing, the spring too dry, the fall too wet, and then an early frost. Napoléon was no longer a spring chicken—he'd turned forty-seven in September— and although his ambition was undimmed, the vagaries of farming were starting to wear him down. How hard did a man have to struggle just to keep from falling back? Besides, there was Clara and a house full of young children to think of. Perhaps it was time to kick things up a notch. According to a recent headline in the *Herald*, the long-awaited rail-way to Port Churchill on Hudson Bay was finally going to be completed, giving Western Canada a new gateway to markets overseas. As a major commercial and distribution center, Saskatoon was going to boom. The smart money was heading for the city.

Still, the decision to leave can't have been easy. Of the Blondin clan who had settled in the Goose Lake Country more than two decades earlier, Napoléon was the last man standing, the family's crowning success. His old man had stayed in the game as long as he could but, in the end, had been driven out by tragedy and old age. Meanwhile, Napoléon's siblings had succumbed to misfortune, each in his or her own way. The farm north of Harris was the fulfillment of an ambition they had pursued together, the dream of landed self-sufficiency that they had inherited from their ancestors. It was no small matter to sell out and turn your back on everything you had achieved: the house and barns, the sheds filled with tools and equipment, the meticulously tilled fields. It was no small matter to start your life all over again in middle age.

But he'd done it before, hadn't he, back when he'd barely had two pennies to rub together? Now he had money in the bank and a track record as a farmer and businessman. God knew he wasn't afraid of hard work. Yes, it was a dramatic step, but when had he ever shied away from a challenge? The move into Saskatoon would be the next exhilarating stage in his life's adventure.

The Blondins weren't the only family to pull up stakes that fall. The Herald was filled with reports of "dainty lunches" held for ladies who, with husbands and children, were bidding the place farewell. One woman was given "two very pretty pieces of ivory" as a memento of her time in Harris; another received a camera and film.[1] But there was no farewell gathering for

Napoléon or Clara Blondin, no eloquent speeches or parting gift. The *Herald* duly reported the sale of the Blondin farm to a Mr. Joe Sexsmith, effective December 1, and that was the end of it. Except for a single quarter-section that Napoléon couldn't bring himself to sell, he and his family were finished with Harris.

I wonder what Clara was thinking the day they pulled down the lane for the last time and said goodbye to the farm. In my mind's eye, she's seated in the McLaughlin-Buick— her children crammed in behind her and her husband at the wheel—gazing out the window at a snowy expanse of fields. She'd been stuck out there, on that bleak plot of land, for seven long years. "I hated the farm every minute I was ever on it," one of her neighbors would later confess. "I hated the fact that we didn't have too many close neighbours... it seemed I was alone so much of the time... [And] the work was terrific, you know... the heavy lifting—carrying pails of water—and being tied down, that was another thing I hated.

"We live in Saskatoon now," that neighbor said, "and, believe me, I haven't missed that farm."[2]

Saskatoon had always been part of the Blondins' lives, maybe even the best part of it, a place of opportunity, friendship, and fun. Napoléon could still remember the grubby, improbable hamlet he had first encountered in the summer of 1904. Back then, the settlement had consisted of two clusters of whitewashed wooden buildings: Nutana, the site of the original Temperance Colony, to the east, and Saskatoon, all false-fronted swagger, to the west. The rival communities glowered at each other across the low-slung valley of the South Saskatchewan River, connected only by an unreliable ferry and a rickety railroad bridge.

Four years later, in 1908, when Napoléon returned to file his homestead papers, the settlement had been transformed. A population of a couple of hundred had mushroomed to several thousand, and the rival enclaves, together with the newly surveyed subdivision of Riversdale, had joined hands in a single municipality, known aspirationally as the City of Saskatoon. Everywhere he'd looked, that out-sized ambition had been taking physical form. The handsome steel Traffic Bridge provided safe passage across the river. ("Walk your horses. Automobiles not to exceed 6 miles per hour," a prominent signboard warned.) The frail railway trestle had been replaced by not one but three substantial crossings, one for each of the national lines—Canadian Northern, Canadian Pacific, and the Grand Trunk Pacific—that now converged in Saskatoon and made it the hub of an enormous commercial area. The city's trading zone was "three times as large as Switzerland [and] two-thirds the size of Turkey," one civic booster crowed.[3] On the main commercial streets downtown, the frontier-style clapboard storefronts that had seemed perfectly serviceable only a few months earlier were being torn down and replaced by stylish modern edifices of stone and brick.

Even more noteworthy, from Napoléon Blondin's point of view, were all the new wholesale outlets that had begun springing up in town. From one lone warehouse in 1906, the number had multiplied to six the following year, and then to two dozen, and then gone off the charts. By 1909, when he began coming into the city regularly as the proprietor of Harris's Pioneer Hardware Store, he'd had his choice of at least ninety suppliers. As he made his rounds, picking up a stock of barn paint here, an order of kerosene or stove pipes there, he must have been astounded, as everyone was, by the brash young community's confidence and explosive progress.

By 1910, construction had begun on the new provincial university, its gray stone elegance rising out of the open prairie on the northeast edge of town. Soon thereafter, a profusion of magnificent churches began sprouting along the river—the brick spire of the Roman Catholics to the south answered with Gothic flourish by the Anglicans and the four-square solidity of the Presbyterians at the other end of the street. Meanwhile, the Methodists, standard-bearers for the community's teetotal founders, were erecting their own monumental sanctuary on prime real estate downtown. With room for 1,200 adherents, Third Avenue Methodist was an expression of faith not only in God but also in the prospects of this up-by-its-bootstraps town.

In the heady years of the early 1910s, Saskatoon's advancement had been almost beyond belief. Riding high on the tide of Western immigration, it was known as Canada's "Magic City" and "the Miracle City of the West." In the modest estimation of the local Board of Trade, the settlement's short history embodied "a record of progress and development that has never yet been approached either within the British Empire, or throughout the entire world."[4] And who could argue with this boast? By 1911, the city's population had topped 12,000, and property assessments stood at $23 million. A year later, a civic census put the count at 28,000, and assessments had nearly doubled. Everywhere you went, people were heady with predictions about the town's continued success, as those upward trends were extrapolated into an infinite future. Even the president of the university was caught up in the excess, foreseeing a metropolis of two million souls within a couple of decades.

And so Napoléon had looked on as the community strutted and preened and congratulated itself on its world-beating progress. He had also been watching in 1913, when those hopes were dashed. As Europe prepared for the onset of war, the British investment that had powered the boom suddenly dried up, and construction came to an abrupt halt. One of the projects left in the lurch was the grand new Anglican cathedral beside the river. That was why, on that memorable summer day in 1916 when Napoléon and Clara had slipped into the city to get married, they'd exchanged their vows under the white wooden steeple of the old English Church next door. As they emerged into the July sunshine as husband and wife, with the soon-to-be-finished cathedral towering above them and the river shining at their feet, they must already have felt like honorary citizens of the city.

TEN YEARS LATER, when Napoléon and Clara pulled into town intent on making it their home, they found a place marked by traces of everything that had happened before. The new gravel highway that brought them east from Harris turned sharply at Avenue H, along the route of the Old Bone Trail, and then led toward downtown, through the narrow, close-packed houses of Riversdale and environs. These were working-class neighborhoods, the kinds of places where immigrants from central and Eastern Europe tended to congregate, people with names like Weinstein or Greschuk or Sachinski. Napoléon's own brother Hercules lived here, a block over on Avenue I, and a few scattered households of the Blondins' distant cousins from Prairie Ronde had also settled in this part of town.

In the heart of the settlement, a few minutes' drive ahead, was the business district, gap-toothed and incomplete since the 1913 collapse, and north of that, the leafy streets of Caswell Hill, home to entrepreneurs and civic leaders. Among them, until his untimely death in 1925, had been Brother W. H. G. Armstrong, Grand Organizer of the Grand Orange Lodge of Saskatchewan. But that's not where the Blondins were headed. From Avenue H, they followed the river east to Nineteenth Street, under the railroad tracks, past the dilapidated shacks of Chinatown, across the Traffic Bridge, and up Long Hill to the top of the east bank. In front of them lay the community of Nutana, the site chosen by the temperance advocates for their utopian community and laid out in the 1880s according to progressive principles. With its generous margins and staunchly loyalist allusions—from Victoria School in the west, via Temperance, Dufferin, and Lansdowne Avenues to Albert School in the east—it was an enclave of soft-spoken Anglo respectability.

"Saskatoon has the Brightest, Happiest Social Life to be found anywhere," one of the city's promotional brochures promised. "Saskatoon for Sociability and for Cultured, Kind-Hearted People."[5] Nowhere in town did this boast ring more true than on the gracious streets of Nutana. As I picture the Blondins pulling up in front of the handsome two-story home that Napoléon had rented for them, I can't help remembering the elation that Diana and I felt, decades later, when we arrived in the same neighborhood. Surely their hearts, like ours, were light with anticipation.

WITHIN MONTHS, IT became clear that Napoléon Blondin's intuition had been exactly correct. The economic tide had indeed turned, and prosperity was rushing back into the city. "During the post-war period of hard times much property came into the hands of the city of Saskatoon through the failure of private owners to continue tax payments," the *Daily Star* acknowledged.[6] But not so anymore. With wheat prices finally on the rise, the city was frantic with construction: $70,000 invested in a stockyard, $300,000 for a brewery, $500,000 for the massive new Robin Hood flour mill. What's more, the *Star* noted, "new stores, garages, lumber yards and warehouses have kept building contractors continually busy since the construction season began." Best of all, residents were getting their swagger back and had started to buy the city's large inventory of abandoned real estate. "About eleven hundred lots have been sold this year," the *Star*'s 1927 report continued, "and the purchasers have included citizens in all walks of life."

Napoléon Blondin made a quick visit to Spokane to visit his father, perhaps in part to check out the prospects south of the border, but returned with new resolve. No place in the world knew how to boom quite like his new hometown. "Saskatoon People Have Many Reasons for Thanksgiving," the *Star* affirmed.[7] Soon Napoléon had purchased a corner lot a few blocks from the family's rental house. The new location had everything you could ask for: proximity to streetcars, schools, and shopping; easy access to the river valley and bridges; even a measure of prestige. The university was a fifteen-minute walk away, along footpaths worn into the prairie, and some of the university's leading figures lived in the neighborhood—the bursar, for example, and the dean of law.

One of the province's most prominent politicians, James Thomas Milton Anderson, lived just down the road, at the intersection of Temperance Street and Albert Avenue. He was not only the MLA for Saskatoon City but also the leader of the province's Conservative caucus. Like Napoléon, he had been born in the bush country of northern Ontario in the 1870s and migrated west, to Saskatchewan, in the early 1900s. Unlike his new neighbor, however, Anderson was a man of professional standing, a former teacher and educational bureaucrat, with advanced degrees in law and pedagogy, and a penchant for bowler hats. He was also a member of the Masons and, perhaps inevitably, an Orangeman.

The Loyal Orange Lodge was not the suffocating presence in Saskatoon that it had been out on the farm. Yet, with eight locals within or immediately around the city, the organization was a pervasive force, influencing both the tone and the vocabulary of political discourse. By the late 1920s, the brethren were in a particularly sour and dyspeptic mood. The focus of their displeasure was, again, the "alien problem." In 1925, hoping to kick-start immigration (which had essentially halted during the war), the federal government negotiated agreements with the national railways, empowering them to recruit agricultural and domestic workers from the "non-preferred countries" of the European continent. The result, in the anguished opinion of the Orange Order, was an influx into Western Canada of "the dregs and off-scourings of Southern and Central Europe."[8] Who could doubt the statistics that seemed to prove these incomers had a propensity for manslaughter and murder?

Nor were the Orangemen alone in sounding the alarm. In 1927, no less a body than the Synod of the Anglican Church in

Saskatchewan raised its voice to condemn this "serious menace to British supremacy" in the province.[9]

It didn't escape the notice of either Anglicans or Orangemen that many of the newcomers, perhaps even most, were
not only irredeemably foreign but also Roman Catholic. It
followed that the Pope was mixed up in this business, probably (or so Orangemen in both Saskatoon and Goose Lake
County suspected) by conspiring behind the scenes to gain
control of the immigration bureaucracy. The French Canadians, too, were up to their usual mischief, or so the Orangemen
said, jockeying for sectarian advantage and sowing division.
What was this insidious trend toward singing "O Canada"—a
"French Catholic Racial Hymn"—in the place of "God Save
the King"?[10] Why had French suddenly appeared on money
orders and official notices in Saskatchewan post offices? "If
[all] these trends continue," an Orange spokesman warned,
"the time is not far distant when people of British stock will
be submerged and may have to ask for permission to live in
this Western country," a country that, by all that was right
and holy, should be entirely theirs.[11]

Dr. Anderson, the Blondins' new neighbor, was an urbane
and generous man, not given to explosive language or outbursts of bigotry, but his views on the crisis facing the country
were uncompromising. In his doctoral dissertation, published
as *The Education of the New Canadian: A Treatise on Canada's
Greatest Educational Problem*, he acknowledged the challenge
of imbuing "the seemingly crude human material" of Eastern
European immigrants with "a true Canadian spirit and attach-
ment to British ideals and institutions."

"We may despise the 'foreigner' and all that is non-English,"
he admitted, "but the fact remains that this element is here

to stay and its presence is bound to make an impress upon our future citizenship. The paramount factor in racial fusion is undoubtedly the education of the children of these non-English races."

It followed that the solution to the problem resided, as the Orange Order had always said, in the "common," or public, school, or as Anderson called it, "the assimilating organon of the masses." Here, children from "cloudy" backgrounds could learn the uses of soap and water, the virtue of sliced bread over hunks of *chorni khlib*, and the joy of singing patriotic selections like "Tipperary" and "Never Let the Old Flag Fall." It almost went without saying that this schooling must be conducted exclusively in "our" language. The King's English.[12]

The future of the nation was at risk, yet Liberal governments in both Regina and Ottawa continued to press down the path of doom. And meanwhile, the Orange Order was losing traction, its membership apathetic, its voice increasingly shrill. Where was the political organization that could lead the country toward its highest destiny, "as a living link in the great earth-girdling imperial chain of the greatest Empire on Earth"?[13] As leader of the Conservative Party, Brother Anderson was fired up for the battle, but he suffered a drastic shortage of means. In the twenty-plus years of the province's history, the Conservatives had never once held power, never sat on the government side of the house. They were ne'er-do-wells, also-rans, perennially in opposition. Anderson presided over a caucus of just four members, three others and himself. But desperate times called for desperate measures, and Dr. J. T. M. Anderson was an increasingly desperate man.

THE INVISIBLE EMPIRE, Knights of the Ku Klux Klan of
Kanada, arrived in the province in the closing week of 1926,
at the behest of the organization's national HQ in Toronto.
Things had gotten a bit sticky for the movement in Ontario
that autumn, when two of its members were found guilty of
setting dynamite in St. Mary's Roman Catholic Church in
Barrie. An ideal moment, the leadership thought, for a change
of venue. Accordingly, a team of experienced operatives was
dispatched to Saskatchewan—a King Kleagle, or chief organizer, named Lewis A. Scott, assisted by his son Hugh and
a Klokard, or Klan lecturer, named "Pat" Emmons. All three
were American citizens who had previously risen to promi-
nence as leaders of the Indiana Klan, where they had peddled
an intoxicating mixture of white supremacy, xenophobia,
anti-Catholic bigotry, "old-time religion," and "pure Amer-
icanism." So potent was their appeal that, by the mid-1920s,
Klan-sponsored candidates had taken control of both the state
assembly and the governor's office. In 1925, however, their
reign came to an abrupt end when the state's leading Klans-
man, Grand Dragon D. C. Stephenson, was convicted in the
abduction, rape, and murder of a female civil servant.

It's possible, I suppose, that word of these atrocities had
not found its way to the scattered towns and cities of the Saskatchewan plains. But even if people were in the dark about
the Klan's recent misdeeds, everybody knew (or should have
known) about its historical infamy. The first full-length American movie shown in Saskatoon had been D. W. Griffith's epic
blockbuster *The Birth of a Nation*, which was screened at the
Empire Theatre on Twentieth Street in the spring of 1916, to
the accompaniment of a twenty-piece orchestra. Admission

was a hefty $1.50, up from the usual twenty-five cents, but that didn't keep the show from playing to enthusiastic audiences. As the music swelled to its martial climax, legions of robed-and-hooded horsemen thundered across the screen, first defeating a mob of African-American insurgents and then rescuing a white maiden from the clutches of a mixed-race man. In case anyone missed the significance of these developments, an intertitle flashed up to provide an explanation: the white race had come together "in common defence of their Aryan birthright."[14]

Although the revitalized "Second Klan"—the movement that rode into Saskatchewan in the 1920s—had officially forsworn violence, it remained unapologetically committed to white, Anglo-Saxon, Protestant domination. The Klan was a religious movement, its promoters cried, motivated solely by a desire to rid society of sin, attributes that made it, in Klokard Emmons's words, "the greatest Christian Benevolent Fraternal Organization... in the world today."[15] But benevolent did not mean spineless. The Klan was tough on non-preferred immigration, tough on Papist interference, tough on sectarian schools. "We fed people anti's," Emmons would later confess, "whatever we found that they could be taught to hate and fear, we fed them. We were out to get the dollars and we got them."[16]

No point in railing against "negroes" in Saskatchewan, since vanishingly few black settlers had ever been allowed in. Similarly, even though the KKK was explicitly anti-Semitic, there was no mileage to be made by attacking Jews since they, too, were few and far between. As for "Indians" and "half-breeds," they had already been swept aside and were of no further interest to Emmons or his audiences. No, what really got the crowds going in Saskatchewan was a rip-roaring sermon on a familiar theme. "One Flag, One Language, One School," the American organizers chorused. "Keep Canada British."[17]

Across the province, voices were raised against the Klan, from the pulpit, in the legislature, and in the press, but it was difficult ground to hold. Even the Klan's most ardent opponents were pro-British and pro-status quo. The standard-bearer for the anti-Klan forces, the Liberal premier, James G. "Jimmy" Gardiner, claimed that the Klan's great evil was getting people riled up about a problem that didn't exist. Let's just calm down, he counseled, and look at the statistics. Roman Catholics made up 20 percent of the population but only 12 percent of the employees in the Department of Education. They were underrepresented in cabinet and across the civil service as a whole. Obviously, there was no Papist threat. But the discrimination the premier had exposed passed without comment.

Meanwhile, the Klan's incandescent call to action spread across the province. Within a matter of weeks, klaverns, or locals, had been established in more than two dozen communities, from Shaunavon in the west to Whitewood and Moosomin in the east. (At its peak, the membership would exceed 25,000, almost as large as that of the Saskatchewan Grain Growers.) With its extravagant titles, secret handshakes, and general folderol, the KKK offered a top-of-the-line experience for anyone who enjoyed ritualized male bonding, and members of other fraternal societies were easy marks for the Klan recruitment drive. In the Blondins' old stomping grounds at Harris, most of the local Orangemen not only forked over the ten-dollar fee for initiation, plus another three dollars in dues, but also sent away for regulation hoods and gowns from the mail-order catalogue. Years later, their disturbing regalia was still hanging, half-forgotten, in the basement of the Orange Temple, each item marked with the name of one of the town's leading citizens.

In May, Emmons addressed a full house at the Grand Theatre in Regina. "If you want to join the Ku Klux Klan you have to be a white Protestant," he told the approving crowd. If the Klan had its way, he continued, "Every man who did not respect the Union Jack would be sent back to the country from which he came. The organization stands for one language and that is English."[18] A couple of weeks later, he delivered a similar message to a throng of seven thousand at an outdoor rally on Moose Jaw's South Hill. As usual, his rhetorical flourishes were lifted from the pages of the Loyal Orange Lodge, but his appeal was enlivened by American razzmatazz. A wooden cross towered above the assembly, more than a hundred feet in height, with arms thirty-five feet across. Before the evening was over, it was set alight, its lurid glow visible across the entire city.

If Emmons's word is to be trusted, some of the province's politicians were envious of the Klan's success and wanted to grab a piece of the action for themselves. The most notable of those supplicants—or so Emmons alleged—was the Blondins' new neighbor, the leader of Saskatchewan's Conservatives. In Emmons's version of events, Dr. Anderson had barged in to see him several times, first at the KKK office in Moose Jaw and then, a few weeks later, at hotels in Regina and Saskatoon. Once, he'd come looking for Klan support in a by-election; later, he'd encouraged Emmons to organize a klavern in Saskatoon, even going so far as to provide a list of potential recruits. Anderson hotly denied these accusations, but some

of his closest associates were not so sure. "I had no idea that
Dr. Anderson had so little discretion," one insider fretted in
private.[19]

In the end, it didn't greatly matter what Anderson had
said or done, because one night in late August of 1927, eight
months into their stay, Klokard Emmons and his colleagues
packed up their belongings, including the small fortune they
had collected in membership and dues, and made a run for it
across the border.

By rights, their defection should have put an end to
the Klan in the province, but that isn't what happened. In
amazingly short order, a new organization rose from the
wreckage, a made-in-Saskatchewan Klan, motivated, or
so its leadership promised, by the very highest values and
the purest intentions. Gone were the terrifying hoods and
gowns; gone too (or so the organizers insisted) was the
Klan's American legacy of civic unrest. "The Klan of Saskatchewan [does] not pattern its work after that of the
United States," asserted its new Imperial Wizard, an accoun-
tant from Regina named John W. Rosborough. "What is
reported to have happened in the United States has no more
connection with the organization here than the flood of
Bible days with the high water of the Mississippi" earlier in
the year.[20] And it was true that the leaders of the resurgent
movement were paragons of bourgeois propriety: an accoun-
tant, a politician, a civil servant. Several were members of
the Orange Order, and everyone on the new provincial exec-
utive leaned far to the right.

The KKK "is the most complete political organization ever
known in the west," the new Imperial Treasurer (a former MP)
confided to the higher-ups within Conservative ranks. "Every

organizer in it is a Tory... I know it for I pay them. And I never pay a Grit. Smile when you hear anything about this organization. And keep silent."[21]

WHILE DR. ANDERSON and his colleagues were slinking around the province, laying the foundations for future success, Napoléon Sureau dit Blondin was back home in Nutana, preoccupied with building a future for his family and himself. All season long, work on his new house had proceeded briskly: the footprint of the building had been staked, the basement dug and poured. By early summer, when the Klan was holding its first public rallies, the exterior walls were framed and sheeted. By autumn, when the American organizers absconded with their ill-gotten gains, the doors and windows were in place. Did Clara and the children move in early, when the shell of the house was completed but before the interior work was done? Is that how random fragments of their everyday lives managed to lodge themselves among the wood shavings behind the wallboards? That torn page of arithmetic calculations. The exotic giveaway from a home-decorating store. A child's handmade valentine bearing a list of intended (and reconsidered) recipients: "Eunice, Kathrine, Gladys, ~~Moma~~, ~~Daddy~~, Teacher."

> Do not trample on my heart—,
> Which has been pierced by Cupid's dart;
> Only for your love I pine,
> Won't you be my Valentine?

Let's say, based on these clues, that the house was finished and the family in place by February of 1928. Napoléon had done his work with skill and, yes, with love. The whole place gleamed, from the varnished trim around the windows to the pale glow of the hardwood floors. A handsome clawfoot tub stood in the bathroom on the main floor—all mod cons!— and upstairs, in lieu of an attic, a loft, lit by a dormer window, offered generous light and space for the older children. Nothing fancy, you understand—this wasn't a two-and-a-half-story edifice like the Andersons' place down the street—but it was quietly pleasing nonetheless. The little house radiated pride and accomplishment.

BUT COZY AS their new home was, it couldn't protect Napoléon and Clara from the storm that was brewing outside their walls. First came the news (leaked to the media by a concerned participant) that a meeting had been held, in secret, to establish a Saskatoon klavern of the Ku Klux Klan and that various committees had been established to conduct a range of "invisible" investigations. For instance, one group, to be led by a Mr. Brouder of the Oldsmobile Company, had been delegated "to find out how many Roman Catholics there were in this city."[22] (Clara Blondin, for one.) The Blondins' former MP, John Evans, was said to have been present, and though their new neighbor, Dr. Anderson, was not in attendance, he was reportedly nominated in absentia to oversee the klavern's political program.

Soon, the movement went public, with a well-attended rally at a fundamentalist church downtown. An electric cross blazed red at the entrance as, inside, the Klan's fiery new spokesman, a seminary dropout from Ontario named J. J. Maloney, set a large crowd on full alert with his denunciations of "the menace of Roman Catholicism."[23] (Two of his favorite themes were

204 the doctrine of transubstantiation and the allegedly torrid sex lives of nuns.) Looking down from his vantage point in Heaven, the late Grand Orange Organizer, Brother Armstrong, would have recognized a fitting successor to himself in the KKK's new "Protestant Lecturer."

From then on, the mood just kept getting darker. In March, as the Blondins were settling into their new home, the Conservatives met in convention downtown to prepare for a provincial election that could be called at any time. Although Maloney himself was not present, the Klan's heavyweights were out in force—some as official delegates, others handing out Klan brochures—as were prominent members of the Orange Order. ("We had some difficulty keeping them in the background," one of the convention organizers admitted in private, "but succeeded in doing so without any incident whatever.")[24] What's more, by one means and another, the organizers pulled strings to ensure that only Protestants were elected to official roles within the party, it being "considered inexpedient that any Catholic should hold office in this organization."[25]

The Conservative Party, the Orangemen, and the Ku Klux Klan now stood arm in arm, confirming each other's delusions and singing the same tune. The statesmanlike solemnity of Conservative policy provided a bass line for the strident call to arms of the Protestant brotherhoods. One central idea echoed through all their proclamations: Saskatchewan was, and indeed had always been, the victim of a French-Catholic plot. "Solid Quebec, with its central authority, can swing either of the major parties in or out of office," they argued, an overbalance that put English Canada in constant jeopardy. Worse yet, since Québec voters were controlled by their priests, and the priests took their orders from Rome, "there was no gainsaying the fact" that the country was "to a great extent in the hands" of the Pope.

"Quebec is French," J. J. Maloney declaimed to audiences around the province, "and Quebec is Rome."[26]

Not convinced? Think back to the shame of 1905 when the federal government, at the behest of the Pope, had imposed a system of separate schools on Saskatchewan. Cast your mind back to the recent war, when French Canadians had opposed conscription, thereby saving their skins and laying the way for Catholic dominance. ("Considering the casualties overseas and the numbers who died since the war of disabilities sustained through active service," J. J. Maloney maintained, "one can readily see the fine Italian hand that said: 'Don't go. Let the Protestants get killed off and we'll rule Canada afterwards.'")[27] Think of the Railway Agreements that were filling the country with Papist scum. Recall the odious concessions that had been made to French speakers in the school system and note the "gradual aggression" with which French was, even then, being forced down English throats.

"The French language is now on our postal money orders, train tickets, [and] paper money," the Klan's Maloney thundered, "and the Canadian Radio Commission is utilizing French on the air by broadcasts, much to the disgust of the West and Ontario.

"Why all this?" he continued. "Simply the hand of Rome. The West will not take any of this French catering. We are British out here."[28]

206   THAT YEAR, 1928, crosses were lit in dozens of locations across the province—including one at Crystal Beach, another at Tessier, and still others on the lawns of Catholics in and around Harris—calling Bible-believing Protestants to the defense of British values. Meanwhile, fumes of Orangiste outrage continued to swirl around the province's pulpits and its press. One of the chief offenders, distressingly, was the bishop of the Anglican Church in Saskatchewan, an institution that had once seemed to offer a kind of sanctuary to Napoléon and Clara. Bishop George E. Lloyd had been fighting for British ascendancy for decades, first as an armed combatant against the Métis in 1885 and subsequently as an aggressive proponent of British settlement and English-only schools. And now here he was, still at the forefront of the battle, decrying a French reader as offensive to Protestants and maligning newcomers from Eastern Europe as "dirty, ignorant, garlic-smelling, non-preferred continentals."[29] Meanwhile, other commentators were objecting to the recent revelation that nuns, dressed in wimples and habits, were teaching Protestant students in a handful of the province's public schools, mostly in Francophone communities.

"Would you like to have a black-skirted 'she-cat' of a Nun teach your children?" an Orange spokesman raged. "Better wake up before it is too late and we have a revolution, for as sure as you are alive, blood will be spilled if the Protestant people don't band together."[30]

Small wonder that the Soeurs de l'Assomption, newly arrived in the province from Nicolet, Québec, were relieved that fall when the fire escapes were completed on their new school in the town of Biggar, northwest of Harris. "Nous *craindrons moins maintenant les fanatiques de Biggar,"* the Mother Superior confided in her journal, *"si toutefois ils s'avisaient de mettre le feu à notre maison."*[31] We will now be less afraid of the local fanatics should they take a notion to set fire to our house.

BACK IN THE Blondins' pretty little home on a gracious street in Saskatoon, a child is huddled on the staircase, listening to his parents shout.

"No French," he hears his mother say. "Don't you dare speak French in this house."

13

— REVELATIONS —

*Les heritages
c'est comme les chromosomes,
ça se choisit pas.*

Heritage is like our chromosomes,
we don't get to choose.

JEAN FOREST, *L'aube de Suse,* 1985

THE LONG-ANTICIPATED PROVINCIAL election was finally held on June 6, 1929. When the last blazing cross had been extinguished and the final tally was in, Brother Anderson was pained to discover that his party had yet again been defeated. Although the Conservatives had made impressive gains, up from four seats to twenty-four, they had been surpassed by the Liberals. On the plus side, however, Anderson's caucus now included such dignitaries as the Klan's go-to attorney; the Grand Master of the Orange Lodge (representing the Goose Lake district); and J. J. Maloney's father-in-law. Better yet, the Conservative surge had deprived the Liberals of an outright majority, and when the legislature convened that fall, the ruling party fell on a vote of nonconfidence. And that is how it happened that the Blondins' near neighbor, Dr. J. T. M. Anderson, was sworn in as the leader of a coalition government.

Saskatchewan's fifth premier continued to insist that he was not now, and never had been, a member of the Ku Klux Klan, but there was no doubt about his standing as an Orangeman. Convinced that the hidden hand of the Pope was interfering in the province's public schools, he threw himself into a program of purification. One of his first moves, in his joint role as minister of education, was to cut off the supply of French-speaking (bilingual) teachers from Québec, on the supposed grounds that their training was deficient. Next, he drafted a law barring religious dress and symbols from all public schools. Never again would a woman wearing a nun's wimple teach impressionable Protestant youth.

With those preliminaries out of the way, he then ordered a quick-and-dirty investigation of the *cours primaire*, the provision, so abhorrent to the Orange Order, that permitted six-year-olds to be taught in French for a single transitional year. The results of this research seemed to confirm his bleakest fears. Students who were subjected to even these few months of bilingual education were prevented from attaining an adequate grasp of English. Not only did this misguided provision place its victims at a disadvantage, but in Dr. Anderson's professional opinion, it put the country's very existence at risk. In remarkably short order, the *cours primaire* was made *ultra vires*.

All those decades of struggle by the Orangemen and their increasingly unsavory allies had finally born dismal fruit. Under Anderson's exacting regime, no language other than English was permitted on school playgrounds. No language other than English could be used during the daily half-hour of religious training. No language other than English could be spoken at meetings of local school trustees. Although a course in French grammar was still on the books as an option, it was limited to one hour per day and it, too, had to be taught in English. There was no provision for teaching any other "foreign" language—no German or Polish, no Ukrainian—and not even a whisper of support for Michif or Saulteaux or Cree. Any school district that failed to observe the English-only rule was deprived of funding.

Like their counterparts in Ontario and Manitoba before them, Saskatchewan's Francophone communities were now among the casualties in the country's culture wars. Their sympathizers began to call them *les blessés*, the wounded ones.

THERE MUST HAVE been times when Clara stood here at her living-room window, with her husband away at work, and watched as their illustrious neighbor sauntered down the block. Or perhaps she was on the boulevard with her children, knee-deep in the potatoes that she had planted there, and saw him striding past, rushing to a meeting at the Red Robin Café on Broadway or heading homeward. He was an unmistakable figure: a slender, upright gentleman with an arresting gaze and slightly oversized ears, who favored tightly buttoned collars and glistening white waistcoats. Did he acknowledge the Blondins' presence with a stiff nod and a tip of his bowler hat? Did Clara swallow her bruised feelings and smile back?

All she and Napoléon had ever wanted to do was fit in and make a good life for themselves. All they had ever wanted was a decent future for their children. Of course, it was unsettling when your most intimate affiliations—your mother tongue, your childhood religion, your ancestry—were disparaged by your own government. But what option did the average person have except to make the best of a bad situation? Clara was not a club woman or a crusader. She was a tiny, fiery being with a grade-four education who loved to argue and to dance. A few weeks before the provincial election, she'd given birth to another baby, a boy whom they'd named Charles, and with a family of five youngsters to look after, all under the age of twelve, she was too busy to concern herself with the wider world. Besides, she was finished with being French. For her, the solution was simple: just get with the program and speak English.

Although Napoléon carried a lingering pride in his ancestry, he expressed it quietly, in offhand remarks to his children and through the S in his signature. The guys at work could call him "Paul," but in his heart, he would always be N. S. Blondin, Napoléon Sureau dit Blondin. That middle initial was a discreet way of giving the finger to Anglo conformity; it was a clandestine gesture of connection with his forebears. But he wanted nothing to do with public squabbles over language and religion. Leave politics to the true believers, to the men of education and standing who spoke for the Church and the French community through their lobby group, l'Association Catholique Franco-Canadienne de la Saskatchewan. Let them petition and protest and wrangle; let them congratulate themselves on winning trivial gains. On the issue of religious garb, for instance, the ACFC had managed to persuade the government that nuns should be permitted to wear their regulation dresses under academic gowns and to replace their wimples with a kind of "French widows' bonnet." On all substantive

212 measures, however, Premier Anderson refused to budge, true to the Orange watchword of "No Surrender."

Win or lose, Orange or *bleu*, Napoléon would roll with circumstances. His main concern, now as always, was economic survival. He had already accomplished so much through sheer determination and hard work, as an entrepreneur, a farmer, a husband and father, a homeowner. He had started out in life with nothing, and now he was a man of means. In addition to putting money into this new house, he had invested some of the proceeds from the sale of his farm in the stock market, and he had a fat wad of brightly colored certificates to testify to his increasing wealth. That very summer, 1929, the Dow Jones average had shot up by 20 percent. Say it in English or say it in French, it was all the same to him. He was *un self-made man*.

WHEN THE NEW YORK stock market crashed late in October, the news flashed around the world. By mid-November, the Dow had lost almost half of its value. But not to worry, the experts said. It was just a natural fluctuation—a "correction," they explained—and things would be back to normal before you knew it. Sure enough, stock values did begin to inch up. Meanwhile, on the banks of the South Saskatchewan River, the economy continued to steam ahead. That year, the City of Saskatoon had issued a record $6 million in permits for new construction. In addition to five new schools, the community now boasted a magnificent new Eaton's department store, a new power plant and police station, and a fancy new movie house, the Capitol Theatre, with room for 1,600 patrons in its exotic Spanish-themed auditorium. Work had begun on the new Federal Building; Macleod's and Massey-Harris had both come to town, and the CNR was preparing to build a luxury hotel, the Bessborough, on a prime location beside the river.

And so Saskatoon embarked on the 1930s with its bumptious self-regard undimmed. Despite the disturbance in the financial system, the community was continuing to progress. Of a total population that now exceeded forty thousand, the vast majority were self-sustaining, with only fifty families on the dole. Although that number had doubled in just twelve months, it was not a reason for concern. As late as midsummer of 1930, the mayor was confidently assuring the public that everything was going to plan.

Then, in faraway Liverpool and Chicago, the export market for wheat began to collapse. A bushel of grain that had sold for $1.24 in 1929 was worth just $0.59 by December of the following year. Twelve months later, the rate had fallen to $0.35, the lowest price for a bushel of wheat since the 1600s. Factor in drought and dust storms. Factor in grasshopper plagues and debt. When the farmers of Saskatchewan went down—and they went down hard—farm-service centers like Saskatoon went down with them.

The final blow was delivered by Wall Street. In the spring of 1931, the Dow Jones average, which had rebounded nicely over the previous weeks and months, tipped into a long, slow, steady descent. By the time things bottomed out, the market had dumped 90 percent of its value, and Napoléon's cache of curlicue-bedecked certificates was essentially worthless. By the autumn of 1932, the number of households on relief in Saskatoon had exploded to almost 1,300, totaling more than 5,000 people in all. Among them were Napoléon and Clara Blondin and their children.

214   WHEN I TELL this story to Diana, she looks stricken, and I know she is imagining her own young brood caught in a similar wreck. "That's harsh," she says finally, then summons a twisted grin. "Now aren't you going to tell me nothing like that could ever happen again?" From outdoors, we hear the high-pitched laughter of her little girls.

THE DEPRESSION HIT Saskatchewan like a punch in the gut. During the boom years of the late twenties, the province had reported some of the highest per capita incomes anywhere in the world. A decade later, its people were among the poorest of the poor, with two-thirds of the rural population on the dole. Even the venerable Grand Orange Lodge was shaken by the catastrophe. At its annual meeting in 1931, its members congratulated themselves on having staged yet another "monster celebration" of the Glorious Twelfth (again in Saskatoon), and they applauded Premier Anderson for asserting the supremacy of English in the province's schools. But even in their moment of victory, their spirits were forlorn. Their membership was in free fall, and their coffers increasingly bare. If one year went down in the annals as "trying," the next was "tough," and the one after that "depressing."[1]

As for the Saskatchewan Klan, it attained official status as a Benevolent Society in the early thirties, but by then, its force was spent. Its de facto leader, J. J. Maloney, had expected a reward from the Anderson government for his role in the campaign, and when nothing of the sort was forthcoming, he packed up his hurt feelings and left the province. His new field of enterprise was Alberta, in particular Edmonton, which had enough French-speaking Catholics to make it, in his estimation, "the Rome of the West."[2] There, he rose to the rank of Imperial Wizard, with eleven klaverns at his command, but his glory days were numbered. Hauled into court for a series of offenses, including defamation and petty fraud, he eventually fled to British Columbia and lived out his days in comparative quiet. Another reprehensible voice was silenced when Anglican bishop G. E. Lloyd gave up his post and subsided into a restless retirement. (A recipient of an honorary doctorate from the University of Saskatchewan in 1929, he continues to be acknowledged as a founder of his namesake city, Lloydminster.)

If the clamor of bigotry had been muted, its key tenets were alive and well. "Canada was, and must always remain, British." For British, read white, Anglo-Saxon, and Protestant. For Saskatoon's civic administration, this meant ensuring that British subjects were first in line for benefits when work-for-welfare jobs were handed out. It meant requiring relief recipients who had been in the country for five years or less to sign forms acknowledging that they could be deported on the slightest pretext. It meant keeping Métis clients under an anxious watch, since they were assumed to be irresponsible and unworthy of trust. Cruelty piled upon cruelty, injustice upon injustice.

By now, many of the people from Prairie Ronde had migrated into the city and taken up residence in shacks or vacant houses, or sometimes merely tents, on the outskirts of the settlement. Alarmed by the suffering of their families, these refugees began to reconnect with one another and rekindle their sense of kinship, even taking the bold step of forming the Saskatoon local of the new Métis Society of Saskatchewan. Yet in this city, as elsewhere around the province, the Métis continued to struggle for recognition and respect, and their repeated demands for education, livelihood, and land rights went unanswered.

THE BLONDINS LOST the house. In 1932, they lost this beautiful little house. In my mind's eye, I see them plodding down the front sidewalk carrying suitcases and cardboard boxes, pieces of furniture, the flotsam of a life reduced to splinters. There was no thrill in this departure, as there had been in leaving Harris. This time, there was nothing but defeat and dislocation. Goodbye to Albert School. Goodbye to the cafés and shops on Broadway Avenue. Goodbye to the promise of being fully respectable. As a particularly painful side note, Napoléon and his family were also bidding a partial farewell to their closest relatives, Hercules and Mabel and their children, who had recently moved into a house just a few doors away.

The new home that Napoléon had found for his family was across the river, on the northern outskirts of town. Like much of the city's housing stock at the time, it did not have indoor plumbing, just an outhouse and a pump, but it was the best he could manage under the circumstances. Fortunately, he and Clara both had a lifetime of experience in the arts of making do. They kept a sheep and chickens in the backyard, sometimes a pig as well. For a while, they had a milk cow, but she kept getting loose and trampling the neighbors' gardens, so they had to get rid of her. At times, Clara supplemented their income by taking in boarders. At times, Napoléon brought in a little cash from one of the business ventures he and Hercules undertook—their bulk-petroleum depot or their woolen mill— but the takings were seldom enough to cover even the basics.

There were days when his children went hungry. They were often ill-clad and cold. They were shamed by the standard-issue clothing that marked them as relief recipients. Their father absorbed all these injuries and compounded them with his own.

The provocations of life on the dole were endless. To qualify for assistance, applicants had to promise to repay the city every cent they'd received "on demand" and to open their homes "at any time" to civic inspection.[3] If the inspector found evidence that a member of the household had committed the slightest deviation—joined a social club, for example, or installed a telephone—the family's benefits were instantly revoked. Hercules and his household suffered this fate in the winter of 1932 because they acquired a radio. Although Hercules wrote to appeal the decision (the offending device belonged to his daughter, he said), the disqualification stood. People who squandered their resources on luxuries did not deserve public help.

Anxiety mutated into resentment. Resentment boiled over in rage. That same November, a group of thirty women marched into council chambers in city hall, accompanied by their kids, and demanded changes to the relief administration. They returned to their homes two days later, having won an assurance that they wouldn't be pressed for immediate repayment of their benefits. By contrast, the crowd of unemployed men who congregated outside the relief office were met by police with force; a newspaper article the next day spoke of arrests and "blood-soaked batons."[4] And when

218 demonstrators marched on city hall, waving a red banner and singing the Communist anthem, "The Internationale," the city responded by hiring special constables and equipping them with tear gas. Thereafter, all such parades were banned, on the pretext that they failed to show due deference to the Union Jack.

The Communist Party of Canada had recently been declared illegal (its leaders locked up in Kingston Pen), but a quiet undercurrent of agitation continued to stir through Saskatoon. In bars, on street corners, and at the relief store, wherever the unemployed met, there were muttered calls for revolution and, failing that, for a program of radical reforms: public health care, unemployment insurance, a minimum wage for women, and price supports for farmers. "The idea of communism is to bring about economic security," one of its local advocates asserted, and who could argue with that?[5] Buried deep in Napoléon Blondin's wallet was a card with a fancy green border that identified him as a Communist, a symbol of the anger that was burning in his stomach.

NAPOLÉON AND CLARA'S youngest son, Charles, was only three when his family fell. But if that trauma left a mark on him, it isn't immediately apparent. At eighty-three, "Chuck" Blondin—Lorena and Fran's Uncle Chick—is cheerful and outgoing, with a glint of mischief in his eyes and a spring to his step that suggests a much younger man. He invites me into his home with hugs, though we've never met before, and introduces me to his wife, Joyce, who offers hugs of her own.

If I've adopted the Blondins as friends and relations, Chuck and Joyce have returned the compliment by greeting me like a long-lost cousin. We sit in their comfortably cluttered kitchen, cups of tea in hand, as Chuck leafs through a binder full of family memorabilia. Here are the originals of the pictures that his nieces had shown me all those months before. "My" house under construction. Chuck's older brothers and sister standing in the potato patch on "my" boulevard. Although he was a toddler when the family was forced to leave, he still knows the address by heart. "The house that Dad built," he calls it, or, simply, "Dad's house."

Here, too, are the familiar pictures of Clara as a young woman, and others, taken later in her life, that I've never seen before. In one she is wearing a Santa hat; in all of them she is grinning so broadly you can almost hear her laugh. "She was a good mother," Chuck says fondly, picking up one of the prints. "Always singing and humming. She loved us all, took care of us." He puts the photo back on the table and gives it a little pat, then gazes down at it in silence.

"There was a lot of fighting," he says, without looking up. "A lot of arguing, between Mom and Dad. About politics. About everything, really." He gestures at a photo of his dad. "He was a hard person to live with, and she was independent, fought back."

A hard person to live with? He nods. "You never knew where you were with my dad," he says, his voice suddenly grave. "You'd just be standing there, and he would walk by and lay a hand print on your face." His hand flies up to his cheek, as if he can still feel the sting. "You'd go to school that way, a red mark. And Mom would just go crazy—don't do that to the kids."

He closes the album softly and looks up at me. "My dad could sell anybody anything," he says evenly, "but it all disappeared when he walked through the door. He left the girls and Mom alone, I think, but he was hard on his boys." He lays his hands on the table and looks me straight in the eye.

There is nothing to say. I'm sorry. I'm not surprised. I'm sorry. Over the noise of my confused thoughts, I hear myself offering excuses for his father's violence. Generations of bigotry, the Ku Klux Klan, the shock of falling on your ass. I tell him about my grandpa Humphrey, on that dried-out Alberta farm, and how he beat his sons, not that the circumstances justified his actions, of course…

But Chuck will have none of my mumbled rationalizations. "I decided early on that when I grew up, I was not going to be like my dad," he says quietly. "I don't like to remember these things, but that's the way it was." He fixes me with a look that permits no further argument.

AND YET, WHEN the pain that was burning in Napoléon's gut turned out to be cancer, it was Chuck and his older brother Ralph who accompanied their father all the way to the Mayo Clinic on the train. And when it was determined that nothing could be done to help him, they were the ones who brought him home again.

Bless us, O Lord, and preserve us from all evil,
and bring us to eternal life;
and may the souls of the faithful departed,
through the mercy of God, rest in peace. Amen.[6]

BUT I AM getting ahead of my story. In the years after the Blondins lost the house, the Depression ground grimly on, bringing down not just individual families but the entire town. In the good old days of the late 1920s, it had not been exceptional for several hundred "modern" homes (those graced with indoor plumbing) to be built annually in Saskatoon. By the mid-thirties, the tally had dropped to five or two and sometimes none at all. Nineteen thirty-four was one of the nothing years, and the appalling economic conditions must certainly have played a part in the outcome of the provincial election that summer. The Conservatives, who had come to power four years earlier amid the smoke from burning crosses, stood for reelection and were completely obliterated. From the premier on down, every single Conservative was defeated. True to form, Anderson blamed this rout on the undue influence of the Catholic Church.

But if Brother Anderson was out of the picture, the bigotry that had helped to bring him to power had not vanished overnight. The incoming Liberals had campaigned on a promise to defend minority rights by repealing Anderson's discriminatory laws. Once in office, however, the new government did nothing but hem and haw. In the late 1930s, when nuns in the community of Prud'homme, Saskatchewan, brazenly resorted to wearing their religious clothing, unaltered and uncloaked, the government came down hard, depriving the school district of its sustaining grants in the fall of 1939 and again the following year.

In public, Liberal politicians defended this action as simple respect for the law, but in their private correspondence, they acknowledged what was really going on. A dozen years after their encounter with the Klan, they were still running scared.

222 "The disruption of the province in the year 1929 furnishes food for thought," a prominent Liberal mused in 1941. "There is... considerable evidence... that the attitude of mind displayed in that controversy still exists," one of his colleagues noted. "Let sleeping dogs lie," another (himself a French Catholic) advised.[7] As long as a majority of voters were committed to WASP dominance, Dr. Anderson's Amendments would be too hot to touch. Even the outbreak of war against European fascists did not cause opinions to shift.

And so the strictures remained in place through the 1940s and beyond. Change could have come in 1944, when Tommy Douglas and his Co-operative Commonwealth Federation swept to power on a promise to put "humanity first." And change certainly should have come in 1947, with the introduction, by the Douglas government, of the Saskatchewan Bill of Rights. The first broadly based human-rights legislation in the country, the Bill not only outlawed discrimination on the basis of race, creed, religion, and ethnicity in specified circumstances but also prohibited the incitement of hatred. For the first time, the dissemination of inflammatory rhetoric, the bigots' stock in trade, was not just abhorrent but actually illegal. And yet the restrictions on language and religious expression in the province's schools (though by now seldom enforced) remained on the statute books, the legacy of the KKK and the Orange Order.

English would remain the only legal medium of instruction in Saskatchewan until the 1960s, when the door was gradually opened to French and then, grudgingly, to other languages. The ban on religious dress and insignias would persist even longer.

"EVERYTHING WAS ENGLISH," Chuck Blondin says, thinking back to those years, the thirties and forties, when he was growing up. "I never heard French, never felt I was French, never any connection there." It was as if his family tree had been hacked off at the roots.

As the 1940s progressed, Napoléon and Clara's little household became increasingly isolated. By now, the old man, Cléophas, was dead and buried in faraway Spokane, and Napoléon's brothers Alex, Télémaque, and Ulysse had each dispersed in his own direction. Even Hercules had finally given up on Saskatchewan and moved away; he died in Edmonton in 1940, at the age of fifty-seven. The deeper family connection lay out East in Lafontaine, and although Clara somehow managed to scrape together enough money for a trip "to Penetang," it would turn out to be a once-in-a-lifetime extravagance. The plain fact was that she and Napoléon had been cast out on their own, with no means of support except their own inner resources.

Clara responded to the ongoing crisis as she had always done, by caring for her six children (her last-born a baby girl), sparring with her husband, and stepping out whenever she could to community dances. "She was a party lady," her son recalls fondly. "She loved dancing, had lots of 'boyfriends.'" Her husband, for his part, thought about nothing but work. Although the Depression had lifted elsewhere in the country, on the prairies, and in Saskatchewan in particular, conditions remained tough. Well into the 1940s, Saskatoon was in a state of paralysis. In 1944, for example, a stunning total of four "modern" homes was added to the city's housing stock. His dalliance with revolutionary politics now behind him, Napoléon relaunched himself into these frigid economic waters as an entrepreneur, first as Blondin and Blondin, in partnership with Hercules, and later as a sole proprietorship: the Blondin Roofing Products Ltd., offering "roof repairing by experienced workmen."[8] One of those experienced workmen was a very young Chuck, who was assigned the task of "firing the kettles"—heating vats of diluted asphalt over open wood fires, high up above the ground.

With the local economy at a standstill, the business was not an immediate success. In fact, when Napoléon and Clara's eldest son, Ralph, enlisted in the Navy in 1941, he felt it necessary to send part of his pay packet home to help his parents. By now, Napoléon was acutely ill and on morphine, but his ambition had not waned. Impatient for opportunity, he moved the family to Winnipeg and then, briefly, to Moose Jaw, before returning to Saskatoon, all in a period of three or four years. ("We [women] can't help what men decide to do," Clara would later observe in a letter to a granddaughter.)[9] When the economy finally began to recover in 1945, the Blondins found themselves in an "unmodern" dwelling in Nutana, a mile or two from the bungalow on which they had once pinned their hopes. From an office in the basement, Napoléon and his sons fanned out across the prairies to apply their "bonded" roofing materials to factories, arenas, and industrial sites, including virtually every grain elevator in Saskatchewan.

NAPOLÉON BLONDIN DIED in St. Paul's Hospital in Saskatoon on September 13, 1946, at the age of sixty-eight, with his family close at hand. One of the visitors to his bedside was his son Ralph, with his brand-new baby daughter.

"My grandfather was a domineering man," that daughter, Lorena, will tell me, "but my own father loved his dad. I think he could see how hard it had been for him to carry on. I think he could see that his father was dying with the cancer. In pain."

Dying. In pain.

Although he had been baptized as an infant and schooled in religion as a child, Napoléon had never been much of a churchgoer. Pressed by a census taker to choose a denomination, he might put himself down as Presbyterian or, just as easily, Church of England, certainly never as a Roman Catholic. But as he lay dying, memories of his childhood faith must have come flooding back. The facade of l'Église de la Sainte-Croix in Lafontaine with its graceful steeple, the peaceful graveyard where his mother and his grandparents had been laid to rest. And beyond that resting place, who knew what or Who might be waiting? In the extremity of his final days, Napoléon called for a priest to say the last rites for him.

Napoléon Sureau dit Blondin was buried, among strangers, in the Roman Catholic section of Saskatoon's Woodlawn Cemetery. His name, too French and "foreign" for English-only ears, is misspelled in the official records.

AND THEN, AS it always does, life carried on. For better or worse, the daughters grew up and married men with names like Tomczak and Gallagher. For richer or poorer, the sons carried on with their father's roofing business. Clara, left with an eleven-year-old daughter to care for and no income, became a sometimes unwelcome guest in the homes of her grown-up children. At her lowest ebb, in her early fifties, she spent several months in the mental hospital in Weyburn. And yet, with the passage of years—scrappy and determined as ever—she achieved a carefully guarded independence. "She'd decide to come for a visit," Chuck's wife, Joyce, remembers with an affectionate smile, "and just show up unannounced. There she'd be at the door with her little suitcase."

In due course, Clara moved into a seniors' residence in High River, Alberta, and it was there she met a widower with an ultra-Anglo name and a pedigree to match: Cecil Arthur Peacock, the man Chuck describes as "the love of her life."

"Oh, she really loved him. She was atwitter all the time."

Asked late in life if she still remembered how to speak her mother tongue, Clara "drew herself up like an indignant hen," as if the very thought gave her offense, and said, "*Most certainly not.*" For her, the loss of identity was a small price to pay for happiness.

CHUCK BLONDIN SITS, teacup in hand, gazing at the humble treasures spread out in front of him: photos of people and places he knew as a child, a flyer for his father's firm, a tiny prayer book that once belonged to his mother. He picks up one of the pictures and spends a long time looking at it.

"Yes," he says, finally, glancing up at me, "that's the house my dad built."

In the photo, the dwelling stands unfinished, the windows framed but open, the doorway empty and beckoning. I think of all the ghosts who have wafted in through those entries since I began calling to them. Men, women, and children.

Adventurers and rebels. Survivors, one and all. *Ton histoire est une épopée des plus brillants exploits,* I think to myself. And then I remember the dark secrets that have risen from under the floorboards or crept out of locked and forgotten rooms. The long shadow of religious intolerance. The smoke of burning crosses. The sting of a father's hand.

Beside me, Chuck is still studying the image as if it has dimensions I will never see. When he looks up, he is smiling. I don't want to break the spell, but there is one last question that I know I have to ask.

"Are you concerned about how I tell this story?" I mean: what I tell and what I don't.

"No, not at all," he says calmly. "Just tell the truth as best you can."

⌂

BACK IN THE house that Napoléon built, I sit at the dining-room table, alone with my thoughts. Just there, on my right, is the place where we once kept Diana's tank of turtles and her cage of mice. Here, at this very table, is where Keith and I first met and started a conversation that has been running ever since. Here, too, the Blondin granddaughters opened their family album and showed me a doorway into the past, an entry point I would not have discovered without their help. The world on the other side of that portal had turned out to be uncomfortable and unnerving, filled with events and players that were familiar but that now appeared unmasked. Institutions that had always seemed normal suddenly became grotesque. My home society had been shaped by bigotry and racism.

The truth: We live in a house of stories bequeathed to us by the past. It's no mansion filled with wonders; in fact, it is a fixer-upper, in need of loving care. When we find cracks in the foundations and rot in the woodwork, then it's good to face up to the defects and bring them out into the light. And it's good, so good, to sit with one another and share our experiences. Stories are living things. They transcend boundaries and divisions; they seek out common ground. There is room in our house of stories for everyone.

ACKNOWLEDGMENTS

THIS BOOK STANDS on a foundation laid by the scholars whose work is included in the bibliography. Additional information was furnished by documents held in public archives and museums, including both the Regina and Saskatoon offices of the Provincial Archives of Saskatchewan; the University Archives and Special Collections, University of Saskatchewan Library; Local History Room, Saskatoon Public Library; City of Saskatoon Archives; Harris and District Museum; the Biggar Museum and Gallery; Provincial Archives of Alberta; Penetanguishene Centennial Museum and Archives; and the Centre du Patrimoine of La Société historique de Saint-Boniface. Sincere thanks to the staff and volunteers at all these institutions and also to Penetanguishene genealogists Hubert Charlebois, Deborah Crawford, and Pamela Brown Tessier.

The manuscript was reviewed at various stages of completion by several expert readers—Harris memory-keeper Art Dunlap, City of Saskatoon archivist Jeff O'Brien, cultural theorist Emma Lind, fiction writer and poet Guillaume Morissette, Métis historian Cheryl Troupe-Strouts, and Saskatchewan chronicler *nonpareil* Bill Waiser—each of whom

230 made valuable suggestions for improvements. The incomparable Maria Campbell was kind enough to share her thoughts and to give me permission to quote from our conversation. Thank you to composer Gérard Jean, who allowed me to reproduce lyrics from his choral work "1916," and to Jean-Guy Pilon and Éditions Typo for permission to quote from his work. I am also grateful to my cousin Linda Bunney for information about our Jack ancestors and to my adorable aunt, Lillian Rideout, for making me tea and sharing her memories.

As always, I owe a huge debt of gratitude to my longtime publisher, Rob Sanders, for his patience, enthusiasm, and steadfast support. Editor Nancy Flight exercised her professional judgment with just the right combination of compassion and precision. Thanks, too, to copy editor Paula Ayer, designer Belle Wuthrich, proofreader Dawn Loewen, and the rest of the team at Greystone Books for their many invaluable contributions.

It is a special pleasure to acknowledge the members of the Blondin clan who have taken a friendly interest in this work, including Faye and Helen Blondin and Fran Zerr. Family archivist Lorena Martens has shared her knowledge with warmth and candor. Thanks, too, to her husband, Jim. An extra measure of appreciation is due to Chuck and Joyce Blondin, who welcomed me into their home, opened their cache of family memorabilia, and trusted me with their stories.

It is an honor to acknowledge the financial support of the Access Copyright Foundation, the Canada Council for the Arts, and the Saskatchewan Arts Board.

Finally, I am grateful to my daughter, Diana, for the initial spark of inspiration that set this project alight. My respect and love for my partner-in-all-things, Keith Bell, is beyond words.

BLONDIN FAMILY TREE (PARTIAL)

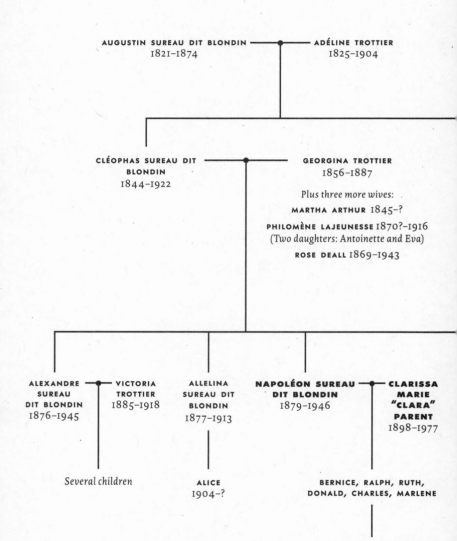

AUGUSTIN SUREAU DIT BLONDIN
1821–1874

ADÉLINE TROTTIER
1825–1904

CLÉOPHAS SUREAU DIT BLONDIN
1844–1922

GEORGINA TROTTIER
1856–1887

Plus three more wives:

MARTHA ARTHUR 1845–?

PHILOMÈNE LAJEUNESSE 1870?–1916
(Two daughters: Antoinette and Eva)

ROSE DEALL 1869–1943

ALEXANDRE SUREAU DIT BLONDIN
1876–1945

VICTORIA TROTTIER
1885–1918

ALLELINA SUREAU DIT BLONDIN
1877–1913

NAPOLÉON SUREAU DIT BLONDIN
1879–1946

CLARISSA MARIE "CLARA" PARENT
1898–1977

Several children

ALICE
1904–?

BERNICE, RALPH, RUTH, DONALD, CHARLES, MARLENE

LORENA, FRAN, AND OTHERS

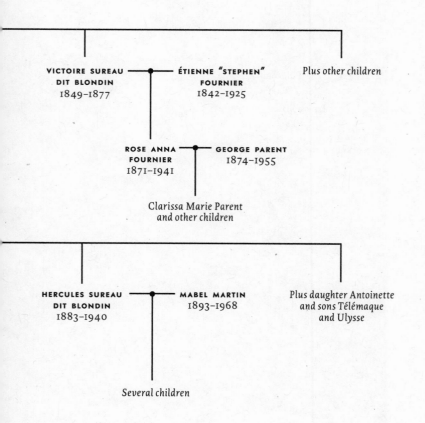

VICTOIRE SUREAU DIT BLONDIN 1849–1877 ——● ÉTIENNE "STEPHEN" FOURNIER 1842–1925

Plus other children

ROSE ANNA FOURNIER 1871–1941 ——● GEORGE PARENT 1874–1955

Clarissa Marie Parent and other children

HERCULES SUREAU DIT BLONDIN 1883–1940 ——● MABEL MARTIN 1893–1968

Plus daughter Antoinette and sons Télémaque and Ulysse

Several children

MAP OF PLACES IN THE TEXT

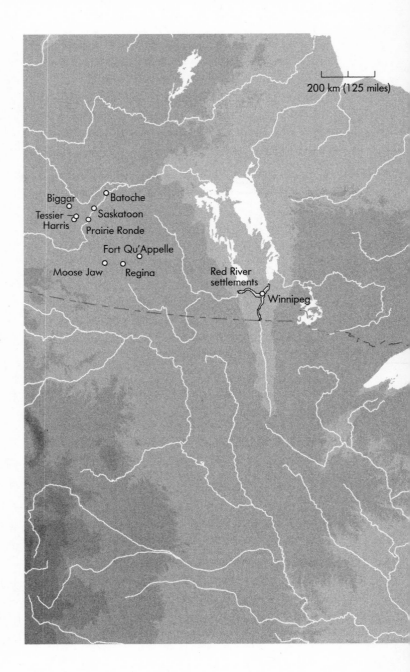

NOTES

NOTES REFER TO direct quotations only. Additional information on sources is provided in the bibliography.

Chapter 1: Little House

1   Henry Youle Hind, *Narrative of the Canadian Red River Exploring Expedition of 1857 and of the Assinniboine and Saskatchewan Exploring Expedition of 1858* (London: Longman, Green, Longman, and Roberts, 1860), as quoted by Jeff O'Brien, "A History of Saskatoon to 1914" (Unpublished paper, City of Saskatoon Archives, July 2005), 4.

2   John N. Lake, "The Temperance Colonization Society and the Foundation of Saskatoon," *Narratives of Saskatoon 1882–1912* (Saskatoon: Committee of the Historical Association of Saskatoon, University Book Store, 1927), 15–17.

3   *Ibid.*

4   *Ibid.*

5   O'Brien, "A History of Saskatoon to 1914," 4.

6   Alexander Muir, "The Maple Leaf Forever," 1867.

7   Jack Kapica, *Shocked and Appalled: A Century of Letters to the Globe and Mail* (Toronto: Lester and Orpen Dennys, 1985), 108–9.

8   "Métis Petition of September 2, 1880," Virtual Museum of Métis History and Culture, Gabriel Dumont Institute of Native Studies and Applied Research, metismuseum.ca/resource.php/14528.

238 **Chapter 2: Tangled Roots**

1   "Bienheureuse Marie-Anne Blondin (1809–1890), Une existence marquée par la croix," Conférence des évêques catholiques du Canada/Canadian Conference of Catholic Bishops, cccb.ca/site/images/Bienheureuse_Marie-Anne_Blondin-FR.pdf.

2   Sieur de Champlain, as quoted by Father Paul Le Jeune, "Relation of What Occurred in New France in the Year 1633," *Jesuit Relations*, vol. 5, moses.creighton.edu/kripke/jesuitrelations/relations_05.html.

3   Louis Hémon, *Maria Chapdelaine: Récit du Canada Français* (Paris: Bernard Grasset, 1954, first ed. 1913), 239, 241.

Chapter 4: An Agitation of Ghosts

1   Paraphrased from Antonine Maillet, "The Great Disturbance According to Bélonie," trans. Solenn Carriou, *Globe and Mail*, July 15, 2000, fawi.net/ezine/vol3no2/Maillet.html.

2   Jacques Lacoursière, Jean Provencher, and Denis Vaugeois, *Canada-Québec, 1534–2000* (Sillery, Québec: Septentrion, 2001), 154.

3   Adam Shortt and Arthur G. Doughty, eds., "Presentments of the Grand Jury of Quebec, October 16, 1764," *Documents Pertaining to the Constitutional History of Canada 1759–1791* (Ottawa: J. de L. Taché, 1918), 155.

4   "Governor J. A. Murray to the Lords of Trade October 29, 1764," ibid., 167.

5   Ernest Gagnon, "J'ai perdu mon amant," *Chansons populaires du Canada* (Québec: Bureau du "Foyer Canadien," 1865), 194–6.

6   John Graves Simcoe, as quoted in Lacoursière et al., *Canada-Québec, 1534–2000*, 193. Back translation from French to English by the author.

7   Lacoursière et al., *Canada-Québec, 1534–2000*, 195.

8   Jonathan Lemire, "Augustin Tassé, aubergiste, patriote de Sainte-Rose," Rébellions et patriotes de 1837–1838, jonathanlemire.com/articles/histoire-de-1837-1838-recueil-2007/augustin-tasse-aubergiste-patriote-de-sainte-rose/; Louis-Joseph Papineau, "Les 92 résolutions de l'assemblée législative du Bas-Canada, février 1834," La bibliothèque indépendantiste, biblio.republiquelibre.org/Les_92_résolutions_de_l%27Assemblée_législative_du_Bas-Canada.

Chapter 5: Township of Tiny

1   *The Montreal Gazette*, April 25, 1849, as quoted by Jacques Lacoursière and Robin Philpot, *A People's History of Quebec* (Montréal: Baraka Books and Sillery, Québec: Septentrion, 2009), 106.

2   "French Schools in County of Simcoe," *Sessional Papers, Fourth Session of Sixth Legislature, Province of Ontario*, Session 1890, vol. XXII, part VI, 3–12.

3   Marie Asselin Marchildon with Louise Mullie, *Ce n'est qu'un au revoir* (privately published, 1988), 33–34.

4   Daniel Marchildon, *De coureur de bois à quoi? L'histoire de la Franco-Huronie* (privately published, 1980), 90. "*Les parents défavorisés toute leur vie dans un marché de travail anglophone parce qu'ils ne parlent pas assez bien l'anglais, ne veulent pas que leurs enfants souffrent du même problème, et ils les encouragent de façon exagérée à apprendre l'anglais.*"

5   Béatrice Mandeville, as quoted by Yves Roby, *Histoire d'un rêve brisée: Les Canadiens français aux États-Unis* (Sillery, Québec: Septentrion, 2000), 31. "*Le monde était heureux aux États-Unis. Il y avait de l'argent, de quoi vivre. Au Canada, c'était la pauvreté.*"

6   Jack Kerouac, letter to Yvonne Le Maître, September 8, 1950, *Jack Kerouac: Selected Letters, 1940–1956*, ed. Anne Charters (New York: Viking, 1995), 228.

Chapter 6: Prairie Fire

1   "Heritage Minutes: Sir John A. Macdonald," Historica Canada, September 12, 2014, youtube.com/watch?reload=9&v=vBGNEJpznNE.

2   John A. Macdonald to George-Etienne Cartier, as quoted in "Canada Buys Rupert's Land," *Le Canada: A People's History/Une Histoire Populaire*, cbc.ca/history/EPCONTENTSEIEP9CHIPA3LE.html.

3   "Mémoire de Louis Schmidt," as quoted by Diane Payment, "Native Society and Economy in Transition at the Forks, 1850–1900" (Ottawa: Canadian Parks Service, 1988), 39. "*Les desseins du Canada devinrent bientôt manifestes. Il voulait s'introduire dans le pays, comme dans une terre déserte, sans plus s'occuper du people qui l'habitait... les arpenteurs... se mirent à tirer des lignes de tous côtés, sans s'occuper s'ils étaient sur des propriétés privées ou non.*"

4   John A. Macdonald, as quoted by Grant W. Grams, "Red River's Anglophone Community: The Conflicting Views of John Christian

Schultz and Alexander Begg," *Manitoba History* 64 (Fall 2010), mhs.mb.ca/docs/mb_history/64/redriveranglophones.shtml; Lovell Clark, "Schultz, Sir John Christian," *Dictionary of Canadian Biography*, biographi.ca/en/bio.php?BioId=40542.

5   Clark, *ibid.*

6   *Ibid.*

7   Suzanne Zeller, "McDougall, William," *Dictionary of Canadian Biography*, biographi.ca/en/bio/mcdougall_william_13E.html.

8   John A. Macdonald, as quoted by D. N. Sprague, *Canada and the Métis, 1869–1885* (Waterloo, ON: Wilfrid Laurier University Press, 1988), 103.

9   Gerhard Ens, "Métis Lands in Manitoba," *Manitoba History* 5 (Spring 1983), mhs.mb.ca/docs/mb_history/05/metislands.shtml.

10 Archbishop Taché to Father Lacombe, 1876, as quoted by Marie-Anna A. Roy, *La Montagne Pembina au temps des colons* (Winnipeg: Canadian Publishers Ltd, 1969), 12. "*Nous sommes débordés de toutes parts par des hommes qui ont la force, l'énergie, le nombre et la haine au coeur.*"

11 Jean Teillet and Jason Madden, "Manitoba Métis Federation v. Canada. Understanding the Supreme Court of Canada's Decision," Pape, Salter, Teillet LLP, pstlaw.ca/resources/PST-LLP-MMF-Case-Summary-Nov-2013-v02.pdf.

12 Douglas O. Linder, ed., "The Indictment of Louis Riel, 20th July 1885," famous-trials.com/louisriel/852-indictment.

13 Charles Lafreniere, as quoted by Deborah Nowak, "A Clear Path to Antoine Lafreniere and Our Metis Heritage," The Livingstone Family History—Alive and Well, July 2012, livingstonaliveandwell. blogspot.com/2012/07/clear-path-to-antoine-lafreniere-and.html.

14 "Le dernier mieux de l'Ouest: Le Canada au vingtième siècle, vastes ressources agricoles, résidences pour des millions" (Ottawa: Department of the Interior, 1908).

Chapter 7: Land Claims

1   Sir Clifford Sifton, "The Immigrants Canada Wants," *Maclean's Magazine*, April 1, 1922, 16.

2   Unidentified critics, as quoted in Robert R. Smale, "For Whose
    Kingdom? Central Canadian Baptists, Watson Kirkconnell, and the
    Evangelization of Immigrants, 1880–1939," *Baptists and Public Life in
    Canada*, eds. Gordon L. Heath and Paul R. Wilson (Hamilton, ON:
    McMaster Divinity College Press, 2012), 351.

3   Joseph-Arthur (Comte de) Gobineau, *Essai sur l'inégalité des races
    humaines* (Paris: Éditions Pierre Belfond, 1967, first published 1853–55,
    Livre premier), 99, classiques.uqac.ca/classiques/gobineau/essai_
    inegalite_races/essai_inegalite_races_1.pdf.

4   *Saskatoon Phenix*, May 22, 1904.

5   John N. Lake, as quoted by Gail A. McConnell, *Saskatoon: Hub City of
    the West, an Illustrated History* (Windsor Publications, 1983), 15.

6   *Saskatoon Phenix*, n.d., spring 1904.

7   *Saskatoon Phenix*, July 22, 1904.

8   Homestead File 847742: Sworn statement by Charles Trottier,
    December 19, 1903, Provincial Archives of Saskatchewan.

9   Homestead File 847742: Sworn statement by Norbert Trottier, June
    8, 1907, Provincial Archives of Saskatchewan.

10 Homestead File 1686787: Internal communication, Department of
    the Interior, June 10, 1907, and Department of Interior to W. Oswald
    Smyth (representing Norbert Trottier), July 12, 1907; Homestead File
    847742: Letter from P. G. Keyes, Department of Interior, to Charles
    Trottier, January 10, 1904, Provincial Archives of Saskatchewan.

Chapter 8: Proving Up

1   Henri Bourassa, as quoted by Richard Lapointe and Lucille Tess-
    ier, *The Francophones of Saskatchewan: A History*, trans. Lucille Tessier
    (Regina: Campion College, 1986), 70–71.

2   Jean Hamelin, "Taché, Alexandre-Antonin," *Dictionary of Canadian
    Biography*, biographi.ca/en/bio/tache_alexandre_antonin_12E.html.

3   Gilles Martel, Glen Campbell, and Thomas Flanagan, eds., *Louis Riel:
    Poésies de jeunesses* (St-Boniface, Les Éditions du Blé, 1977), 105–8.

4   Donatien Frémont, *Les Français dans l'ouest Canadien*, 3rd ed. (St-
    Boniface, Les Éditions du Blé, 2002), 20. "Ils excitèrent surtout l'hila-
    rité des jeunes snobs de l'endroit, qui n'en pouvaient croire leurs yeux."

242

5   Madame Tessier, as quoted in *Tales and Trails of Tessier* (Tessier, SK: Tessier Celebrate Saskatchewan Book Committee, 1982), 293.

6   Homestead File 923844: Sworn statement by N. S. Blondin, July 25, 1905, Provincial Archives of Saskatchewan.

Chapter 9: Crystal Beach

1   Grand Secretary's Report, Annual Report Grand Orange Lodge, N. W. T., 1904, 21; Grand Orange Lodge, Report of Proceedings, 1892–1925, Provincial Archives of Saskatchewan R.2.434.

2   Address of Welcome from Pile-o-Bones Black Preceptory, Annual Report Grand Orange Lodge, N. W. T., 1904, 41, Provincial Archives of Saskatchewan R.2.434.

3   Grand Secretary's Report, Annual Report Grand Orange Lodge of Saskatchewan, 1906, 13, Provincial Archives of Saskatchewan R.2.434.

4   Copy of Telegram, Annual Report Grand Orange Lodge, N. W. T., 1904, 16, Provincial Archives of Saskatchewan R.2.434.

5   Réverend Père H. Leduc, O. M. I., *Hostilité démasquée: Territoires du Nord-Ouest. Ordonnance Scolaire No 22 de 1892 et ses néfastes conséquences* (Montréal: C. O. Beauchemin et Fils, 1896), 5, 58.

6   Jean Lionnet, *Chez les français du Canada*, 4th ed. (Paris: Librairie Plon, 1910), 227.

7   Geo. D. Braid to Ella, April 8, 1905, as quoted in *Tales and Trails of Tessier* (Tessier: Tessier Celebrate Saskatchewan Book Committee, 1982), 19.

8   "Goose Lake District, Saskatchewan Canada, The Finest Land of a Fine Country" (St. Paul, MN: Godart Land Co., 1913), Special Collections, University of Saskatchewan.

9   W. H. G. Armstrong, Grand Organizers Report, Annual Report Grand Orange Lodge of Saskatchewan, 1911, 10, Provincial Archives of Saskatchewan R.2.434.

10 "Harris Continues to Grow, and Changes Take Place during the Years 1910–11," *Early History of the Village of Harris*, Harris and District Museum, Harris, SK.

Chapter 10: Battle Grounds

1   *Goose Lake Herald*, September 14, 1916.

2   *Goose Lake Herald*, August 10, 1916.

3   *Goose Lake Herald*, May 4, 1916.

4   Supplement, *Goose Lake Herald*, September 13, 1914, Harris and District Museum, Harris, SK.

5   Homestead File 2120495: Inspector's report, April 12, 1917, Provincial Archives of Saskatchewan.

6   "The First World War, Canada and the First World War, Canada Enters the War," Veterans Affairs Canada, last modified October 23, 2014, veterans.gc.ca/eng/remembrance/history/first-world-war/canada/Canada3.

7   "The Voice," August 1914, as quoted by John Herd Thompson, *The Harvests of War: The Prairie West, 1914–1918* (Toronto: McClelland and Stewart, 1978), 24.

8   "Saskatchewan's Big Year," in *Production and Thrift: Agricultural War Book*, Canada Department of Agriculture, 1916, 17.

9   Homestead File 2849: Cléophas S. Blondin to the Edmonton Land Office, ca. 1917, Alberta, Canada, Homestead Records, 1870–1930.

10 Georges Bugnet, *La forêt* (Montréal: Typo, 1993), 25.

11 *Ibid.*, 202.

12 Georges Bugnet to his brother Maurice, as quoted by Jean Papen, "Georges Bugnet, homme de lettres canadien, sa vie, son oeuvre" (PhD dissertation, Université Laval, 1967), 28.

13 *Goose Lake Herald*, March 9, 1916.

14 Registration of Marriage Record No 2308 1916, marriage of Napoléon Sureau dit Blondin and Clarsey Mary Parent, July 19, 1916.

15 *Goose Lake Herald*, August 3, 1916.

16 "Early Morning Fire Scorches Blondin Warehouse," *Goose Lake Herald*, March 23, 1918, Harris and District Museum, Harris, SK.

17 *Goose Lake Herald*, September 5, 1918.

18 Grand Organizer's Report, Annual Report Grand Orange Lodge of Saskatchewan, 1915, 17, Provincial Archives of Saskatchewan R.2.434.

244

19 "Goose Lake Orangemen Have Big Day: Thousands Celebrate the Glorious Twelfth at Crystal Beach," *Goose Lake Herald*, Thursday, July 16, 1918, 1.

20 Grand Master's Report, Annual Report Grand Orange Lodge of Saskatchewan, 1912, 12, Provincial Archives of Saskatchewan R.2.434.

Chapter 11: Hard Times

1 "Clearing Sale of Horses, Cattle & Machinery, on the farm of N. S. Blondin...," *Goose Lake Herald*, March 6, 1919.

2 Elk Valley School Division, Provincial Archives of Saskatchewan R-177.10/7.

3 Report of Committee on Correspondence, Annual Report Grand Orange Lodge of Saskatchewan, 1919, 33, Provincial Archives of Saskatchewan R2.435.

4· Grand Organizer's Report, Annual Report Grand Orange Lodge of Saskatchewan, 1921, 27, Provincial Archives of Saskatchewan R.2.434.

5 Grand Master's Address, Annual Report Grand Orange Lodge of Saskatchewan, 1920, 18, Provincial Archives of Saskatchewan R.2.434.

6 Report of Committee on Correspondence, Annual Report Grand Orange Lodge of Saskatchewan, 1918, 35, Provincial Archives of Saskatchewan R.2.434.

7 Grand Master's Address, Annual Report Grand Orange Lodge of Saskatchewan, 1919, 13, Provincial Archives of Saskatchewan R.2.434.

8 "1916," words and music by Gérard Jean, from *L'Article 23/Section 23* by David Arnason, Claude Dorge, and Gérard Jean, 1985.

9 Grand Master's Address, Annual Report Grand Orange Lodge of Saskatchewan, 1921, 14, Provincial Archives of Saskatchewan R.2.434.

10 *Ibid.*

11 Report of Resolutions Committee, Annual Report Grand Orange Lodge of Saskatchewan, 1924, 39, Provincial Archives of Saskatchewan R.2.434.

12 *Goose Lake Herald*, September 15, 1921.

13 *Goose Lake Herald*, February 1, 1923.

Chapter 12: Invisible Empire

1   *Goose Lake Herald*, October 14 and 21, 1927.

2   Alice Dunlap, in Allan Anderson, *Remembering the Farm: Memories of Farming, Ranching, and Rural Life in Canada Past and Present* (Toronto: Macmillan, 1977), 11.

3   Don Kerr and Stan Hanson, *Saskatoon: The First Half Century* (Edmonton: NeWest, 1982), 77.

4   "Saskatoon," Saskatoon Board of Trade, 1913, Special Collections, University of Saskatchewan Library.

5   Ibid.

6   "Saskatoon People Have Many Reasons for Thanksgiving," *Saskatoon Daily Star*, November 4, 1927, Clipping file, Local History Room, Saskatoon Public Library.

7   Ibid.

8   Grand Master's Address, Annual Report Grand Orange Lodge of Saskatchewan, 1928, 18, Provincial Archives of Saskatchewan R.2.435.

9   Ibid., 19.

10 Report of Resolutions Committee, Annual Report Grand Orange Lodge of Saskatchewan, 1924, 40, Provincial Archives of Saskatchewan R.2.434.

11 Grand Master's Address, Annual Report Grand Orange Lodge of Saskatchewan, 1928, 19, Provincial Archives of Saskatchewan R.2.435.

12 J. T. M. Anderson, *The Education of the New Canadian: A Treatise on Canada's Greatest Educational Problem* (Toronto: J. M. Dent and Sons, 1918), 171, 189, peel.library.ualberta.ca/bibliography/4362/9.html.

13 Ibid., 8.

14 D. W. Griffith, dir., *The Birth of a Nation* (David W. Griffith Corp., 1915), youtube.com/watch?v=13kmVgQHIEY.

15 "Pat" Emmons, as quoted by Martin Robin, *Shades of Right: Nativist and Fascist Politics in Canada, 1920–1940* (Toronto: University of Toronto Press, 1992), 30.

16 Rabbi Ferdinand Isserman, "The Klan in Saskatchewan," *Canadian Jewish Review*, June 15, 1928, Provincial Archives of Saskatchewan, Gardiner Papers, 13,791–92.

246   17 James M. Pitsula, *Keeping Canada British: The Ku Klux Klan in 1920s Saskatchewan* (Vancouver: University of British Columbia Press, 2013). *See also* Grand Master's Address, Annual Report Grand Orange Lodge of Saskatchewan 1919, 12; Report of Committee on Correspondence, Annual Report Grand Orange Lodge of Saskatchewan 1918, 35, Provincial Archives of Saskatchewan R.2.434.

18 "Pat" Emmons, as quoted by Anthony Appleblatt, "The Ku Klux Klan in Saskatchewan," 13 (unpublished research paper, 1971), University of Saskatchewan Library.

19 J. F. Bryant to R. B. Bennett, as quoted by Pitsula, *op. cit.*, 78. One of the places where Anderson was alleged to have met with KKK officials was the Flanagan Hotel, now the Senator. Later, he was also said to frequent the KKK office in room 405 of the Connaught Building, around the corner from the hotel. See Robin, *Shades of Right*, 71.

20 John W. Rosborough, as quoted by Robin, *Shades of Right*, 42.

21 Dr. W. D. Cowan to R. B. Bennett, January 16, 1928, as quoted by Pitsula, *Keeping Canada British*, 220.

22 William Calderwood, "The Rise and Fall of the Ku Klux Klan in Saskatchewan" (Master's thesis, University of Saskatchewan, Regina Campus, 1968), 84–85.

23 J. J. Maloney, *Rome in Canada* (Vancouver: Columbia Protestant Publications, c. 1934), 17.

24 J. F. Bryant to R. B. Bennett, March 16, 1928, as quoted by William Calderwood, "Pulpit, Press and Political Reaction to the Ku Klux Klan in Saskatchewan," in Samuel D. Clark, J. Paul Grayson, and Linda M. Grayson, eds., *Prophecy and Protest: Social Movements in Twentieth Century Canada* (Toronto: Gage, 1975), 210–11.

25 Hearn to Bennett, March 28, 1928, as quoted by Calderwood, *ibid.*, 212.

26 Maloney, *Rome in Canada*, 23.

27 *Ibid.*, 11.

28 *Ibid.*, 23–24, 25.

29 George E. Lloyd, *Regina Daily Star*, June 5, 1929, as quoted by Calderwood, "The Rise and Fall of the Ku Klux Klan in Saskatchewan," 187-8.

30 Unidentified Orangeman, as quoted by Patrick Kyba, "Ballot Boxes
    and Burning Crosses," in Norman Ward and Duff Spafford, eds.,
    Politics in Saskatchewan (Toronto: Longmans, 1968), 115.

31 Entry for October 26, 1928, Régistre pour servir à l'inscription des
    Chroniques des Soeurs de l'Assomption de la S. V., Biggar, Saskatch-
    ewan, Provincial Archives of Alberta PR 1973.0080/000 SASV/3/I.

Chapter 13: Revelations

1   Grand Orange Lodge of Saskatchewan Annual Report, 1931, 15; Report
    for 1932, 14; Report for 1934, 18, Provincial Archives of Saskatchewan
    R.2.393.

2   Maloney, *Rome in Canada*, 79.

3   "The Agreement," November 19, 1932, City of Saskatoon Archives
    1200-0356-002.

4   "Police Augmented to Handle Mobs," [Regina] *Evening Star*, Novem-
    ber 21, 1932, City of Saskatoon Archives 1009-2.

5   Communists: Re-engaging King and Palmer in Parks Dept [1932],
    City of Saskatoon Archives 1013-III vol. 2.

6   Prayer from *Key of Heaven*, Charles Blondin personal collection. On
    the endpapers, Clara Blondin has written, "This is the same little
    pray[er] book like I used to have when I was a little girl."

7   Dr. J. M. Uhrich, Minister of Public Health (himself a Catholic),
    1941; H. Stains, Minister of Education, 1942; and Omers Demers,
    MLA for Shellbrook (also a Catholic), 1941; as quoted by Raymond
    Huel, "The Anderson Amendments: A Half Century Later," *Cana-
    dian Catholic Historical Association Study Sessions* 47 (1980), 5–21.

8   Blondin Roofing Products Co. Ltd. flyer, 1945–46, Charles Blondin
    personal collection.

9   Clara Blondin to Lorena Martens, March 29, 1977, Lorena Martens
    personal collection.

BIBLIOGRAPHY

Recommended Reading

Begley, Lloyd L. "The Foreign Threat: Nativism in Saskatchewan 1896–1930." Master's thesis, Universities of Winnipeg and Manitoba, 1996.

Jones, David C. *Empire of Dust: Settling and Abandoning the Prairie Dry Belt.* Calgary: University of Calgary Press, 2002.

Kerr, Don, and Stan Hanson. *Saskatoon: The First Half Century.* Edmonton: NeWest, 1982.

Lacoursière, Jacques, Jean Provencher, and Denis Vaugeois. *Canada-Québec, 1534–2000.* Sillery, Québec: Les éditions du Septentrion, 2001.

Lapointe, Richard, and Lucille Tessier. *The Francophones of Saskatchewan: A History.* Translated by Lucille Tessier. Regina: Campion College, 1986.

McNichol, Dustin. "You Can't Have It All French, All at Once: French Language Rights, Bilingualism, and Political Community in Saskatchewan, 1870–1990." PhD dissertation, University of Saskatchewan, 2016.

Owram, Doug. *Promise of Eden: The Canadian Expansionist Movement and the Idea of the West, 1856–1900.* Toronto: University of Toronto Press, 1992.

Painchaud, Robert. *Un rêve français dans le peuplement de la Prairie.* St-Boniface: Éditions des Plaines, 1987.

Palmer, Howard. *Patterns of Prejudice: A History of Nativism in Alberta.* Toronto: McClelland and Stewart, 1982.

Pitsula, James M. *Keeping Canada British: The Ku Klux Klan in 1920s Saskatchewan.* Vancouver: University of British Columbia Press, 2013.

250   Roby, Yves. *Histoire d'un rêve brisée: Les Canadiens français aux États-Unis.* Sillery, Québec: Septentrion, 2000.

Thompson, John Herd. *The Harvests of War: The Prairie West, 1914–1918.* Toronto: McClelland and Stewart, 1978.

Troupe, Cheryl Lynn. "Métis Women: Social Structure, Urbanization and Political Activism." Master's thesis, University of Saskatchewan, 2009.

Waiser, Bill. "The Myth of Multiculturalism in Early Saskatchewan." In *Perspectives of Saskatchewan,* edited by Jene M. Porter. Winnipeg: University of Manitoba Press, 2009.

———. *Saskatchewan: A New History.* Calgary: Fifth House, 2005.

Chapter 1: Little House

Black, Norman Fergus. *History of Saskatchewan and the Old North West.* Regina: North West Historical Co., 1913.

Blakely, F. L. Letter of instruction to surveyor, July 6, 1883. Provincial Archives of Saskatchewan GR 15. Individual Surveyor's Files No 39.

Lake, John N. "The Temperance Colonization Society and the Foundation of Saskatoon." In *Narratives of Saskatoon 1882–1912.* Saskatoon: Committee of the Historical Association of Saskatoon and University Book Store, 1927.

Manual of Instructions for the Survey of Dominion Lands, 1st to 10th Editions. Ottawa: Natural Resources Canada. clss.nrcan.gc.ca/standards-normes/toc-domlan-terredom-1-3-vi-eng.php.

Morton, Arthur S., ed. John N. Lake's Diary. Special Collections, University of Saskatchewan.

Musée Virtuel Francophone de la Saskatchewan. "Jules Décorby, o.m.i." Société historique de la Saskatchewan. musee.societehisto.com/jules-decorby-o-m-i-n372-t792.html.

O'Brien, Jeff. "A History of Saskatoon to 1914." Saskatoon: City of Saskatoon Archives, 2005.

Peel's Prairie Provinces. *Henderson's Saskatoon Directory.* Winnipeg: Henderson Directories, 1908–2000. peel.library.ualberta.ca/bibliography/3177.html.

Sullivan, Fr. John L., and Diane Paré Szabo. "Family Names and Nicknames in Colonial Québec." Sussex-Lisbon Area Historium,

March 24, 2017, kellerhistorymuseum.org/genealogy/reilly-miller/ canadian-dit-names-2/.

Thomas, Lewis H. "Saskatoon, 1883–1920: The Formative Years." In *Town and City: Aspects of Western Canadian Urban Development*, edited by Alan F. J. Artibise. Regina: Canadian Plains Research Center, 1981.

Virtual Museum of Métis History and Culture. "Biographies of Petitioners at Fort Qu'Appelle: Metis Petition of August 29, 1882." Gabriel Dumont Institute of Native Studies and Applied Research. http://www.metismuseum.ca/resource.php/14180.

———. "Métis Petition of September 2, 1880." http://www.metismuseum. ca/resource.php/14528.

———. "Simon Blondeau (Blondin) Sr. (b. 1827)." http://www. metismuseum.ca/resource.php/13859.

Whitecap Dakota First Nation. "History and Culture." whitecapdakota. com/history-culture/.

———. *Wapaha Ska: Whitecap Dakota First Nation.* whitecapdakota.com/ documents/WDFN-OTC-remake-final.pdf.

Chapter 2: Tangled Roots

Beaucourt, Marquis de. *Revue des quéstions historiques.* Paris: Librairie de Victor Palmé, 1866. Bibliothèque nationale de la France. gallica.bnf. fr/ark:/12148/bpt6k16919h/f9.image.r=.

"Bienheureuse Marie-Anne Blondin (1809–1890)." cccb.ca/site/images/ Bienheureuse_Marie-Anne_Blondin-FR.pdf.

Blondin, Yves. "Hilaire Sureau dit Blondin." unicaen.fr/mrsh/prefen/ notices/60706hs.pdf.

Burton, Edwin, Edward D'Alton, and Jarvis Kelley. "Penal Laws." *The Catholic Encyclopedia.* New York: Robert Appleton Company, 1911.

Chénier, Rémi. *Québec: A French Colonial Town in America, 1660 to 1690.* Studies in Archaeology, Architecture and History, National Historic Sites. Ottawa: Environment Canada, 1991.

Fromhold, Joachim. *The Western Cree (Pakisimotan Wi Iniwak) Archange L'Hirondelle c1806–1891.* N.p.: First Nations Publishing, 2012.

Geni. "Gustav Anjou, Fraudulent Genealogist." Accessed May 25, 2012. geni.com/projects/Gustav-Anjou-Fraudulent-Genealogist/4449.

252   Hémon, Louis. *Maria Chapdelaine: Récit du Canada Français.* 1913. Reprint. Paris: Bernard Grasset, 1954.

Lee, Grace Lawless. *The Huguenot Settlements in Ireland.* Baltimore: Baltimore Genealogical Publishing, 1999.

Le Jeune, Fr. Paul. "Relation of What Occurred in New France in the Year 1633." *Jesuit Relations* 5. moses.creighton.edu/kripke/jesuitrelations/relations_05.html.

Le Programme de recherche en démographie historique/The Research Program in Historical Demography, Université de Montréal. prdh-igd.com/en/le-prdh.

Matthiessen, Diana Gail. "Peter Carrico I." dgmweb.net/FGS/Car/CarricoPeterI-_.html.

Shannon, Timothy J. "Native American-Pennsylvania Relations, 1754–89." The Encyclopedia of Greater Philadelphia, Rutgers University, 2015. philadelphiaencyclopedia.org/archive/native-american-pennsylvania-relations-1754-89-2/.

Sherk, Thomas A. *The Sherk Family.* Baltimore: Gateway Press, 1982.

Voyageur Contracts Database. Centre du patrimoine, Société historique de Saint-Boniface. shsb.mb.ca/en/Voyageurs_database.

Wiener, Roberta, and James R. Arnold. "Maryland's Battles—Battles with the Native Americans." *Maryland: The History of Maryland Colony, 1634–1776.* Chicago: Raintree, 2005.

Chapter 3: Making Connections

Lizotte, Marjorie. "Percheron Immigration." A point in history and a few acres of snow (website). apointinhistory.net/percheron-immigration.php.

Parent, Guy. *Pierre Parent: Le pionnier. Boucher, carrier, chaufournier et fermier.* Société de généalogie de Québec, Contribution no. 105. Sainte-Foy, Québec, 2005.

Chapter 4: An Agitation of Ghosts

De Stephano, Luke. *Vaudreuil-Soulanges, un lieu de convergence.* Québec: Les Éditions GID, 2008.

Gagnon, Ernest. *Chansons populaires du Canada.* Québec: Bureau du "Foyer Canadien," 1865.

Globensky, Charles Auguste Maximilien. *La rébellion de 1837 à Saint-Eustache.* 1889. Montréal: Éditions du Jour, 1974.

Lacoursière, Jacques, and Robin Philpot. *A People's History of Quebec.* Montréal: Baraka Books and Sillery, Québec: Septentrion, 2009.

Lemire, Jonathan. "Augustin Tassé, aubergiste, patriote de Sainte-Rose." *Rébellions et patriotes de 1837-1838.* jonathanlemire.com/articles/historie-de-1837-1838-recueil-2007/augustin-tasse-aubergiste-patriote-de-sainte-rose/.

Maillet, Antoinine. "The Great Disturbance According to Bélonie." Translated by Solenn Carriou. *Globe and Mail,* July 15, 2000. fawi.net/ezine/vol3no2/Maillet.html.

Papineau, Louis-Joseph. "Les 92 résolutions de l'assemblée législative du Bas-Canada. février 1834." *La bibliothèque indépendantiste.* biblio.republiquelibre.org/Les_92_résolutions_de_l%27Assemblée_législative_du_Bas-Canada.

Salles d'exposition de la Maison de la culture et du patrimoine Saint-Eustache, Québec. "La rébellion de 1837 à Saint-Eustache." *Virtual Museum.ca.* virtualmuseum.ca/sgc-cms/histoires_de_chez_nous-community_memories/pm_v2.php?id=exhibit_home&fl=0&lg=English&ex=00000580.

Shortt, Adam, and Arthur G. Doughty, eds. *Documents Pertaining to the Constitutional History of Canada 1759–1791.* Ottawa: J. de L. Taché, 1918.

Chapter 5: Township of Tiny

Bayfield, John, and Carole Ferow. *This Was Yesterday: A Pictorial History of the Early Days of Penetanguishene.* Privately published, 1982.

Blondin, C. S. dit. "Hear Both Sides and Then Decide." Privately published. Charles Blondin personal collection.

"Captured in Lowell: Napolean Blondin Brought Here on the Charge of Non-Support." *North Adams Transcript,* June 29, 1897.

Charters, Anne, ed. *Jack Kerouac: Selected Letters 1940–1956.* New York: Penguin, 1995.

"French Schools in County of Simcoe." *Sessional Papers, Fourth Session of Sixth Legislature, Province of Ontario,* Session 1890, vol XXII, part VI.

Marchand, Micheline. *The Settlement of Penetanguishene by the Voyageurs and Métis 1825–1871, the French Settlement in Huronia.* Translated from French

254

by Daniel Marchildon. Sudbury: La Société historique du Nouvel-Ontario, 1989.

Marchildon, Daniel. *De coureur de bois à quoi? L'histoire de la Franco-Huronie.* Privately published, 1980.

Marchildon, Marie Asselin, with Louise Mullie. *Ce n'est qu'un au revoir.* Privately published, 1988.

Marchildon, Fr. Thomas. *Le loup de Lafontaine.* Documents historiques no. 29, Collège du Sacré-Coeur, Sudbury, 1955.

Morissonneau, Christian. *La terre promise: Le mythe du Nord québécois.* Montréal: Hurtubise HMH, 1978.

Ontario Heritage Trust. The French Presence in Lafontaine. heritagetrust .on.ca/user_assets/documents/Lafontaine-ENG.pdf.

Penetanguishene Centennial Museum and Archives. *The Descendants of Alexis Tessier.* Penetanguishene, ON: Friends of the Penetanguishene Centennial Museum and Archives, 2010.

"Public Institutions Maintenance," *Sessional Papers, Legislature of the Province of Ontario,* vol. 4. books.google.ca/books?id= ZXZOAAAAMAAJ&lpg=PA175&dq=blondin%2C%20c.%20s.%20 schools&pg=RA5-PA176#v=onepage&q&f=false.

Saint-Pierre, Stéphanie. "Étienne Brûlé, The First Franco-Ontarian." Encyclopedia of French Cultural Heritage in North America. ameriquefrancaise.org/en/article-451/Ã‰tienne_BrÃ»lÃ©,_The_ First_Franco-Ontarian_.html.

Chapter 6: Prairie Fire

Barkwell, Lawrence. "The Reign of Terror against the Métis of Red River." independent.academia.edu/LawrenceBarkwell.

Clark, Lovell. "Schultz, Sir John Christian." *Dictionary of Canadian Biography.* biographi.ca/en/bio/schultz_john_christian_12E.html.

"Le dernier mieux de l'Ouest: Le Canada au vingtième siècle, vastes ressources agricoles, résidences pour des millions." Ottawa: Department of the Interior, 1908.

Descriptive Atlas of Western Canada, issued by direction of Hon. Clifford Sifton. Ottawa: Minister of the Interior, 1900.

Devine, Heather. *The People Who Own Themselves: Aboriginal Ethnogenesis in a Canadian Family, 1660–1900.* Calgary: University of Calgary Press, 2004.

Duhaime, Lloyd. "1874, Louis Riel, M. P., Outlaw." Canadian Legal History. duhaime.org/LawMuseum/CanadianLegalHistory/LawArticle-152/1874-Louis-Riel-MP-Outlaw.aspx.

Ens, Gerhard. "Métis Lands in Manitoba." *Manitoba History* 5 (1983). mhs.mb.ca/docs/mb_history/05/metislands.shtml.

Grams, Grant W. "Red River's Anglophone Community: The Conflicting Views of John Christian Schultz and Alexander Beggs." *Manitoba History* 64 (2010). mhs.mb.ca/docs/mb_history/64/redriveranglophones.shtml

"Heritage Minutes: Sir John A. Macdonald." Historica Canada. youtube.com/watch?v=VBGNEJpznNE.

Linder, Douglas O., ed. "The Indictment of Louis Riel." Famous Trials. famous-trials.com/louisriel/852-indictment.

Louis Riel Institute. "Canada Buys Rupert's Land." *Le Canada: A People's History/Une Histoire Populaire.* cbc.ca/history/EPCONTENTSEIEP9CHIPA3LE.html.

"The Murder of Thomas Scott." Canadian Orange Historical Site. canadianorangehistoricalsite.com/MurderofThomasScott.php.

Nowak, Deborah. "A Clear Path to Antoine Lafreniere and Our Metis Heritage." The Livingstone Family History—Alive and Well. livingstonaliveandwell.blogspot.com/2012/07/clear-path-to-antoine-lafreniere-and.html.

Payment, Diane. *The Free People—Li Gens Libres: A History of the Métis Community of Batoche, Saskatchewan.* Calgary: University of Calgary Press, 2009.

———. "Native Society and Economy in Transition at the Forks, 1850–1900." Ottawa: Canadian Parks Service, 1988.

Rea, J. A. "Scott, Thomas." *Dictionary of Canadian Biography.* biographi.ca/en/bio/scott_thomas_1870_9E.html.

Reid, Jennifer. *Louis Riel and the Creation of Modern Canada: Mythic Discourse and the Postcolonial State.* Winnipeg: University of Manitoba Press, 2012.

Roy, Marie-Anna A. *La Montagne Pembina au temps des colons.* Winnipeg: Canadian Publishers Ltd., 1969.

Sprague, D. N. *Canada and the Métis 1868–1885.* Waterloo, ON: Wilfrid Laurier University Press, 1988.

256 Sprague, D. N., and R. P. Frye. *The Genealogy of the First Metis Nation.*
Winnipeg: Pemmican Publications, 1983.

Teillet, Jean, and Jason Madden. "Manitoba Métis Federation v. Canada. Understanding the Supreme Court of Canada's Decision." Pape, Salter, Teillet LLP. pstlaw.ca/resources/PST-LLP-MMF-Case-Summary-Nov-2013-v02.pdf.

Zeller, Suzanne. "McDougall, William." *Dictionary of Canadian Biography.*
biographi.ca/en/bio/mcdougall_william_13E.html.

Chapter 7: Land Claims

Gobineau, Joseph-Arthur (Comte de). *Essai sur l'inégalité des races humaines.* Paris: Éditions Pierre Belfond, 1967. First published 1853–55, Livre premier. classiques.uqac.ca/classiques/gobineau/essai_inegalite_races/essai_inegalite_races_1.pdf.

Homestead Files 847742 and 1686786. Provincial Archives of Saskatchewan.

McConnell, Gail A. *Saskatoon: Hub City of the West, an Illustrated History.*
[Saskatoon]: Windsor Publications, 1983.

McCormick, P. L. "Transportation and Settlement: Problems in the Expansion of the Frontier of Saskatchewan and Assiniboia in 1904." *Prairie Forum* 5 (1980): 1–18.

Palmer, Howard. "Reluctant Hosts: Anglo-Canadian Views of Multiculturalism in the Twentieth Century." In *Readings in Canadian History Post-Confederation,* edited by R. Douglas Francis and Donald B. Smith. Toronto: Nelson Learning, 2002.

Reed, Leila. "Pioneer Courage on the Prairie." *Saskatchewan History* 39 (1986): 107–13.

Saskatoon Phenix, 1904. University of Saskatchewan Library.

Sifton, Sir Clifford. "The Immigrants Canada Wants." *Maclean's Magazine,* April 1, 1922, 16, 32–34.

Smale, Robert R. "For Whose Kingdom? Central Canadian Baptists, Watson Kirkconnell, and the Evangelization of Immigrants, 1880–1939." In *Baptists and Public Life in Canada,* edited by Gordon L. Heath and Paul R. Wilson. Hamilton, ON: McMaster Divinity College Press, 2012.

St-Onge, Nicole, Carolyn Podruchny, and Brenda Macdougall, eds. *Contours of a People: Metis Family, Mobility and History.* Norman, OK: University of Oklahoma Press, 2012.

Chapter 8: Proving Up

Bernier, Noël. *Fannystelle: Une fleur de France éclose en terre Manitobaine.* St-Boniface: Société Historique de St-Boniface, 1939.

Denis, Wilfrid B. "Francophone Education in Saskatchewan: Resisting Anglo-Hegemony." In *A History of Education in Saskatchewan: Selected Readings,* edited by Brian Noonan, Dianne Hallman, and Murray Scharf. Regina: Canadian Plains Research Center, 2006.

Frémont, Donatien. *Les Français dans l'ouest Canadien.* St-Boniface: Les Éditions du Blé, 1980.

Groulx, Lionel. *L'enseignment du français au Canada. Tome II. Les écoles des minorities.* Montréal: Librairie Granger Frères, 1933.

Guitard, Michelle. "La Rolanderie." *Saskatchewan History* 30 (1977): 110–14.

Hamelin, Jean. "Taché, Alexandre-Antonin." *Dictionary of Canadian Biography.* biographi.ca/en/bio/tache_alexandre_antonin_12E.html.

Harris History Book Committee. *Harris, Heritage and Homage.* Harris, SK: Harris History Book Committee, 1982.

Homestead Files 923844 and 934217. Provincial Archives of Saskatchewan.

Lamarre, Jean. *Les Canadiens français du Michigan: Leur contribution dans le développement de la vallée de la Saginaw et de la peninsula de Keweenaw 1840–1914.* Sillery, Québec: Septentrion, c2000.

Martel, Gilles, Glen Campbell, and Thomas Flanagan, eds. *Louis Riel: Poésies de jeunesses.* St-Boniface, Les Éditions du Blé, 1977.

Painchaud, Robert. "French-Canadian Historiography and Franco-Catholic Settlement in Western Canada, 1870–1915." *Canadian Historical Review* 59 (1978): 447–66.

———. "Les origines des peuplements de langue française dans l'Ouest canadien, 1870–1920, mythes et réalités." *Mémoires de la Société royale du Canada,* Série IV, Tome xiii (1975): 109–21.

Reed, Leila. "Pioneer Courage on the Prairie." *Saskatchewan History* 39 (1986): 107–13.

Sebasky, Marlys. "Breaking the Prairie Sod." *Janson Family History.* jansonfamilyhistory.blogspot.com/2010/02/breaking-prairie-sod.html.

Shillington, C. Howard. "The Old Bone Trail." *Historic Land Trails of Saskatchewan.* West Vancouver, BC: Evvard Publications, 1985.

258   Silver, A. I. "French Canada and the Prairie Frontier, 1870–1890." *Cana-dian Historical Review* 50 (1969): 11–36.

"Snapshot of Canadian Agriculture." *Farm and Farm Operator Data.* Ottawa: Statistics Canada, 2011. statcan.gc.ca/pub/95-640-x/ 2011001/p1/p1-01-eng.htm.

Sullivan, Kristian Ira William. "The French Counts of St. Hubert: An Archaeological Exploration of Social Identity." Master's thesis, University of Saskatchewan, 2009.

Tessier Celebrate Saskatchewan Book Committee. *Tales and Trails of Tessier.* Tessier, SK: Tessier Celebrate Saskatchewan Book Committee, 1982.

Weber, Bob. "The Old Bone Trail for Settlers Going Out, Bones Coming In." *Saskatchewan History Along the Highway.* Red Deer, AB: Red Deer College Press, 1998.

Chapter 9: Crystal Beach

"Goose Lake District, Saskatchewan Canada, The Finest Land of a Fine Country." St. Paul, MN: Godart Land Co., 1913, Special Collections, University of Saskatchewan Library.

Grand Orange Lodge, Report of Proceedings, 1892–1925. Provincial Archives of Saskatchewan R.2.434.

"Harris Continues to Grow, and Changes Take Place during the Years 1910–11." *Early History of the Village of Harris.* Harris, SK: Harris and District Museum Collection, n.d.

Harris History Book Committee. *Harris, Heritage and Homage.* Harris, SK: Harris History Book Committee, 1982.

Homestead Files 923844, 934217, 1675571, and 2120495. Provincial Archives of Saskatchewan.

Houston, Cecil J., and William J. Smyth. *The Sash Canada Wore: A Historical Geography of the Orange Order.* Toronto: University of Toronto Press, 1980.

Kaufman, Eric. "The Orange Order in Ontario, Newfoundland, Scotland and Northern Ireland." In *The Orange Order in Canada*, edited by David A. Wilson. Dublin: Four Courts Press, 2007.

Lapointe, Richard. "Effritement d'une colonie française." *La Saskatchewan de A à Z.* Regina: La société historique de la Saskatchewan, 1987.

Leduc, Fr. H. *Hostilité démasquée: Territoires du Nord-Ouest. Ordonannce Scolaire No. 22 de 1892 et ses néfastes conséquences.* Montréal: C. O. Beauchemin et Fils, 1896.

Lionnet, Jean. *Chez les français du Canada,* 4th ed. Paris: Librairie Plon, 1910.

Malcomson, W. P. "Riding the Goat." *Secret Societies Exposed.* evangelicaltruth.com/chapter6-html.

Pennefather, R. S. *The Orange and the Black: Documents in the History of the Orange Order, Ontario and the West, 1890–1940.* [Toronto]: Orange and Black Publications, c1984.

Senior, Hereward. *Orangeism: The Canadian Phase.* Toronto: McGraw-Hill Ryerson, 1972.

Tessier Celebrate Saskatchewan Book Committee. *Tales and Trails of Tessier.* Tessier, SK: Tessier Celebrate Saskatchewan Book Committee, 1982.

Troupe, Cheryl Lynn. "Métis Women: Social Structure, Urbanization and Political Activism, 1850–1980." Master's thesis, University of Saskatchewan, 2009.

Wilson David A., ed. *The Orange Order in Canada.* Dublin: Four Courts Press, 2007.

Chapter 10: Battle Grounds

Bugnet, Georges. *La forêt.* Montréal: Typo, 1993.

"Canadian Northern Railway: The Edmonton and Slave Lake Railway." *Atlas of Alberta Railways,* University of Alberta. railways.library. ualberta.ca/Chapters-8-3/.

Champ, Joan. "The Impact of the First World War on Saskatchewan's Farm Families." Prepared for Saskatchewan Western Development Museum's Winning the Prairie Gamble 2005 Exhibit.

"The First World War, Canada and the First World War, The Aftermath." Veterans Affairs Canada. veterans.gc.ca/eng/remembrance/history/ first-world-war/canada/Canada19.

Friesen, Gerald. *The Canadian Prairies: A History.* Toronto: University of Toronto Press, 2004.

Goose Lake Herald, 1914–1919. Provincial Archives of Saskatchewan.

Grand Orange Lodge of Saskatchewan, Report of Proceedings 1892– 1925. Provincial Archives of Saskatchewan R.2.434.

260 Homestead Files 1704444, 1743155, 2209680, and 2214052. Alberta, Canada, Homestead Records, 1870–1930. search.ancestry.ca/search/db.aspx?dbid=60865.

Homestead File 2120495. Provincial Archives of Saskatchewan.

Papen, Jean. "Georges Bugnet, homme de lettres canadien, sa vie, son oeuvre." PhD dissertation, Université Laval, 1967.

Saskatchewan Virtual War Memorial. svwm.ca.

"Saskatchewan's Big Year." In *Production and Thrift: Agricultural War Book.* Ottawa: Canada Department of Agriculture, 1916.

"Saskatoon." Saskatoon: Saskatoon Board of Trade, 1913. Special Collections, University of Saskatchewan Library.

Chapter 11: Hard Times

"Alberta Orange Lodges to 1919." Canadian Orange Historical Site. canadianorangehistoricalsite.com/index-232.php.

Armstrong, W. H. G. *Separate Schools: Introduction of the Dual System into Eastern Canada and Its Subsequent Extension to the West.* [Saskatoon]: Provincial Grand Orange Lodge of Saskatchewan, 1918.

Arnason, David, Claude Dorge, and Gérard Jean. *L'Article 23/Section 23* (musical theater). 1985.

Backhouse, Constance. *Colour-Coded: A Legal History of Racism in Canada, 1900–1950.* Toronto: University of Toronto Press (Osgoode Society for Canadian Legal History), 1999.

Blay, Jacqueline. *L'Article 23: Les péripéties législatives et juridiques du fait français au Manitoba 1870–1986.* Winnipeg: Les Éditions du Blé, 1987.

Elk Valley School Division. Provincial Archives of Saskatchewan R-177.10/7.

Goose Lake Herald/Tessier Times, 1921–1928. Provincial Archives of Saskatchewan.

Grand Orange Lodge of Saskatchewan, Report of Proceedings 1892–1925. Provincial Archives of Saskatchewan R.2.434.

Hébert, Raymond N. *Manitoba's French-Language Crisis: A Cautionary Tale.* Montreal: McGill-Queen's University Press, 2005.

Kitzan, Christopher. "The Fighting Bishop: George Exton Lloyd and the Immigration Debate." Master's thesis, University of Saskatchewan, 1996.

Maclean, Nancy. *Behind the Mask of Chivalry: The Making of the Second Ku Klux Klan*. New York: Oxford University Press, 1994.

McLeod, Keith A. "Politics, Schools and the French Language, 1881–1931." In *Politics in Saskatchewan*, edited by Norman Ward and Duff Spafford. Don Mills, ON: Longmans Canada, 1968.

Robin, Martin. *Shades of Right: Nativist and Fascist Politics in Canada, 1920–1940*. Toronto: University of Toronto Press, 1992.

Chapter 12: Invisible Empire

Anderson, Allan. *Remembering the Farm: Memories of Farming, Ranching, and Rural Life in Canada Past and Present*. Toronto: Macmillan, 1977.

Anderson, J. T. M. *The Education of the New Canadian: A Treatise on Canada's Greatest Educational Problem*. Toronto: J. M. Dent and Sons, 1918.

Appleblatt, Anthony. "The Ku Klux Klan in Saskatchewan." Unpublished research paper, 1971.

———. "The School Question in the 1929 Saskatchewan Provincial Election." *Canadian Catholic Historical Association Study Sessions* 43 (1976): 75–90.

Archer, John H., and J. C. Bates. *Historic Saskatoon: A Concise Illustrated History of Saskatoon*. Saskatoon: Junior Chamber of Commerce, 1947.

Calderwood, William. "Pulpit, Press and Political Reaction to the Ku Klux Klan in Saskatchewan." In *Prophecy and Protest: Social Movements in Twentieth Century Canada*, edited by Samuel D. Clark, J. Paul Grayson, and Linda M. Grayson. Toronto: Gage, 1975.

———. "The Rise and Fall of the Ku Klux Klan in Saskatchewan." Master's thesis, University of Saskatchewan, Regina Campus, 1968.

Clubb, Sally Potter. *Saskatoon: The Serenity and the Surge*. Saskatoon: City of Saskatoon, c1966.

Delainey, William P., and William A. S. Sarjeant. *Saskatoon: The Growth of a City*. Saskatoon: Saskatoon Environmental Society, 1974.

East, Melville A. *The Saskatoon Story 1882–1942*. Saskatoon: Privately published, 1952.

262 Huel, Raymond J. A. "J. J. Maloney: How the West Was Saved from Rome, Quebec and the Liberals." In *The Developing West: Essays on Canadian History in Honor of Lewis H. Thomas*. Edmonton: University of Alberta Press, 1983.

Kyba, Patrick. "Ballot Boxes and Burning Crosses." In *Politics in Saskatchewan*, edited by Norman Ward and Duff Spafford. Don Mills, ON: Longmans Canada, 1968.

Maloney, J. J. *Rome in Canada*. Vancouver: Columbia Protestant Publications, c1934.

O'Brien, Jeff, Ruth W. Millar, and William P. Delainey. *Saskatoon: A History in Photographs*. Regina: Coteau Books, 2006.

"Old Knox Church—An Alliance Connection." The Alliance in Saskatoon. collegeofprayer.ca/saskatoon/content/Knox.html.

Rees, R. "The 'Magic City on the Banks of the Saskatchewan': The Saskatoon Real Estate Boom 1910–1913." *Saskatchewan History* 27 (1974): 51–59.

Régistre pour server à l'inscription des Chroniques des Soeurs de l'Assomption de la S. V., Biggar, Saskatchewan. Provincial Archives of Alberta PR 1973 0080/000 SASV/3/1.

Robin, Martin. *Shades of Right: Nativist and Fascist Politics in Canada, 1920–1940*. Toronto: University of Toronto Press, 1992.

Rothman, Joshua. "When Bigotry Paraded Through the Streets." *The Atlantic*, December 4, 2016. theatlantic.com/politics/archive/2016/12/second-klan/509468/.

Thomas, Lewis H. "Saskatoon, 1883–1920: The Formative Years." In *Town and City: Aspects of Western Canadian Urban Development*, edited by Alan F. J. Artibise. Regina: Canadian Plains Research Center, 1981.

Tucker, Richard K. *The Dragon and the Cross: The Rise and Fall of the Ku Klux Klan in Middle America*. Hamden, CT: Archon Books, 1991.

Chapter 13: Revelations

City Relief Board, newspaper clippings, 1932–1933. City of Saskatoon Archives 1009-2.

Communists. Re-engaging King and Palmer in Parks Dept [1932]. City of Saskatoon Archives 1013-III vol. 1–3.

Denis, Wilfrid B. "Francophone Education in Saskatchewan: Resisting Anglo-Hegemony." In *A History of Education in Saskatchewan: Selected Readings*, edited by Brian Noonan, Dianne Hallman, and Murray Scharf. Regina: University of Regina Press, 2006.

Gladish, W. F. "Theatre Design in Canada." *Exhibitors Herald World*, July–September, 1930. archive.org/stream/exibitorsheraldw1ounse#page/n107/mode/1up.

Grand Orange Lodge of Saskatchewan, Report of Proceedings, 1929–1933 and 1936–1939. Provincial Archives of Saskatchewan R.2.393.

Hoffman, George. "The Arid Years." *Legion: Canada's Military History Magazine*, March 1, 1997. legionmagazine.com/en/1997/03/the-arid-years/.

Huel, Raymond. "The Anderson Amendments: A Half Century Later." *Canadian Catholic Historical Association Study Sessions* 47 (1980): 5–21.

——. "French Canadians and the Language Question, 1918." *Saskatchewan History* 23 (1970): 1–15.

——. "The Public School as a Guardian of Anglo-Saxon Traditions: The Saskatchewan Experience, 1913–1918." In *Ethnic Canadians: Culture and Education*, edited by M. L. Kovacs. Regina: Canadian Plains Research Center, 1978.

"A Human Rights Landmark: The Saskatchewan Bill of Rights, Human Rights in Canada: A Historical Perspective." Canadian Human Rights Commission. chrc-ccdp.gc.ca/historical-perspective/en/timePortals/milestones/51mile.asp.

Kitzan, Chris. "Lloyd, George Exton." *Dictionary of Canadian Biography*. biographi.ca/en/bio/lloyd_george_exton_16E.html.

Lawton, Alma. "Relief Administration in Saskatoon During the Depression." *Saskatchewan History* 22 (1969): 41–59.

Maloney, J. J. *Rome in Canada*. Vancouver: Columbia Protestant Publications, c1934.

Minutes of Civic Relief Board. City of Saskatoon Archives CRB 1009, folders 1–8.

O'Brien, Jeff. "Saskatoon, the Great Depression, and the Civic Relief Board." Saskatoon: City of Saskatoon Archives, 2005.

264   Relief—Complaints and investigations (14 vols.), 1931–1944, 1946–1949. City of Saskatoon Archives 1200-0361.

Relief—Deportation of Applicants, 1933. City of Saskatoon Archives 1069-1133.

Relief—Direct (9 vols.), 1932–1942, 1946. City of Saskatoon Archives 122-0356.

Strikwerda, Eric. *The Wages of Relief: Cities and the Unemployed in Prairie Canada, 1929–39.* Edmonton: Athabasca University Press, 2012.

Thompson, Robert H. "Boyhood Memories of Saskatoon in the 1930's." Unpublished manuscript, Local History Room, Saskatoon Public Library.

Weir, H. McI. "City of Saskatoon Engineering Department, Historical Treatise." Unpublished report, City of Saskatoon Archives, 1963.

INDEX

OTHER BOOKS
BY CANDACE SAVAGE

A Geography of Blood: Unearthing Memory from a Prairie Landscape, 2012

Prairie: A Natural History, 2004, 2011

Bees: Nature's Little Wonders, 2011

Crows: Encounters with the Wise Guys of the Avian World, 2005

Curious by Nature: One Woman's Exploration of the Natural World, 2005

Witch: The Wild Ride from Wicked to Wicca, 2000

Beauty Queens: A Playful History, 1998

Mother Nature: Animal Parents and Their Young, 1997

Cowgirls, 1996

The Nature of Wolves: An Intimate Portrait, 1996

Bird Brains: The Intelligence of Ravens, Crows, Magpies and Jays, 1995

Aurora: The Mysterious Northern Lights, 1994

Wild Cats, 1993

Peregrine Falcons, 1992

Grizzly Bears, 1990

Wolves, 1988

Eagles of North America, 1987

The Wonder of Canadian Birds, 1985

Wild Mammals of Western Canada, co-authored with Arthur Savage, 1981

Our Nell: A Scrapbook Biography of Nellie L. McClung, 1979

A Harvest Yet to Reap: A History of Prairie Women, co-authored with Lorna
and Linda Rasmussen and Anne Wheeler, 1976

For Young Readers

Hello, Crow!, 2019

Wizards: An Amazing Journey through the Last Great Age of Magic, 2002

Born to Be a Cowgirl: A Spirited Ride through the Old West, 2001

Eat Up! Healthy Food for a Healthy Earth, 1992

Get Growing! How the Earth Feeds Us, 1991

Trash Attack! Garbage and What We Can Do about It, 1990

DAVID
SUZUKI
INSTITUTE

THE DAVID SUZUKI INSTITUTE is a non-profit organization founded in 2010 to stimulate debate and action on environmental issues. The Institute and the David Suzuki Foundation both work to advance awareness of environmental issues important to all Canadians.

We invite you to support the activities of the Institute. For more information please contact us at:

David Suzuki Institute
219 – 2211 West 4th Avenue
Vancouver, BC, Canada V6K 4S2
info@davidsuzukiinstitute.org
604-742-2899
www.davidsuzukiinstitute.org

Cheques can be made payable to The David Suzuki Institute.